Conflict Management
and the Apostle Paul

Conflict Management and the Apostle Paul

Edited by
SCOT MCKNIGHT
and
GREG MAMULA

CASCADE *Books* · Eugene, Oregon

CONFLICT MANAGEMENT AND THE APOSTLE PAUL

Copyright © 2018 Wipf and Stock Publishers. All rights reserved. Except for brief quotations in critical publications or reviews, no part of this book may be reproduced in any manner without prior written permission from the publisher. Write: Permissions, Wipf and Stock Publishers, 199 W. 8th Ave., Suite 3, Eugene, OR 97401.

Cascade Books
An Imprint of Wipf and Stock Publishers
199 W. 8th Ave., Suite 3
Eugene, OR 97401

www.wipfandstock.com

PAPERBACK ISBN: 978-1-5326-5066-6
HARDCOVER ISBN: 978-1-5326-5067-3
EBOOK ISBN: 978-1-5326-5068-0

Cataloging-in-Publication data:

Names: McKnight, Scot, editor. | Mamula, Greg, editor.

Title: Conflict management and the apostle Paul / edited by Scot McKnight and Greg Mamula.

Description: Eugene, OR : Cascade Books, 2018 | Includes bibliographical references.

Identifiers: ISBN 978-1-5326-5066-6 (paperback) | ISBN 978-1-5326-5067-3 (hardcover) | ISBN 978-1-5326-5068-0 (ebook)

Subjects: LCSH: Paul, the Apostle, Saint. | Conflict management.

Classification: LCC BS2505 C58 2018 (print) | LCC BS2505 (ebook)

Manufactured in the U.S.A.   04/23/18

Contents

Contributors | vii

Paul and Conflict: Example or Not? | ix
    By Scot McKnight

An Introduction to Modern Conflict Management | xiii
    By Lauren Visser and Greg Mamula

1 Hello, Goodbye! Paul and Barnabas as a Model
    of Healthy Separation—Acts 15:36–41 | 1
    By Lauren Visser and Chandler Vinson

2 Paul Pleads with Philemon: Paul as Master Mediator—Philemon | 20
    By Amanda Hecht and Shawn O'Brien

3 Crucial Conversations at the Jerusalem Council: Paul Submits
    to Higher Authority—Acts 15:1–33 | 39
    By Randy Johns and Ray Miller

4 Learning to Love in Faith, Rather than Fight with Power:
    Paul as Mediation Teacher—1 Corinthians 8–11 and Romans 14–15 | 52
    By Doug McPherson and Ben Tertin

5 All Too Human: Leader Loyalties and Spiritual Unity
    Paul as Arbiter—1 Corinthians 1–3 | 72
    By Michael C. Thompson and Greg Mamula

6 The Corinthian Conflict and the Collection: Paul Builds Relationships
    through Wise Agreements—2 Corinthians 8–9 | 89
    By Andrew Gleddiesmith and Ric Strangway

7 The Table and the Cross: Paul Calls for Unity Around the Table
—1 Corinthians 11 | 101
By Jeff Blair and Derwin Gray

8 Mission in Tension: Paul as Ministry Advocate
—Galatians 2:1–10 | 129
By Brett Sanner and Paul Trainor

9 Addressing False Teaching and Heresy: Paul as Guardian
of the Gospel—1–2 Timothy and Titus | 145
By Kristen Bennett Marble and Jared Willemin

Contributors

Scot McKnight, Julius R. Mantey Professor of New Testament, Northern Seminary

Greg Mamula, Associate Executive Minister, American Baptist Churches of Nebraska, Omaha, NE

Jeff Blair, Pastor, Locus Grove Freewill Baptist Church, Locus Grove, OK

Andrew Gleddiesmith, Lead Pastor, Fraserview Church, Richmond, BC, Canada

Derwin Gray, Lead Pastor, Transformation Church, Charlotte, SC

Amanda Hecht, Pastor, Faith Community Church, Wakaw, SK, Canada

Randy Johns, Preaching Minister, Mayfair Church of Christ, Oklahoma City, OK

Kristen Bennett Marble, Senior Pastor, West Morris Street Free Methodist Church, Indianapolis, IN

Doug McPherson, Family Pastor, Mayfield Road Baptist Church, Arlington, TX

Ray P. Miller, Pastor, Crievewood Baptist Church, Nashville, TN

Shawn O'Brien, Pastor of Shred, Torrance, CA

Brett Sanner, Lead Pastor, LifePoint Church, Quincy, IL

Ric D. Strangway, Lead Pastor, North Point Community Church, Calgary, Alberta, Canada

Ben Tertin, Lead Pastor, Central Bible Church, Portland, OR

Michael C. Thompson, Pastor, New Life Baptist Church, Bellevue, NE

Paul Trainor, Director of Las Vegas Extension and Associate Professor of New Testament Theology, Lincoln Christian University

Chandler Vinson, Senior Pastor, Rutledge Baptist Church, Rutledge, TN

Lauren Anders Visser, Adjunct Professor of Communication Arts, Trinity Christian College, Palos Heights, IL

Jared Willemin, Pastor to Children and Their Families, Cross Pointe Church of the Nazarene, Salisbury, MD

Paul and Conflict
Example or Not?

Buried into the back of your copy of Paul's letter to the church of the Roman colony, Philippi, is an apostolic urging that may well be the precise reason Paul wrote this short (in Pauline standards) letter. Two women, Euodia and Syntyche, are urged "to be of the same mind in the Lord" (Phil 4:2; NRSV). Lynn Cohick, in her commentary on Philippians, observes some argue the situation in Philippians 4:1–3 about Euodia and Syntyche is "minor, unimportant, or incidental." She's right, and one could create a long list of scholars who agree. But Lynn turns the corner noting, "most recent commentators hold that Paul's concern for unity between these [two female leaders and] believers is central to the letter."[1]

The story repeats itself. Bible read by males, Bible read for males, women in the Bible ignored or silenced or unnoticed. In a letter about unity shaped by the word "same" (1:27; 2:2; 3:15; 4:2), in a letter justly famous for the Christ hymn (2:6–11) but which is provoked into appearance in this letter to teach Christoformity and sacrifice for others in order to maintain unity (2:1–5), and in a letter where fellowship (1:5; 2:1; 3:10), the first real mention of anyone in particular is these two women. What are they told? To have the "same mind" (3:2). I am of the view, with many others, that the division between Euodia and Syntyche both shapes the problems at Philippi and represents the problem. The problem is division and the need is unity.

Granting that non-controversial conclusion, I want to approach this from another angle, one I have not seen or heard. How do you think Euodia and Syntyche responded to Paul's putting them on the spot? To Paul's degrading of their status in the community by calling them out in this letter, which would have been performed publicly for all in the congregation and house churches to hear?

---

1. Cohick, *Philippians*, 208.

So let's imagine what they might have said in their defense, and we'll get to what he said that they surely needed to be of the same mind about below. It would not have been a stretch of imagination for the Christians of Philippi to know, first, about some of the Apostles Behaving Badly. I'm speaking here of the public outburst of Paul against Peter and Peter's rather obvious failure to live up to the gospel that includes gentiles. The story is told from Paul's angle in Gal 2:11–14. Details aside—was Peter eating pork? Were the Jewish believers demanding circumcision?—the incident itself is enough to tell the story of apostles. "One mind, Paul?" Euodia and Syntyche ask.

And, second, we can reasonably think that Paul was not himself of "one mind" with either Barnabas or John Mark. One can read up about Paul's strong disagreement with Barnabas over taking John Mark on the mission trip subsequent to the Council in Jerusalem (Acts 15:37–40). Earlier John Mark had jumped the mission trip ship and headed back to Jerusalem (13:13) and Paul didn't like it. Barnabas, correctly it turns out, saw more in John Mark than did Paul at the time. Euodia and Syntyche could have looked Paul square in the eyes and said, "One mind, Paul?"

It takes no imagination to know that what festered between Paul and the Corinthians was anything but unity, fellowship, and one mind. In a close reading of his letters, and maybe it will take more than one close reading, we encounter one communication after another. We find 1 Corinthians, and then what is called the severe letter, then we get 2 Corinthians, which may be more than one letter. In addition to the letters, we also discover that Paul crossed the Aegean from Ephesus to Corinth one trip after another. We learn it was not just Paul travelling but also Timothy and Titus each trying to work things out. Any reading with sensitivity can see that 2 Cor 10–13 is Paul's response to accusations made against him by the Corinthians. They couldn't be entirely wrong, could they? "One mind, Paul?"

These three examples could at least have flashed through the mental screens of Euodia and Syntyche when they, sitting in the house church—one of theirs?—heard their names and heard as well Paul's urging of them to be of "the same mind." Did they even hear Paul continue with "help these women since they have contended at my side in the cause of the gospel, along with Clement and the rest of my coworkers, whose names are in the book of life" (4:3)? And who is this "companion"? Perhaps Epaphroditus, perhaps Luke, perhaps Timothy. Whoever it is, he is being urged to work with Euodia and Syntyche to come to agreement. There are many things we don't know—including what the point of their dispute was. What we do know is that they were fractured and they were contributing to fracturing in the Philippian house churches.

If they continued to listen, however, they heard Paul affirm them publicly, and that was noteworthy and valuable in a world driven by status and public honor. If they listened they heard him tell the whole church that they have been companions with Paul in gospel work—which means evangelism and teaching and discipline and suffering. If they listened they heard him label them with his most noble term: "coworkers." If they listened they heard they were to be classed with the leader Clement. Most noticeable, they heard him say they—in spite of their tension—were names listed in the "book of life." This is Paul's way of saying they are on God's side all the way.

Whatever they heard they knew that the tension at work between them, however, was at work in Paul's own life and mission. Paul could surely point to fractured relationships now healed—which is the case with Barnabas (1 Cor 9:6), Peter (9:5; 15:5), and John Mark (Col 4:10; Phlm 24; 2 Tim 4:9, 11), and it is noticeable that Peter is now getting along with John Mark too (1 Pet 5:13). I am not suggesting directly that Paul could respond to their flashing mental screens with his stories of fractured relationships now made healthy again, but we could.

What I am saying is that Paul is not perfect; only Jesus gets that place in our minds and hearts. What I am saying is that Paul is not a perfect pastor and his approach to conflict is not always consistent with Jesus' or even with his own gospel of reconciliation (2 Cor 5:16–21). What I am saying is that in the book that follows we will take conflict management theory at its best, which for pastors at least is Christian principles put to use in management theories, and examine the Apostle Paul. He comes out pretty well, but not unscathed.

What I am saying is that Paul is like us and he needs to grow just as we do.

This collection of essays around a given theme—conflict management—and using a theory of conflict management to provoke questions about the Apostle Paul's management style emerged from a Doctor's of Ministry course at Northern Seminary. My hope for the papers that were presented in class was that they would be solid enough for publication was realized. The opening sketch of recent studies on conflict management by Lauren Visser and Greg Mamula set the tone but also gave to the rest of the students categories by which to assess Paul. The week-long intensive revealed to me that pastors, who often live weekly with conflict in the church setting, see dimensions of Paul's own ministry that non-pastors often do not see. So, as the papers were presented and the discussions followed I sat back and watched veterans in conflict management ply their trade with skill and wisdom.

I asked Greg Mamula, who as a church administrator for the American Baptist Churches is called routinely into conflict situations in local churches, to edit this book with me and I did so for this major reason: I knew he could make suggestions for each chapter on how conflict management theory might apply to a specific incident in the life of the Apostle Paul. I am grateful for his wisdom and careful attention to the details of bringing our book to completion.

Northern Seminary deserves our gratitude for the freedom it is giving to this professor to chart some unexplored waters in some of our classes. I want to express my thanks to President of Northern, William Shiell, for his enthusiasm and support of this book.

Scot McKnight
Julius R. Mantey Professor of New Testament
Northern Seminary
Lisle, Illinois

Bibliography

Cohick, Lynn H. *Philippians*. Story of God Bible Commentary. New Testament Series 11. Grand Rapids: Zondervan, 2013.

An Introduction to Modern Conflict Management

By Lauren Visser and Greg Mamula

Pastor X has been the pastor of her church for three years. She thought she had a good working relationship with her congregation, but after the last committee meeting, she is now unsure. The committee is composed of six members, and the meeting started the same as always: pray, review minutes from previous meeting, and work through the agenda items. At the very end of the meeting, one of the committee members added a last-minute agenda item: education. He was adamant that children's ministry should be the most important focus for the next month, and since Christmas was coming, they should create a children's Christmas program. Pastor X immediately responded that while involving children is a wonderful idea, there was not enough time to pull together an entire Christmas program on such short notice. The committee member then loudly proclaimed that Pastor X was disengaged from the community, disrespectful, and did not care about the church or its future. The other members remained silent until the tirade was done and the committee chair responded, "Okay. Let's be done for now and pray." As soon as the prayer was done, the angry committee member stormed out of the room. Everyone else left in silence without looking at each other. Hurt and confused, Pastor X now wonders, "What do I do next?"

The situation above is fictional, but it represents very real, hurtful conflicts that many pastors have experienced in ministry. Conflict is inevitable. People have different goals, views, and personalities, and the church is full of imperfect people. But conflict does not have to be destructive. The Chinese character for "conflict" is the combination of two characters: "danger" and "opportunity." With this realization, conflict can be seen as a challenge that can lead to new opportunities. For pastors like Pastor X, who are wondering where to start after experiencing conflict and how to move from danger to opportunity, this book will provide insight into what Paul says about conflict. Before we listen to Paul, though, there are many other helpful conflict management resources. Some deal with general contexts while others specifically relate to church contexts. All provide a framework for managing conflict, and this introduction will provide a brief overview of various conflict management strategies.

Research on Conflict

Some of the best research regarding conflict and conflict management comes from the Harvard Negotiation Project. For the past three decades, Roger Fisher and William Ury (of the Harvard Negotiation Project) have had a dramatic impact on conflict management. Their book *Getting to Yes: Negotiating Agreement Without Giving In* is an international bestseller in its third edition.[2] The principles of *Getting to Yes* have inspired many other conflict managers and their teachings. Their greatest contribution to conflict management is their perspective on what is actually being negotiated in the negotiation process. Many conflicts center around what Fisher and Ury call "positional bargaining," where each side takes a position, argues for it, and compromises those positions until an agreement is reached or an impasse occurs. Taking a position is helpful in that it informs the other party in the conflict what you want and helps guide you into producing terms for an agreement. However, positional bargaining has several weaknesses. It does not guarantee an agreement can be reached, sometimes produces hostile actions outside of the negotiation process, hinders the ability for an ongoing relationship once the negotiations are over, and, when multiple parties are involved the issues become even more complicated.

What makes Fisher and Ury's approach different and effective is how they view the process of a good negotiation. For them, "Any method of negotiation may be fairly judged by three criteria: It should produce a wise agreement if possible. It should be efficient. And it should improve or at least not damage the relationship between the parties."[3] The ability to look beyond positions and begin looking toward substance is important. In other words, begin to focus on the issue itself and not the individual personalities involved. Then begin to develop procedures for dealing with the issue in partnership with the other parties involved in the conflict. This is called "principled negotiation" by Fisher and Ury. The good thing about this type of alternative to conflict management is that it can be done unilaterally. One

2. Fisher, Ury, and Patton, *Getting to Yes*.
3. Ibid., 4.

side can begin to deal with the issue in this manner and it will begin to affect the approach of the other parties involved in the conflict.

Fisher and Ury's Basic Four

There are four basic points that summarize all of Fisher and Ury's teaching on principled negotiation. *First*, separate the people from the problem. People often have difficulty with effective communication, especially when strong emotions are involved. When people take a positional bargaining approach, it exacerbates the problem because our emotions get connected to their positions. A good conflict manager must learn to be able to separate the individual personalities involved in the conflict from the issue at hand. At some point, they also seek to help the parties involved begin to see themselves as working side by side, attacking the problem together. A simple action I have found helpful in separating people from the problem is once gathered in the negotiation room to put the opposing parties on the same side of a table facing a white board with the main issue written on it. When the parties involved are not looking across a table at one another they begin to see each other less as combatants and more as partners facing the problem together.

Next, focus on interests, not positions. To really resolve a conflict, understanding the deeper interest is of paramount importance. Positions are usually indicative of underlying issues. Making both parties aware of their interests helps them better understand where each side is coming from. When all the parties involved better understand the ultimate interests of those involved it helps them begin to frame possible solutions that meet the interests rather than a hardline position.

Third, the conflict manager is also invited to help the parties involved create multiple options for mutual gain. Searching for one right solution can be a roadblock to the conflict management process. Developing a wide range of possible solutions that advance the shared interests and creatively reconcile differing interests is a creative way to get the parties involved working together.

The *fourth* and final task of principled negotiation is insisting on using objective criteria. Developing a fair standard on how to reach an agreement is helpful. All good negotiation should include the three principles of wisdom, efficiency, and relationship building. However, to give shape to those principles, an outside standard that speaks to the issue at hand might be helpful such as market value, cultural contexts, legal standing, or even an outside expert opinion.

These four principles from Fisher and Ury and their larger implications and detailed applications have been lifted up across cultures and contexts as standard practices when approaching conflict situations. These principles have been used in global politics, business deals, peace negotiations, community debates, and even church struggles.

A Conversational Perspective

While Fisher and Ury approached conflict management from a negotiation standpoint, other members of the Harvard Negotiation Project focused on conflict management from a conversational perspective. In the book *Difficult Conversations: How to Discuss What Matters Most*, Douglas Stone, Bruce Patton, and Sheila Heen offer "a way to deal creatively with tough problems while treating people with decency and integrity."[4] The authors start by explaining that all difficult conversations share the same structure, which breaks into three categories: the "what happened?" conversation, the feeling conversation, and the identity conversation.[5] Managing conflict means managing these three underlying conversations.

When discussing the first conversation, *"what happened?,"* Stone, Patton, and Heen warn against three assumptions. The first is the truth assumption, which often leads people to argue about whether or not they are right. But the authors warn that difficult conversations are not about what is true; they are about what is important. This thinking thus causes a shift from proving the truth toward understanding different perceptions, interpretations, and values.[6] The second assumption is the intention invention, which is an assumption that one person can judge another's intentions or motives. The authors issue another warning: intentions are invisible and inventing them leads to unfounded assumptions. The third assumption is the blame frame, which seeks to discover who is at fault. Unsurprisingly, the authors warn yet again that this distracts people from discussing what is actually important and prevents them from correcting errors and moving forward.[7]

In the second category, *the feeling conversation*, one acknowledges that conflict involves emotions. While it is sometimes unproductive to discuss feelings, there are also times when it is essential. Therefore, one needs to learn how to discuss feelings as a part of managing conflict.[8] Whether

---

4. Stone, Patton, and Heen, *Difficult Conversations*, xxx.
5. Ibid., 7–8.
6. Ibid., 9–10.
7. Ibid., 10–12.
8. Ibid., 13–14.

feelings are shared or left unexpressed, they can still affect a conversation. Therefore, the authors urge those managing conflict to explore their emotional footprint and to learn to acknowledge that others' feelings are just as important as their own.[9] When describing feelings, the authors also helpfully suggest that feelings should be described carefully, be connected to the problem, and be shared without evaluation.[10]

The third category is the *identity conversation*, and it is perhaps the most challenging category. This category causes one to look inward, to discover who they are, and to ascertain how they see themselves. When managing conflict, one must also manage one's inner dialogue and discover what one believes the conflict is saying about their own self.[11] One of the fundamental questions one must ask is, "What is at stake?" Three core identities that often seem threatened by difficult questions are: am I competent?; am I a good person?; and am I worthy of love?[12] A key to managing these questions is to become aware of them and then to adopt the "and stance," which allows for people's identities to be complex, such as making wise *and* unwise choices or having noble *and* less noble intentions. When unpacking one's identity, three realities one ought to accept are that one will make mistakes, intentions are complex, and all parties have contributed to the problem.[13]

In order to effectively manage conflict and embrace difficult conversations, all three categories need to be balanced. Once a balance is present, Stone, Patton, and Heen state that the nature of the conversation changes. One is no longer focused on proving their point, getting their way, or convincing the other person that they are wrong; instead, the conversation is focused on learning. Once this is a learning conversation, participants focus on "what has happened from the other person's point of view, explain your point of view, share and understand feelings, and work together to figure out a way to manage the problem going forward."[14] Throughout their book, Stone, Patton, and Heen provide real life examples and alternative solutions to difficult conversations. They also provide a concise checklist, summarizing the five steps one takes when engaging with difficult conversations:

9. Ibid., 91–94.
10. Ibid., 102–4.
11. Ibid., 14–15.
12. Ibid., 111–12.
13. Ibid., 116–21.
14. Ibid., 16.

Step 1: Prepare by walking through the three conversations.

Step 2: Check your purposes and decide whether to raise the issue.

Step 3: Start from the third story.

Step 4: Explore their story and yours.

Step 5: Problem-solving.[15]

At the crux of the book is the reminder that one cannot change other people, but one can change the way they converse with them.[16] By starting with acknowledgment of the structure and forces underneath conflict, and then finding a way to share stories, difficult conversations can become less difficult and more productive.

General-situation theories are always helpful for laying foundations of understanding, and the Harvard Negotiation Project has done a masterful job of providing tools for effectively managing conflict and handling difficult conversations. But for those pastors who are steeped in church conflicts, theories with practical applications toward the church are often desired. Thankfully, there are many scholars who have applied different conflict management theories specifically to managing church conflict.

This book will focus on church conflict and on the Apostle Paul. In the chapters that follow, one issue will become clear: we need to use common sense. Since we do not have records of Paul's conflicts with his churches and their church leaders, a lot of the information we would like to have is not available. Therefore, we will be tasked at times to use our common sense to fill in the gaps by applying common human experience and current understandings of conflict and conflict management. Such an endeavor builds on one of the trends of modern scholarship, which is that exploring modern social-scientific models has value for comprehending first century realities. Despite the lack of information regarding the exact conflicts Paul experienced, we believe that the models developed by contemporary scholars provide a set of categories that will enable us to better understand Paul's conflicts and help us assess how he handled them.[17]

Family Systems Approach

In their book, *Church Conflict: The Hidden Systems Behind the Fights*, Charles H. Cosgrove and Dennis D. Hatfield employ family systems theory as a way

---

15. Ibid., 233–34.
16. Ibid., 294.
17. One good example is Rambo, *Understanding Religious Conversion*.

of understanding and managing church conflict. Their thesis is that "behind the official systems of the local church (its offices, boards, committees, etc.) there is another system, a *family-like* system, which powerfully determines the way that church members relate to one another, do business together, care for one another, and fight with one another."[18] Through using family systems theory, Cosgrove and Hatfield explain that people repeat the family patterns they learned while growing up, and this affects the way they function in all areas of life, including the church.[19] Family systems theory thus provides a framework for understanding choices, interactions, and conflict.

Cosgrove and Hatfield helpfully provide definitions and a mapping technique for those church leaders who are interested in working through conflict with a greater understanding of family systems and how they are at play in the church. The foundation for using family systems theory is first to start by looking at two aspects of boundaries: structure of authority and quality of communication. Structure of authority refers to whether people are acting as parents or as children (which will be discussed in the next paragraph); quality of communication refers to whether communication is clear and honest.[20] Both types of boundaries need to be assessed if they are open or closed. Open boundaries allow free-flowing interaction and communication between groups; closed boundaries lead to rigid and strained interactions.[21]

A parent in the family system theory does not necessarily have to be a biological parent, just like a child does not have to be a biological child. Instead, these designations refer to patterns of leadership and patterns of deferral. In other words, parents are the formal or informal leaders of the church while children are the followers. The main difference between church parents and church children is recognized power.[22] There are also two types of children: independent children and parental children. Independent children are not controlled by any church parent; they hold to their own thoughts and opinions, but they do not have any followers. Parental children are those who have power delegated to them from parents. They exercise leadership and care toward others, but they take their cues from the parents and defer to them for decision-making.[23]

---

18. Cosgrove and Hatfield, *Church Conflict*, 5.
19 Ibid., 12.
20. Ibid., 33.
21. Ibid., 35–37.
22. Ibid., 46–47.
23. Ibid., 55–57.

From this brief overview of family systems theory, Cosgrove and Hatfield offer four truths related to church conflict management: "First, the congregational system is interconnected. . . . Second, the congregational system is both dynamic and stable. . . . Third, the congregational family is already organized to care for its own members. . . . Fourth, the psychic life of the individual is not only private ('internal') but also social."[24] From these principles, Cosgrove and Hatfield then offer several different strategies pastors can employ when engaging with their congregation under the umbrella of family systems theory. One, they can employ strategic insider action, which is acting from within the family system to suggest change. Two, they can use the focused strategy, which aims at getting to the root of the problem since the seemingly most pressing issues are not also the most significant ones. Three, they can affiliate, which means decreasing the distance between different people or groups by positively identifying with them. Four, they can use unbalancing tactics to form new coalitions that restructure the system and eliminates conflict.[25] The fifth and last strategy that Cosgrove and Hatfield offer is that of joining, through affirmation and identification. They state, "Affirmation means expressing appreciation and praise to others for the things we value about them. Identification means discovering and matching similarities between ourselves and others."[26] Cosgrove and Hatfield reiterate that all these strategies must be covered in faith. Such faith trusts that the Holy Spirit is indeed working to turn church families into God's family, and it is believing that all parents and children in family systems can truly grow up to become image bearers of Christ.

Reconciliation Approach

Like Cosgrove and Hatfield, John Paul Lederach also believes in the importance of faith when working to manage conflict. His background, however, comes from intense work in peacemaking and reconciliation rather than from working within a specific congregation. He believes in sharing stories and creating space to hear other people's stories, and he describes conflict as a journey, where people travel in and out of messy situations.[27] From his experience, Lederach provides another framework for managing conflict in the church.

24. Ibid., 125.
25. Ibid., 126–39.
26. Ibid., 179.
27. Lederach, *Journey Toward Reconciliation*, 14.

In describing his process of peacemaking and reconciliation, Lederach shares his own stories, and he cautions against forming enemies. He lays out three steps that go into creating enemies: "First, to construct the image of the enemy, I must separate myself from them. . . . [Second,] I see myself as superior. . . . Third, separation and superiority lead to dehumanizing the other person(s)."[28] Lederach cautions against such distancing, and he reminds Christians in conflict that if they look to find God in others, they will be unable to turn them into an enemy.

As do many other writers, Lederach affirms that conflict is natural. Cosgrove and Hatfield stated, "As all handbooks on conflict management stress, the best way to manage conflict is to treat it as something normal and bring it out into the open where it can be handled fairly and constructively."[29] Lederach also adds that conflict is not a sin. However, there are signs of when sin has entered into a conflict. For example, this can be seen when someone acts like God or wants to be God or when someone assumes superiority. This can also be seen through oppressing others, elevating one's position or ideas over others, or refusing to listen to others' views and opinions. Lederach also adds that it is unhelpful to hold back deep feelings, project blame, and resist self-reflection.[30]

In order to provide practical steps for managing conflict from a biblical perspective, Lederach unpacks Matt 18. His four steps are: go directly to the person with whom you have a problem, bring two or three witnesses along, tell the problem to the church, and relate as with a Gentile or tax collector. Lederach comments how the first two steps are found in family systems theory, as described above by Cosgrove and Hatfield.[31] Lederach also emphasizes Acts 15 as a source for biblical principles, and he notes six steps for managing conflict from this passage: "recognize and define the problem . . . create the appropriate forum for processing matters . . . let diverse viewpoints be represented . . . document diversity . . . use the gifts of the community . . . [and] decide, then implement decisions."[32]

Perhaps most importantly for Lederach is to continue to dream of peace and to believe that peace is part of God's plan for his people. Lederach states a list of his beliefs, and one of his core beliefs is that God has chosen to work through the weak and the foolish. God invites all people to work

---

28. Ibid., 47–48.
29. Cosgrove and Hatfield, *Church Conflict*, 42.
30. Ibid., 117.
31. Ibid., 120–35.
32. Ibid., 143–50.

in his kingdom and to see others through his eyes.[33] Conflict can be painful, scary, and damaging. But by sharing stories, refusing to create enemies, and confronting sin, conflict can also lead to transformed relationships and strengthened systems.

Starting With the Bible

Christian conflict manager Karl Slaikeu takes the principles from Fisher and Ury,[34] and like Lederach, he interacts with Matt 5 and Matt 18 as a way of managing conflict. Slaikeu uses these two Scripture passages as the foundation for his *Preferred Path* process of interpersonal conflict management.[35] Slaikeu and others in Christian conflict management have taught and expounded on these two passages in very helpful ways recently. For them the passages create a template for dealing with interpersonal conflicts. The goal in modeling these passages of Scripture as conflict management process is for reconciliation between the parties and restoration of relationships.

The Matt 5 and Matt 18 template can be explained as follows: first, if you are aware you are in conflict with another person, it is your responsibility to go to them and seek reconciliation. This is something that is done unilaterally. The Matt 5 passage hints that if I know my horizontal relationships with my fellow humans are in disarray then my vertical relationship with God is also in disarray. One must seek earthly restoration before one can be in proper relationship with God.

If going one-on-one does not resolve the conflict and bring about reconciliation and restoration, you are invited to bring in outside help. In the case of Matt 18 it would imply someone from the church since those who are in conflict are "brothers and sisters." As Slaikeu and others teach, those who are brought into the conflict initially are to serve as silent witnesses to the efforts of the one seeking reconciliation. They are not there to gang up on the other party involved in the conflict. The goal is for the extra presence to persuade the other to repent.

If bringing observers does not work, you are to bring in the church body. This is a stage where modern conflict management fits. The idea that an extra voice can be brought into the procedure sometimes helps to resolve the conflict. There are three outcomes to this type of outside involvement. The first is mediation, where the church conflict manager seeks to resolve the issue in a wise and efficient manner while restoring the relationships of

---

33. Ibid., 200–201.
34. Slaikeu, *When Push Comes to Shove*, 23–51.
35. Preferred Path Conflict Resolution, http://www.preferredpathministry.com/.

those in conflict with one another and the rest of the church. The second possible solution is arbitration. Arbitration is the process of an outside party listening to all the parties involved and then casting a ruling on future steps. The final possible outcome is that of litigious settlement. Some sort of outside legal ruling party will settle the matter. The problem with arbitration and litigation is that while it might result in a fair or even wise verdict, it does little to maintain the relationship between the conflicted parties. If the offending party does not listen to the voice of the church, then the third and final solution is separation, to treat them like a "pagan or tax collector." While on the surface this sounds harsh and has at times been used as a motive for excommunication, or what might now be more accurate expressions, separation or temporary separation. Slaikeu would argue it is a form of grace. Jesus treated tax collectors and pagans with a gentle touch. Jesus had fellowship meals with them and in so doing he taught through action and parables about the kingdom of God to them. So too today if the church is treating the offending party like a tax collector in the way Jesus did, it would imply we remain in fellowship with them, not excommunicating them. If the offender is being treated as a tax collector it implies they do not fully understand the kingdom teachings of Jesus. They are to remain in fellowship but must be taught from the very beginning the teachings of Jesus.

While both Slaikeu and Lederach engage with Matt 5 and Matt 18, these are not the only Scripture passages available as resources for conflict management. James Christensen and Thomas Johnson remind us of the complexities of New Testament conflict and the various methods of conflict management in *Healing Church Strife in the New Testament and Today: Beyond Matthew 18:15–17*.

There are some common themes found in the New Testament outside of Matthew that point to how conflict was handled. In other words, Christensen and Johnson argue there is no single consistent procedure for handling conflict among the followers of Jesus. Nor are there different processes for different types of conflict. The instructions provided in the New Testament are partial or situational and include moral and spiritual ramifications.[36]

Christensen and Johnson share several New Testament conflict management themes. The *first* is the dictum or *arbitration*, where a defined announcement by a recognized authority seeks to settle the matter with a ruling. Relationships between those involved are a lower priority than the integrity of the church. Dictum is not always successful. 1 Cor 5 is an example of Paul commanding a church to cast out a wicked person from the

---

36. Christensen and Johnson, *Healing Church Strife*, 8–9.

congregation. He has little concern for the current relationship with the offender; there is no call for repentance and no opportunity for reconciliation. His focus is on the immorality of the church. However, a dictum is also used in Acts 8:20–23 when Peter demands that Magnus repent of trying to purchase the gift of the Holy Spirit so that he might be forgiven and restored. Here Peter issues a command to repent, but it is so that Magnus might be forgiven and reconciled.

The *second* way the New Testament deals with conflict is through the process of *separation*. Separation ends the dispute but does not lead to reconciliation. An example is that of the parting of ways between Paul and Barnabas in Acts 15:39. Though later there is reconciliation between Paul and Barnabas and John Mark in Col 4. In 1 John and 2 John we see entire groups leaving the church over teaching matters. In 2 Thess 3 Paul encourages the church to have nothing to do with a member. And again in 1 Cor 5 the excommunication of the offender is proposed. These separations might stop the immediate fighting but they do not solve the issue.

A *third* New Testament conflict management theme is *avoidance*. Avoidance includes accepting the wrong of others without retaliation. Jesus urged followers to turn the other cheek. Paul encourages the Corinthians to keep the peace by being wronged rather than instigate a new conflict through a lawsuit in 1 Cor 6. James encourages the church to allow differences to exist side by side and let God judge in Jas 4:10–12.

Fourth, conflict is dealt with through the process of *negotiation*. Negotiation requires a trained, neutral third party who facilitates a process. This is most like Matt 5 and 18. Negotiation took place at the Jerusalem Council in Acts 15. The letter to Philemon is an artfully crafted negotiation between Paul and Philemon regarding Onesimus.

Finally, some form of arbitration in the form of *official church action* is described in the New Testament. Some sort of outside authority makes a decision. The Jerusalem Council in Acts 15 is a type of official church action. After the negotiations between Paul, Barnabas, Peter and the council take place, the rulers made a decision and everyone lived by the edict of that decision.

Although it is helpful to turn to books, methods, and theories about conflict management, as pastors, it is also crucial that we examine Scripture. While Matt 5 and 18 have often been held up as models for conflict management, they are not the only options. One voice and source of information regarding biblical conflict management that has often been ignored is that of Paul. The purpose of this book is to examine how Paul handled conflict and what we as a church can learn from him today.

Bibliography

Christensen, James, and Thomas F. Johnson. *Healing Church Strife in the New Testament and Today Beyond Matthew 18:15–17*. Eugene, OR: Wipf & Stock, 2016.

Cosgrove, Charles H., and Dennis D. Hatfield. *Church Conflict: The Hidden Systems Behind the Fights*. Nashville: Abingdon, 1994.

Fisher, Roger, William L. Ury, and Bruce Patton. *Getting to Yes: Negotiating Agreement Without Giving In*. 3rd ed. New York: Penguin, 2011.

Lederach, John Paul. *The Journey Toward Reconciliation*. Scottdale, PA: Herald, 1999.

Rambo, Lewis R. *Understanding Religious Conversion*. New Haven: Yale University Press, 1993.

Slaikeu, Karl A. *When Push Comes to Shove: A Practical Guide to Mediating Disputes*. Jossey-Bass Conflict Resolution Series. San Francisco: Jossey-Bass, 1996.

Stone, Douglas, Bruce Patton, and Sheila Heen. *Difficult Conversations: How to Discuss What Matters Most*. New York: Penguin, 1999.

1

Hello, Goodbye!
Paul and Barnabas as a Model of Healthy Separation

ACTS 15:36–41

By Lauren Visser and Chandler Vinson

John Lennon and Paul McCartney are considered by many to be one of the best songwriting teams of all time. Yet these two iconic musicians could not have been more different. In his memoir, engineer Geoff Emerick wrote, "Paul was a natural communicator; John couldn't articulate his ideas well. Paul was the diplomat; John was the agitator. Paul was soft-spoken and almost unfailingly polite; John could be a right loudmouth and quite rude. Paul was willing to put in long hours to get a part right; John was impatient, always ready to move on to the next thing."[1] Yet this partnership did not last forever, and hearts broke when the Beatles separated. Paul and Barnabas are also a famous pair from history, and they, too, were very different from each other. Despite their differences, they were able to collaborate for tremendous success. Yet just like Lennon and McCartney, Paul and Barnabas also separated, and one can imagine how hearts broke in ancient times as well.

1. Shenk, "Power of Two."

"Don't cause division." "You need to reconcile." "Fight the good fight." These are familiar prescriptions pastors hear when dealing with conflict. They are guided by principles of love, unity, perseverance, and reconciliation, which are wonderful values. However, these same, well-intentioned adages can also cause guilt, shame, and frustration for the pastor when someone leaves the church, when reconciliation is not possible, or when the pastor herself or himself needs to depart from the congregation. In times of intense conflict, we believe that Acts 15:3–41, as difficult as it is, is a source of empowerment and encouragement for every pastor who has ever had to go say good-bye to a congregation or watch a relationship end with a parishioner, friend, family member, or colleague. Sometimes, despite all the literature and research regarding conflict management and mediation, the best way to manage conflict is to walk away from it.

Paul and Barnabas

Paul and Barnabas are the first missionary team in Acts, and like Lewis and Clark, they explored unknown territory. In Acts 13:1–2, while prophets and teachers are worshiping and fasting in Antioch, the Holy Spirit tells them to set apart Barnabas and Paul (still called Saul in this passage) for the work that has been prepared for them. After fasting and praying, Barnabas and Paul start their missionary work with a holy commissioning. They are then guided by the Spirit to Seleucia, Cyprus, and Salamis.[2] In Paphos, they confront a false prophet,[3] and in Pisidian Antioch, they teach in the synagogue and encourage people to continue in the grace of God.[4] Even when they are threatened with stoning in Iconium,[5] these men continue to work together, facing all trials and tribulations as a team.

With such an auspicious beginning, it is hard to imagine that these two giants of the faith would ever disagree or be in conflict, but this is exactly what one sees in Acts 15:36–41. Not only is it hard to imagine, but it can also be difficult to believe. After all, many people have been taught to place Paul on a pedestal and removing him from that vaunted status can be personally challenging. Roy D. Bell commiserates with such people and agrees that reading such a passage can be trying. He writes:

It is hard to believe that those two men would quarrel. They had been through so much together. . . . It was Barnabas who gave Saul credibility

---

2. Acts 13:4–5.
3. Acts 13:6–12.
4. Acts 13:13–43.
5. Acts 14:1–7.

after his remarkable conversion on the way to Damascus. When Saul, later known as Paul, returned to Jerusalem, there was real fear that his conversion was not real and that its purpose was for him to infiltrate the Christian community. Barnabas introduced him to the apostles, took him into his own house and became his colleague.[6]

It is extra difficult to digest such a disagreement because it comes after a great triumph. In Acts 15:1–35, Paul and Barnabas argue with the Jerusalem council over whether or not Gentile converts need to be circumcised. They are presented as a unified front, and in response to their passionate testimony, "the whole assembly became silent as they listened to Barnabas and Paul telling about the signs and wonders God had done among the Gentiles through them."[7] Not only does the assembly convert to Barnabas's and Paul's way of thinking, but they also deliver a letter of support and send men to help with the missionary journeys. This victory represents a monumental milestone for the duo and for the nascent Christian movement. Yet it leads directly to heartbreak. In Acts' very next section, Christianity's first great missionary team dissolves.

Not the WWE

We are secure enough in our identities to admit that we enjoy watching the WWE. We know it is scripted and the drama is manufactured; that is why it is sports entertainment. And there is *plenty* of entertainment. New plot lines are constantly unfolding as factions are created and feuds ignite. Disagreements are a huge impetus for new storylines: friends turn on each other, teams break up, and chairs are thrown. Most commonly, the motives for the breakups are jealousy or ego. Sometimes there is no motive at all; it just happens. Unlike the WWE, though, the disagreement between Paul and Barnabas is not manufactured or lacking motivation. The conflict between Paul and Barnabas is personal, complex, and theologically significant. They are not splitting on a whim, and they do not take this decision lightly. Before examining aspects of the rift, it is first important to note how serious the conflict is. New Testament scholar and professor Darrell L. Bock notes:

> The term (*paroxysmos*), when used negatively, describes anger, irritation, or exasperation in a disagreement. . . . In Heb 10:24 it is used positively of stimulating or stirring someone to love, but it is also used of God's wrath

---

6. Bell, *Biblical Models of Handling Conflict*, 86.

7. Acts 15:12. All Bible quotations are from the New International Version (NIV), unless otherwise indicated.

and of how Paul was provoked at seeing idols. The uses for God's wrath show how strong in force the term can be—this is a major disagreement.[8]

Pastor R. Kent Hughes agrees with Bock's conclusion about the seriousness of the disagreement and colorfully adds, "This was not a mild gentleman's disagreement but an intense and passionate conflict!"[9] Another New Testament scholar, Craig S. Keener, also affirms that this was an emotionally charged conflict.[10] It cannot be stated enough how deeply rooted and important this conflict was. A dean of pastors, Lloyd J. Ogilvie, further explains how determined both men were in their positions:

> The Scripture is very pointed in the Greek and our English translation, telling us *"Barnabas was determined to take with him John called Mark"* (v.37). The Greek word for "determined" is from *boulomai*, meaning to be minded with strong purpose. This is the same root we noted in chapter 2 of Acts for the immutable, irrevocable purpose of God. Barnabas was intractable in his position. Paul was equally strong-minded. He did not want a missionary drop-out again![11]

Through these analyses, one can see how significant and complex this conflict is. One also knows the result of the conflict: a separation. Now we examine what caused the conflict.

Who Broke Up the Beatles?

The Beatles are one of the greatest rock groups—if not *the* greatest rock group—of all time. If you asked the average person to explain in one word why this iconic band broke up, they would say, "Yoko." For years, Yoko Ono has been vilified and blamed by fans as the reason why the Beatles broke up. From the very beginning of her relationship with John Lennon, she was treated with contempt, insulted with racial slurs, and threatened physically.[12] There was also clear tension between Ono and the other members of the band when Lennon brought her in as a collaborator, so the perception that Ono's presence led to the dissolution of the iconic band seems plausible.

The surface conclusion, however, is not the most accurate one. In an interview with Sir David Frost, Sir Paul McCartney said, "She [Yoko Ono] certainly didn't break the group up. The group was breaking up and I think she attracted John so much to another way of life that he went on to, very

---

8. Bock, *Acts*, 519.
9. Hughes, *Acts*, 202.
10. Keener, *Acts*, 114.
11. Ogilvie, *Acts*, 237.
12. Gilmore, "Why the Beatles Broke Up."

successfully, add a sort of second part to his career, writing things like 'Imagine' and 'Give Peace a Chance.' I don't think he would have done that without Yoko."[13] Furthermore, if one takes the time to look at the bigger picture, different reasons arise and become clearer. In an article in *Rolling Stone*, Mikal Gilmore lists other causes for the separation. For example, the partnership had been fraying for a year before the breakup, and the strong friendship between Lennon and McCartney was stretched. While the two iconic singer-songwriters represent one of the greatest collaborations in rock and roll's history, they had an uneven partnership and very different writing styles.[14] As Gilmore points out, "McCartney was orderly and meticulous, and placed a high premium on craft; Lennon was unruly, less prone to lingering over a song, and despite his cocky front, less secure in his work than his writing partner."[15] Just as Ono has been wrongfully accused of breaking up the Beatles, so we believe that John Mark has borne an unfair burden as the reason why Paul and Barnabas ended their partnership.

At first glance, the conflict between Paul and Barnabas seems like a simple one. Barnabas wants John Mark to travel with them; Paul does not want him. New Testament professor Gerhard A. Krodel states, "John Mark, who had quit during their first journey and returned to Jerusalem, became the bone of contention."[16] One of the leading scholars of the previous generation, C. K. Barrett, singles out John Mark as the cause of the separation, arguing that Luke "leaves no doubt about the connection between the quarrel [over John Mark] and the separation, and the importance of the result. No other cause is given for the separation."[17] Likewise, another Bible scholar, David G. Peterson, concurs that the split revolved around John Mark.[18] Through this overview it is easy to see how scholars commonly believe that John Mark was the reason that Paul and Barnabas went their separate ways. In more modern parlance, John Mark is the Yoko Ono of ancient apostles; it is he who notoriously breaks up the band.

As mentioned above, there is clear tension between Paul and Barnabas over John Mark, just like with Lennon, McCartney, and Ono. But we believe there is much more simmering under the surface. When one looks deeper, one sees that there are differences in priority, personality, and sense of calling. We will first look at Paul and then examine Barnabas.

13. "Paul McCartney: Still Prancing."
14. Gilmore, "Why the Beatles Broke Up."
15. Ibid.
16. Krodel, *Acts*, 394.
17. Barrett, *Acts 15–28*, 755–56.
18. Peterson, *Acts of the Apostles*, 448.

Paul: Let It Be

Paul is very clear about his sense of calling. In Eph 3:8–9 he states, "Although I am less than the least of all the Lord's people, this grace was given me: to preach to the Gentiles the boundless riches of Christ, and to make plain to everyone the administration of this mystery, which for ages past was kept hidden in God, who created all things." Paul is trying to share the gospel with *everyone*, and such an ambitious goal requires constant movement. William Barclay observes that Paul is a man of action who never seems to stay in one place.[19] He is dedicated to his mission, and he will not allow anything or anyone to deter him from it.

Philippians 3:13–14 paints a clear picture of Paul's focus and determination to reach his goal: "Brothers and sisters, I do not consider myself yet to have taken hold of it [my goal]. But one thing I do: Forgetting what is behind and straining toward what is ahead, I press on toward the goal to win the prize for which God has called me heavenward in Christ Jesus." Professor Stephen E. Fowl notes that in contrasting "Paul's current situation and where he plans to end up . . . he show[s] how it [striving for the goal] directs his current ways of thinking and acting."[20] Well-known New Testament scholar Gordon D. Fee calls attention to the importance of Paul's emphasis on "'not being there yet' and on his straining every nerve 'to get there.'"[21] By highlighting these words, Paul is also stressing the importance of perseverance, and for Paul, the prize "belongs only to those who persevere."[22] Therefore, from this passage and overview, one can see that Paul does not want anyone or anything to distract him from accomplishing what God has laid before him. Not only is he determined to persist and strive to accomplish his goal, he wants everyone else to persevere alongside him.

Before one judges Paul too harshly and labels him as someone who is too strict and unforgiving, one must remember that his missionary calling is a battle. For example, in 1 Tim 6:12, he tells Timothy, "Fight the good fight of the faith." And in 2 Tim 4:7, Paul describes himself as having "fought the good fight." Not only is fighting part of Paul's mentality, but so is a sense of duty, courage, loyalty, and willingness to face danger for the sake of Jesus Christ. Therefore, his emphasis on perseverance and a single-minded pursuit aligns with a battle mentality, and loyalty becomes paramount for accomplishing the tasks at hand. If Paul cannot trust his ministry partners

---

19. Barclay, *Acts of the Apostles*, 138.
20. Fowl, *Philippians*, 161.
21. Fee, *Paul's Letters to the Philippians*, 341.
22. Ibid., 345.

implicitly, then he does not want them travel with him. Anyone who has ever been betrayed by a person they previously trusted understands the time and energy it takes to engage the risk and offer a second chance. In a battle, that calculated risk often does not carry enough reward, especially if the time and energy needed to reestablish trust with someone diverts one from accomplishing the task at hand. Peterson further explains:

> Sometimes disagreements among Christians seem to be intractable because they arise from differences of experience, insight, or character. In this case the partners disagreed about the wisdom of taking a colleague on a long and arduous journey, with a small team requiring unanimity, trust, and mutual support, when the person himself had previously proved to be unreliable in the course of a similar undertaking. Marshall describes it as "a classic example of the perpetual problem of whether to place the interests of the individual or of the work as a whole first, and there is no rule of thumb in dealing with it."[23]

For Paul, the decision was to keep the work as a whole at the forefront, which is consistent with his character, passion, and drive. Paul is wholeheartedly committed to fulfilling his calling, and he needs all his time and energy to be focused on accomplishing his goals.

Not only does Paul's personality and sense of calling affect his reaction to John Mark's desertion, but so does the New Testament context. David E. Frederickson studies ancient philosophers and notes that according to scholars like Cicero and Plutarch, risking danger is necessary for the sake of friendship. Plutarch and Diogenes Laertius also state that a willingness to suffer and die is the ultimate demonstration of friendship. The one caveat, though, was that if you suffered and died for someone, that person must be good and virtuous.[24] Paul was dedicated to his mission and to his missionary partners. Yet in ancient eyes, John Mark did not demonstrate that same level of commitment. By abandoning Paul and walking away from their friendship, John Mark is essentially saying that Paul is not good and virtuous; he is not worth suffering and dying for. For a man who has worked tirelessly to change his reputation after his conversion from Saul to Paul, this nonverbal message would be a stunning blow.

The contextual insult to his character may have been compounded by Paul's relationship with Gamaliel. Gamaliel was an honored *rabban* who was one of the most celebrated teachers of his day. He was one of the first to receive the title *rabban*, which means "our great one." This title is more

---

23. Peterson, *Acts of the Apostles*, 447–48.
24. Frederickson, "Paul, Hardships, and Suffering," 178.

lofty than "rabbi," which means "my great one."[25] Joseph Trafton also notes, "Later Jewish tradition said of him, 'From the time that Rabban Gamaliel died, respect for the Torah ceased, and purity and abstinence died at the same time.'"[26] From these descriptions, one can deduce that Gamaliel was a person of character, and people followed his wisdom, example, and advice. In his testimony in Acts 22:3, Paul states that he studied under Gamaliel. Therefore, one cannot help but wonder if Paul felt that he needed to follow his former teacher's example and be a person who others wanted to follow. The specialist in rabbinic traditions, David Instone-Brewer, explains how he cannot think of any example in early sources that records a disciple who abandoned or deserted his rabbi. He further expounds by saying, "However, it isn't the kind of thing you'd expect to have recorded, because most of the stuff about rabbis is similar to hagiography in the Christian world—i.e., it is honorific and sometimes unbelievably so, and it would not add honour to a rabbi's memory to have it recorded that a disciple left."[27] It is difficult to determine if Paul learned a standard policy regarding a disciple's abandonment. It is equally difficult to conclude authoritatively if Paul's lack of patience with John Mark was normative or not. Yet it is entirely possible that being steeped in a tradition of loyalty and faithfulness and being mentored by a great *rabban* affected how he dealt with desertion.

From descriptions of himself and how others have described him, one can see that Paul is fully committed to spreading the gospel. He has a clear sense of call, is single-minded in reaching his goal, and is determined to fight a good fight. Due to the cultural influences of the time and his tutelage under Gamaliel, one also sees how Paul values trust and loyalty, and he strives to be a person who inspires trust and loyalty in others. All these factors combined to lead to Paul's one strike rule when it comes to desertion. When John Mark walked away in Pamphylia, he not only walked away from Paul and Barnabas, but in Paul's eyes, he also walked away from God. Such an action cannot be tolerated, and such a man does not create an effective missionary partner or deserve a second chance.

Barnabas: Give Peace a Chance

Barnabas demonstrates a different perspective and sense of calling. While he is equally passionate and committed, his ardor manifests differently than Paul's. Acts 4:36 says that Barnabas is named Joseph, and he is a Levite from

25. Trafton, "Gamaliel," 316.
26. Ibid.
27. David Instone-Brewer, personal communication, May 18, 2017.

Cyprus. The apostles called him Barnabas, though, which means "son of encouragement." His new name speaks to his gift of encouragement, and the same verse also illustrates his generosity, as he sold a field he owned and brought the money to the apostles. He is also described in Acts 11:24 as "a good man, full of the Holy Spirit and faith."[28]

When trying to understand Barnabas's character, mission, and perspective, one should not gloss over the fact that he is a Levite. David A. deSilva, a specialist in New Testament social realities, explains how a person's identity, self-perception, and expectations all come from their lineage and from the reputation of their ancestors.[29] While Levites at this time were relatively inactive and indistinguishable,[30] identifying Barnabas as a Levite connects him to certain expectations. One example comes from the book of Numbers. Numbers 18:1 records, "The Lord said to Aaron, 'You, your sons and your family are to bear the responsibility for offenses connected with the sanctuary, and you and your sons alone are to bear the responsibility for offenses connected with the priesthood.'" Thus, if Barnabas is identified as part of the lineage of Aaron, then he is also connected to the expectation of bearing responsibility for others' offenses against God. Furthermore, if Barnabas sees the work he and Paul are doing as dedicated to God, then he would be even more inclined to intercede on behalf of John Mark. Just as the Levites were accountable for the offenses committed by others, so Barnabas might feel responsible for the offense committed by John Mark. While we do not know the exact extent of Barnabas's connection to Levite responsibilities, the Levite lineage cannot be ignored as a potential contributing factor when considering Barnabas's perspective in handling John Mark.

As mentioned earlier, Scripture does not record why John Mark left Paul and Barnabas in Pamphylia. Hughes suggests, "Most likely it was a combination of things—the realities of missionary life with its ongoing conflict and discomforts, sickness in Pamphylia, Paul's growing ascendancy over Barnabas, a pampered upbringing, homesickness. Whatever the reason, Paul considered it desertion!"[31] But Barnabas seems to have considered it something else. Since Acts does not record Barnabas's motivations for wanting John Mark to travel with them, New Testament and Greek professor William J. Larkin offers some potential reasons. Perhaps Barnabas is demonstrating sympathy or has more grace.[32] Another possibility men-

---

28. Acts 11:24.
29. DeSilva, *Honor, Patronage, Kinship, and Purity*, 158.
30. Ellison, "Levite," 467.
31. Hughes, *Acts*, 202.
32. Larkin, *Acts*, 230–31.

tioned above is his sense of duty as a member of the Levite lineage. It is also possible that Barnabas was more strongly inclined to take a risk on John Mark due to the fact that they are biologically related.[33]

Colossians 4:10 notes that Barnabas and John Mark are cousins, and family connections in second-temple Judaism and early Christianity cannot be underestimated. "Family" often not only meant immediate family but rather referred to kin-based groups that had more extensive family connections. According to ancient Israel scholar, Leo G. Perdue, such kin-based groups consisted "of two or three families living in a residential complex where two or three houses were connected together."[34] Roland da Vaux, the earliest student of Israel's social realities, adds that "the members of the family worked together and cultivated a sense of obligation to help and protect one another."[35]

This family connection would have cultivated a deeper sense of obligation in Barnabas to help John Mark than it would have in Paul. DeSilva supplements, "Where kin understood themselves to be in cooperation with one another—partners in a common quest to advance the family's honor and its components, to advance one another's interests—there could be trust, a commodity rarely extended to those outside of one's family."[36] While Paul needs John Mark to earn his trust, Barnabas already has trust established through family ties. Therefore, it is not as easy for Barnabas to walk away from John Mark as it is for Paul, especially since John Mark trusts Barnabas. Furthermore, there is a deeply rooted family obligation to help John Mark become a part of the mission since relatives were supposed to work together to advance the family. This issue is further complicated by the fact that this request occurs in Jerusalem, which is John Mark's hometown and where there are other family members present, adding to the pressure of the request.

Whether one is familiar with or is part of the Jewish tradition or not, anyone who has ever had a request from a family member understands the complexities of Barnabas's situation. Chan shares an example from his ministry:

> I am an only child, and while I have a small biological family, I have a lot of "aunts" who helped raise me. One "aunt" is Charlotte. She was there the day I was born, and she has supported me throughout my life. One day, she called to ask me to

33. Ibid.
34. Perdue, "Israelite and Early Jewish Family," 166.
35. Da Vaux, *Ancient Israel*, 21.
36. DeSilva, *Honor, Patronage, Kinship, and Purity*, 168.

baptize her granddaughter. I had grown up with her son, and I knew that he had not attended church regularly in years. Yet Charlotte's son thought it would be special for his old friend to baptize his daughter. Special, indeed, but also complicated. As a Baptist pastor, I was not supposed to officiate infant baptisms. The family did not know how complex and loaded their request was; all they knew was that if I said "no," a person they knew and loved was rejecting them. So, one Sunday morning, I found myself sprinkling a baby.

Families sometimes ask a lot, and they often do not fully understand what they are asking. Whether they are intentionally leveraging relationships and connections or not, family pressure was just as real for Barnabas as it is today.

The importance of preserving family connections is well established in this context, but it is not the only influence on Barnabas's decision to give John Mark a second chance. Perhaps another deciding factor was that Barnabas considers this an opportunity to encourage one who had fallen away. He is willing to take John Mark along with them and spend time with him day after day. Luke Timothy Johnson, a professor of New Testament, observes, "The verb *symparalamban* ('to take along with,' see 3 Macc 1:1) is the same as used for John-Mark's initial recruitment in 12:24. Paul uses it himself for his taking Titus with him to Jerusalem (Gal 2:1)."[37] Just as Paul was willing to guide, mentor, and train Titus, so Barnabas is willing to guide, mentor, and train John Mark, despite John Mark's previous failure. F. F. Bruce agrees that Barnabas "probably discerned promising qualities in his young cousin which could be developed under his care rather than under Paul's."[38]

By examining how Barnabas is described, and by considering the context of the time, one gleans a better understanding of why Barnabas supported John Mark. His lineage as a Levite possibly led him to bear responsibility for John Mark's offenses, and their family connection contributed to a greater tolerance for mistakes. Barnabas is a man who is oriented toward encouragement, so working with John Mark allows him to live fully into his mission and calling. Therefore, Barnabas decides to give John Mark another chance. When John Mark walked away in Pamphylia, he never fully walked away from Paul and Barnabas because he was still connected through biological family ties and through the family of God. In Barnabas's eyes, he is still a part of their family and their mission. Such an action can be forgiven,

---

37. Johnson, *Acts of the Apostles*, 282.
38. Bruce, *Book of the Acts*, 301–2.

and such a man can be encouraged and redeemed to become an effective missionary partner.

Clearing John Mark's Name

Paul was called to reach new people; Barnabas was called to encourage, equip, mentor, and atone for others. Paul wants to continue moving forward to accomplish his calling, but Barnabas insists on giving John Mark a second chance in order to fulfill his own calling. With these different goals, their conflict is not merely over whether John Mark should join them on their mission or not. Rather, the conflict is over what their mission is. Is it to travel most effectively, encouraging the current churches and then moving to new areas? Or is it to work with this one leader, developing *him* to help encourage current churches and then move to new areas?

Mentoring and training people is an investment. Lauren shares an example from when she was recently helping her twin sister Lindsey prepare the baby's room for her soon-to-arrive second child:

> As we were moving books and furniture, my three-year-old niece (interestingly, she is also named Charlotte) wanted to help. Charlotte was so excited to help her mom and her baby brother that she wanted to be as involved as possible. So I sprayed the bookshelf and Charlotte "dusted" it—and then I had to dust it after her. And Charlotte carried one book at a time from one room to another—and then Lindsey and I had to carry some books back to the first room. But we knew that teaching Charlotte how to help, and seeing the joy on her face as she sweated and struggled to carry books for "baby brother" was worth the slower pace. Both of us invested in the relationship and in the adorableness rather than focusing solely on completing the room preparations.

Whether one is training a three-year-old or an adult, it takes time. However, many pastors still choose to develop new leaders. While it takes more time in the short run, training and empowering others often pays off in the long run. Yet investing in another person often means completing an activity at a slower pace. Herein lies another conflict. As mentioned earlier, Paul is resolutely focused on sharing the gospel with everyone while Barnabas is more invested in developing John Mark. Krodel postulates that Barnabas argued that "people are at least as important, if not more, than the tasks that have to be performed."[39] The conflict between Paul and Barnabas, therefore, is not truly about John Mark. It is about focus and function. It is about whether they are called to accomplish the task at hand or whether they are called to delay accomplishing the task in favor of training others.

These different priorities reflect the tension in Acts, but this is not the only place where there is discord between Paul and Barnabas. There is also some stress recorded in Galatians. Galatians 2:11–13 hints at a previous problem that might have contributed to the breach. In this passage, Paul writes, "When Cephas came to Antioch, I opposed him to his face, because he stood condemned. For before certain men came from James, he used to eat with the Gentiles. But when they arrived, he began to draw back and separate himself from the Gentiles because he was afraid of those who belonged to the circumcision group. The other Jews joined him in his hypocrisy, so that by their hypocrisy even Barnabas was led astray." While many scholars have tried to connect the dispute in Galatians with the separation in Acts, there is no mention of John Mark in the Galatians account. This has led other scholars to conclude that these were probably separate arguments, which further mitigates John Mark's blame.

Peterson notes, "If the incident described in Galatians 2 occurred before the Jerusalem Council, as seems most likely . . . these disagreements were separated by some time and were over different matters."[40] Barrett agrees that this passage lays a different foundation of controversy than what happened in Acts and states, "When Peter withdrew from table fellowship with Gentile Christians in Antioch even Barnabas was carried away by his hypocrisy, and though only Peter is addressed in the words quoted in Gal 2.14–18(21) they would apply equally to Barnabas. Nothing is said here about [John] Mark."[41] William H. Willimon also points out that Paul himself emphasizes that the disagreement regards hypocrisy and a doctrinal matter.[42] Scot McKnight agrees that Paul sees the scene as "theologically wrong and dangerous."[43] The argument in Galatians was a theological issue that was unrelated to John Mark's desertion. Therefore, disagreement recorded in Galatians seems to be a separate source of friction between Paul and Barnabas and has absolutely nothing to do with John Mark.

Despite strong research by scholars such as Peterson, Barrett, Willimon, and McKnight, the connection between the confrontation in Galatians

---

39. Krodel, *Acts*, 294–95.
40. Peterson, *Acts of the Apostles*, 448.
41. Barrett, *Acts 15–28*, 757.
42. Willimon, *Acts*, 133.
43. McKnight, *Galatians*, 99.

and the separation in Acts is still unclear. By noting the differences in the two conflicts, it opens the possibility that there was more tension brewing before Barnabas ever suggested that John Mark rejoin them. If there was previous friction, and since John Mark was not mentioned in the Galatians account, then he can hardly be held responsible for rifts that he was never around to cause. Just as Yoko Ono was revealed to not be the true cause of the Beatles' breakup, so John Mark is vindicated as the sole cause of Paul and Barnabas's separation.

Who Was Right?

When studying the perspectives of both Paul and Barnabas, one can see that both men are equally determined to live out their callings in the way they feel called, and there does not seem to be any way to resolve these very different views and methods. This is not to say that either person is wrong. While Paul and Barnabas are different people with diverse temperaments, foci, and skill sets, there is no place in Scripture where it says that one person's mission is superior to the other. Paul and Barnabas worked well as a team because their different temperaments, foci, and skill sets complemented each other. In an analysis of Chrysostom, William Kurz points out how both Paul and Barnabas offer positive attributes from their disparate personalities: "Chrysostom understands this parting as due to complementary differences in personality and as resulting in a greater good. . . . Luke has already described the apostles' character to us, showing that one [Barnabas] was more tender and forgiving than the other [Paul] more strict and severe. For the gifts bestowed on them were different. That this is itself a gift is clear."[44]

As observed by Chrysostom, it is important to remember that the different personalities and perspectives are gifts. Both are needed for the kingdom. Yet this also means that the goals that aligned with these missionaries' distinct gifts were incompatible. In this case, Paul and Barnabas agree to disagree and part ways, and God blesses their efforts. In the end, they are both proven correct in their decision to separate.[45] Paul starts a successful

44. Kurz, *Acts of the Apostles*, 248.

45. "Luke does not pass judgment on either party, but indicates that good came out of the separation, because two mission teams were formed." (Peterson, *Acts of the Apostles*, 448). Cf. Bruce, *Book of the Acts*, 301; Fernando, *Acts*, 431. However, some commentators have seen Luke as siding with Paul. Cara, "Ambiguous Characterization," argues that Acts is "pro-Paul." Johnson, *Acts of the Apostles*, 282, concurs, "Luke obviously shares Paul's hard judgment on the nature of the original departure, since *touton* ('this one') holds a place of emphasis at the end of the Greek sentence. The verb,

second missionary journey, and Barnabas is successful in mentoring John Mark until John Mark becomes an effective apostle. Under Barnabas's guidance, John Mark's "latent qualities reached full maturity and were appreciated in due course by Paul himself."[46] One sees this appreciation in 2 Tim 4:11 when Paul writes, "Get [John] Mark and bring him with you, because he is helpful to me in my ministry." Paul also sends greetings from John Mark in Col 4:10, and he again sends greetings from John Mark in Phlm 24, as he calls him a "fellow worker."

In the conflict between Paul and Barnabas, there was no "winner," and there was no "right way" of doing things. Both men were equally gifted, yet gifted in different ways. Both men were equally called and equipped by the Holy Spirit, yet they followed the Spirit in different ways. Although they separated, the conflict was still managed, and the kingdom was expanded.

Learning from Ancient Conflict Management

When managing conflict, Fisher and Ury would recommend that when framing the disagreement, the people should be separate from the problem.[47] Charles H. Cosgrove and Dennis D. Hatfield would suggest using family systems theory as a framework for understanding the disagreement, identifying who is in a parent role and who is in a child role.[48] Karl A. Slaikeu would offer that having an extra voice would be helpful.[49] And Douglas Stone, Bruce Patton, and Sheila Heen would recommend discovering a third story.[50] But none of these options are the ones chosen by Paul and Barnabas. Acts 15:36–41 demonstrates a different model of conflict management, which is one of healthy separation. In other words, they "agree to disagree," and they go their individual ways.

In our culture today, "agree to disagree" is often seen as throwing in the towel. When those engaged in conflict reach the point where their voices are

---

aphistemi, furthermore, has the clear sense of 'apostasy' in the present context (compare Acts 5:37–38). Codex D expands the sentence and puts Paul's sentiments in indirect discourse. Its addition of 'work for which they had been sent' probably derives from 14:26, but represents a good sense of the basis for Paul's position: the mission was not a matter of human whim but of divine commission; commitment to it was therefore not a matter of personal taste (see 1 Cor 9:16–18)." Krodel, *Acts*, 295, argues that Acts sides with Paul by the virtue of writing Barnabas out of the text.

46. Bruce, *Book of the Acts*, 301–2.
47. Fisher, Ury, and Patton, *Getting to Yes*, 17–39.
48. Cosgrove and Hatfield, *Church Conflict*, 46–47.
49. Slaikeu, *When Push Comes to Shove*, 23–51.
50. Stone, Patton, and Heen, *Difficult Conversations*, 233–34.

hoarse from yelling and their brains are mushy from analytic gymnastics, when they cannot dialogue anymore, they "agree to disagree." This is often a way of leaving the conflict with a tentative truce, but both parties often realize that the conflict is still unresolved. Yet this is not in the case for Paul and Barnabas. When they "agree to disagree," they disagree about the best way to accomplish the mission that God has laid before them, but they still agree on the primacy of God's mission and on following the Holy Spirit. God is always the focus, and even though they separate, that does not mean that the conflict is unmanaged, even though there is still a note of uncertainty.

Conflict management theories are wonderful and supremely helpful, but they do not always lead to perfectly understandable conclusions. The text does not explain if Paul and Barnabas planned on working together again in the future, nor does it explicitly state that they did not have such a hope. The later affirmations of and greetings from John Mark points to some sort of acknowledgement on Paul's part that he was too quick to dismiss John Mark, although there is no explanation as to what caused his change of thinking. Scripture also does not overtly explain any type of reconciliation process between Paul and Barnabas. However, John Mark's eventual restoration offers a hope for reconciliation in the midst of separation, a powerful reassurance for anyone who has had to abandon an old path without a new, clear path laid before them. Paul and Barnabas did not know what the future would hold, but they faithfully followed God despite the uncertainty. They were willing to make a difficult decision, leaving a successful partnership with potentially unresolved issues, and submit to the Holy Spirit. In doing so, their division led to a multiplication as more people were reached with the good news of Jesus Christ.

While separation is not always the best course of action, and it should rarely be the first choice, it is still a viable option. Trusting and seeking the Lord should be at its core, and if God is at work, great things can happen. Gangel draws attention to the continued work of the Holy Spirit, even after the separation: "Notice Paul does not intend a second journey for missionary evangelism, though that is precisely what God will do with this proposed trip. His initial motivation, however, was just to go back to towns where they had been to check on the believers and *encourage* [emphasis added] them."[51] The emphasis on encouragement is perhaps why Paul wanted to partner with Barnabas. However, after they agree to disagree, an entirely new mission is launched. With this second mission, Paul and Barnabas focus on different geographical areas. This means that even more people are reached, which is in alignment with Paul's personal mission from Eph 3. As Bock

---

51. Gangel, *Acts*, 254.

points out, "God will do far more than Paul plans."[52] Through Barnabas's mentoring of John Mark and through Paul's partnering with different co-workers, new leaders are developed and encouraged. This is in alignment with Barnabas's personal mission, as alluded to through his nickname in Acts 4. Through these new missions, both Paul and Barnabas are able to honor their callings and convictions, and both men accomplish more than the original partnership planned.

Paul and Barnabas were two very different people who were equally committed to serving God and advancing his kingdom. They offered different perspectives, skill sets, temperaments, and passions. They disagreed over whether or not they should give John Mark a second chance, and they disagreed over table fellowship in Galatians. While they experienced conflict, as all humans do, they never surrendered the work of God. Just as Lennon and McCartney continued to write music, so Paul and Barnabas continued to seek God and follow the calling he had placed before them. Due to their desire to be led by the Holy Spirit, God honored their work, even in the midst of division. When Paul and Barnabas chose the conflict management model of healthy separation, God took a difficult situation and used the division to multiply the positive impact.

Healthy separation is not the answer for every trying situation. It requires humility and a deep reliance on the guidance of the Holy Spirit. While Acts 15 does not illuminate Paul's or Barnabas's thought process, Paul later demonstrates how he exercises wisdom in whether to accept this solution or not. After all, the situation in Acts is not the only time when one reads of a separation associated with Paul. A second split involves Philemon and Onesimus, and while Paul is not overtly connected to Onesimus's departure, he is intimately involved in the mediation process. The separation between Philemon and Onesimus is less mutual than Paul's and Barnabas's but is no less complicated. Through this interaction, one sees yet another conflict management model chosen by Paul.

Bibliography

Barclay, William. *Acts of the Apostles*. The New Daily Study Bible. Louisville: Westminster John Knox, 2003.

Barrett, C. K. *Acts 15-28*. International Critical Commentary. Edinburgh: T&T Clark, 1998.

Bell, Roy D. *Biblical Models of Handling Conflict*. Vancouver, BC: Regent College Publishing, 1987.

---

52. Bock, *Acts*, 519.

Bock, Darrell L. *Acts*. Baker Exegetical Commentary on the New Testament. Grand Rapids: Baker Academic, 2007.

Bruce, F. F. *The Book of the Acts*. Rev. ed. The New International Commentary on the New Testament. Grand Rapids: Eerdmans, 1988.

Cara, Robert James. "The Ambiguous Characterization of Barnabas in Acts 15:36–41." PhD diss., Westminster Theological Seminary, 2001.

Cosgrove, Charles H., and Dennis D. Hatfield. *Church Conflict: The Hidden Systems Behind the Fights*. Nashville: Abingdon, 1994.

Da Vaux, Roland. *Ancient Israel: Its Life and Institutions*. Translated by John McHugh. New York: McGraw-Hill, 1961.

DeSilva, David A. *Honor, Patronage, Kinship, and Purity: Unlocking New Testament Culture*. Downers Grove, IL: InterVarsity, 2000.

Ellison, Henry Leopold. "Levite." In vol. 2 of *New International Dictionary of New Testament Theology*, edited by Colin Brown, 467–68. Grand Rapids: Zondervan, 1976.

Fee, Gordon D. *Paul's Letters to the Philippians*. The New International Commentary on the New Testament. Grand Rapids: Eerdmans, 1995.

Fernando, Ajith. *Acts*. NIV Application Commentary. Grand Rapids: Zondervan, 1998.

Fisher, Roger, William Ury, and Bruce Patton. *Getting to Yes: Negotiating Agreement Without Giving In*. 2nd ed. New York: Penguin, 1991.

Fowl, Stephen E. *Philippians*. Grand Rapids: Eerdmans, 2005.

Frederickson, David E. "Paul, Hardships, and Suffering." In *Paul in the Greco-Roman World: A Handbook*, edited by J. Paul Sampley, 172–97. Harrisburg, PA: Trinity Press International, 2003.

Gangel, Kenneth O. *Acts*. Holman New Testament Commentary. Nashville: Holman Reference, 1998.

Gilmore, Mikal. "Why the Beatles Broke Up. *Rolling Stone*. http://www.rollingstone.com/music/news/why-the-beatles-broke-up-20090903.

Hughes, R. Kent. *Acts: The Church Afire*. Preaching the Word. Wheaton: Crossway, 1996.

Johnson, Luke Timothy. *The Acts of the Apostles*. Sacra Pagina. Collegeville, MN: Liturgical, 1992.

Keener, Craig S. *Acts: An Exegetical Commentary*. Vol. 3, *15:1—23:35*. Grand Rapids: Baker Academic, 2014.

Krodel, Gerhard A. *Acts*. Augsburg Commentary on the New Testament. Minneapolis: Augsburg, 1986.

Kurz, William S. *Acts of the Apostles*. Catholic Commentary on Sacred Scripture. Grand Rapids: Baker Academic, 2013.

Larkin, William J., Jr. *Acts*. The IVP New Testament Commentary Series. Downers Grove: InterVarsity, 1995.

MacArthur, John F. *Acts 13–28*. The MacArthur New Testament Commentary. Chicago: Moody, 1996.

McKnight, Scot. *Galatians*. The NIV Application Commentary. Grand Rapids: Zondervan, 1995.

Ogilvie, Lloyd J. *Acts*. Mastering the New Testament. Dallas: Word Publishing, 1983.

"Paul McCartney: 'Still Prancing.'" *Aljazeera*, Nov. 10, 2012. http://www.aljazeera.com/programmes/frostinterview/2012/11/2012113843381122420.html.

Perdue, Leo G. "The Israelite and Early Jewish Family: Summary and Conclusions." In *Families in Ancient Israel*, edited by Leo G. Perdue, Joseph Blenkinsopp, John J. Collins, and Carol Meyers, 163–222. Louisville: Westminster John Knox, 1997.

Peterson, David G. *The Acts of the Apostles*. Pillar New Testament Commentary. Grand Rapids: Eerdmans, 2009.

Phillips, John. *Exploring Acts: An Expository Commentary*. The John Phillips Commentary Series. Grand Rapids: Kregel, 2001.

Shenk, Joshua Wolf. "The Power of Two." *The Atlantic*, July/August 2014. https://www.theatlantic.com/magazine/archive/2014/07/the-power-of-two/372289/.

Slaikeu, Karl A. *When Push Comes to Shove: A Practical Guide to Mediating Disputes*. 1st ed. Jossey-Bass Conflict Resolution Series. San Francisco: Jossey-Bass, 1996.

State Historical Society of North Dakota. "Corps of Discovery—Did Meriwether Lewis and William Clark Get Along?" North Dakota State Government. http://history.nd.gov/exhibits/lewisclark/lcrelations.html.

Stone, Douglas, Bruce Patton, and Sheila Heen. *Difficult Conversations: How to Discuss What Matters Most*. New York: Penguin, 1999.

Trafton, Joseph. "Gamaliel." In *Mercer Dictionary of the Bible*, edited by Watson E. Mills, 316–17. Macon, GA: Mercer University Press, 1990.

Willimon, William H. *Acts*. Interpretation: A Bible Commentary for Teaching and Preaching. Atlanta: John Knox, 1988.

2

Paul Pleads with Philemon
Paul as Master Mediator

PHILEMON

By Amanda Hecht and Shawn O'Brien

In the letter to Philemon, Paul demonstrates that he was a master mediator, using skills that applied to his first century world that we can learn from even today. As we consider this slim New Testament letter, let us sit back and watch Paul, the master mediator at work.

As a mediator, Paul was well aware of the people that he was working with. He was able to identify both the personalities and the needs/concerns of Philemon (the slave master), and also of Onesimus (the runaway slave); not to mention the interests of people like Apphia, Archippus, and the others involved in this house church. Putting ourselves in the shoes of the people involved in all sides of a conflict is one way that we, as modern-day mediators, can learn from Paul.

Put yourself in Philemon's shoes. He is a prominent citizen who has become a follower of Jesus Christ through the witness of the great Apostle Paul. As part of his obedience to his new allegiance to Jesus, he has opened up his considerable estate to host a community of Christ followers in his own home, placing his home as well as his (considerable) financial resources at the disposal of the church. He is well regarded in the city and in the church. As a wealthy man, Philemon owns slaves to run his household and look after his affairs. This has not changed as a result of becoming a follower of Jesus Christ, because, like many Christians, Philemon "saw no incongruity in proclaiming simultaneously his status as a leader in the church and his identity as a slaveowner."[1] "After all, for Philemon (and Paul, and probably even Onesimus) it was impossible to imagine a slave-less society, except in a utopian dream-world where food cooked itself and doors opened of their own accord."[2] When it came to slaves, he didn't think it was a problem to own them, but he did do his best to punish them only when it was necessary, and not to be too harsh about it. He had always believed that it was a sound business practice to treat one's slaves reasonably—to feed, shelter, and clothe them well. After all, well-maintained tools work well, and ones that were neglected did not. But, despite all of the care he took with his slaves, recently one of his slaves had run away from him. Slaves did this often, so this was not the first (nor the last) time that Philemon believed he would encounter this problem. That's all it was, really. A minor problem, an annoyance, an irritation that he would have to deal with when the time came. He'd offered the normal reward for a runaway slave, and was confident that one of these days the fugitive would be spotted by someone who needed money (and who didn't?), that he would eventually locate this runaway, ironically named "Onesimus" ("Useful"[3]—ha!), and he would punish him appropriately when he returned.[4] Rumor had it, however, that Onesimus, that useless irritant, had made his way to Paul, Philemon's own mentor and teacher about Jesus Christ, that great man who had showed him how to worship Jesus as his Lord. And the people who had spotted this fugitive in Paul's company, though he was in prison, had noted that Paul had also begun to teach Onesimus about Jesus. And Onesimus himself was going about the motions, while with Paul, of also being a follower of Jesus. Philemon didn't really know what all of this meant—to have a slave who might also be someone who was a brother in Jesus. And, he might not necessarily care—a slave is a

---

1. Glancy, *Slavery in Early Christianity*, 9.

2. Barclay, "Paul, Philemon and the Dilemma," 177. As much as we would like to do so, "we must not assume that Christianity was inherently better disposed towards slaves than other earlier forms of ancient thought." Falx and Toner, *How to Manage Your Slaves*, 202.

3. Keener, *IVP Bible Background Commentary*, 645.

4. Punishment could have been anything from a beating, cutting off a limb, up to and including crucifixion, and it usually included branding or being fitted with a collar to indicate that the slave had run away. (Wright, *Paul and the Faithfulness*, 19; Falx and Toner, *How to Manage Your Slaves*, 110–11; Glancy, *Slavery in Early Christianity*, 12–13).

slave, after all, and would be treated as he had always treated them. He did not consider himself to be an unjust or brutal master. But, the rumors continued that people had seen Onesimus (why had they not caught him and brought him back, he did not know) journeying back to Philemon's house, with a letter from Paul in his possession. What would the great (though sadly imprisoned, he must remember to continue to send supplies to him) Paul have written him about? And why would this slave, who had behaved so shamefully, be carrying this letter to him? And, what would this mean, not just for Onesimus himself, but for the other slaves in the house? Would they get some kind of lofty ideas above their station from this troublemaker Onesimus?

Onesimus

Put yourself in Onesimus' shoes. Being a slave defined everything in his life. A slave-owner had complete control over a slave's body, and could do anything with it. Anything. Everything in a slave's life depends on the master and what kind of man he is. And, as much as his friend Paul had praised Philemon, calling him a "fellow-worker" and describing him as a man of faith in the Lord Jesus, who loves the saints in his church, even calling Philemon a man of love, the fact is that you don't run away from a master who is good and kind and loving all of the time. Onesimus knew Philemon as a slave-master. He had heard his cruel words, felt the harsh lash of his tongue and the sting of the whip. Yes, Philemon was a good man, a man who was a follower of Jesus and who even hosted the gathering of the saints in his house. But, he was still a slave-owner who held the lives of other humans in his hand and who profited from their unpaid work. Philemon had both gone to slave markets to purchase a human being who had been stripped naked for all to examine, with a list of their characteristics and work habits hung around their necks, and bartered money for their purchase; and at times had taken his own slaves to this same market, treating them to this demeaning and soul-harrowing experience. After Onesimus ran away from Philemon, he found himself thrown together with Paul, and Paul was important in the Christian movement. Even though he was in prison, Paul had things that needed doing. Maybe Onesimus was not useful to Philemon, but after spending time with Paul and learning about Jesus, he endeavored to be very useful to Paul. He helped Paul in caring for his needs while in bondage, and maybe even advanced to helping Paul with his ministry, sharing the good news of Jesus Christ with others just as Paul had instructed and shared this good news with him.

As much as this was a boon for Onesimus, the slave, to be an assistant to the Apostle Paul, one problem remained. He was still at odds with the man that he had run away from. And Paul didn't want to let that stand. And so, he had written a letter, and had instructed Onesimus to carry this letter back to the lion's den of his old household, the place where he had run away from and was trying his best to forget. What would Philemon do when he heard this letter read out loud? What about Apphia and Archippus? What about the other slaves, who would also be listening? Did Onesimus stand a chance of being forgiven by Philemon, let alone being received as if he were a brother of his owner, Philemon?

Paul

Put yourself in Paul's shoes. While he is in prison, Paul encounters (and converts and teaches) a slave named Onesimus (a common slave name, which roughly translates as "Mr. Useful."[5]) Although the overall story of events that led Paul and Onesimus to connect with one another is debated,[6] a plain reading leads us to believe that Onesimus was afraid to return to Philemon's household. The most likely scenario is that he fears to return to Philemon because he is a runaway slave who seems to have harmed Philemon in some way (v. 18).[7] Paul is not dealing in a faceless, nameless debate about the place of slaves in the church of Jesus Christ, or how a slave-master should relate to his/her slaves; this is the real life of a man named Onesimus. How would Paul reconcile this wronged and powerful man who was on the right side of the law, and this trembling, uncertain, newly-minted-Christian slave?

Paul's solution to this messy, real-life interpersonal conflict sends Onesimus back to Philemon's household, carrying a letter from the apostle himself, expressing his desire for Philemon to be reunited with Onesimus, not as a runaway slave who is bound to his master, but as a brother in the family of Jesus Christ, of which they are all a part. And that letter is, as you probably have guessed, the slim little New Testament book by the name of Philemon. Philemon is the shortest of all of Paul's letters that we have. Despite the brevity of Philemon, and the fact that it addresses such a specific and seemingly personal problem, the fact is that our ancestors in the faith of Jesus Christ saw fit to read this letter enough that it has been preserved and incorporated in our New Testament canon. If "Philemon was the only document we had

---

5. Wright, *Kingdom New Testament*, 440.
6. Bartchy, "Philemon," 306.
7. Wright, *Paul and the Faithfulness of God*, 9.

from early Christianity, we would still know that something very different was happening, different from the way the rest of the world behaved."[8] This light little letter packs a powerful punch when it comes to determining how people who love and follow Jesus Christ should live their lives, especially in the midst of conflict. Onesimus carries the letter, and either reads the letter himself or stands there as the letter is being read to the church, all the while watching Philemon to see if he will favorably receive the news in the letter that is all about him. If we think Paul is asking a lot of Philemon, it is also "a heavy thing that Paul is asking of Onesimus, just as it is a heavy thing that he is asking of Philemon."[9] Philemon's reception of this letter will determine the very fate of Onesimus himself.

That World

People in different times and places approach conflict differently.[10] It is crucial for mediators to understand their world, that is their cultural context, in order to provide solutions that will best work in the world they (and those who find themselves in conflict) inhabit; and to work within the boundaries created by this world in order to find a solution that will work in the long term for these people in this particular time and place. Understanding the time, place, and situation of the world in which the conflict occurs will enable modern-day mediators to provide a clear and focused restoration process, which Paul, the master mediator, demonstrated in his work with this church in Colossae.

Put yourself in Colossae in the first century. In order to put yourself in Paul's shoes, you would have to understand a little bit about the world that Onesimus, Philemon, and Paul inhabited. The world in which we live is not the world in which Paul (and Onesimus and Philemon) lived, wrote, and ministered. In dealing with this situation, Paul runs up against a reality present in the culture in which they walked and breathed, that of social separation on a level we would be unfamiliar with today. "Greco-Roman culture and early Judaism were deeply penetrated by layers of social status. Not only legal categories of free, freed, and slave, but also relative wealth and pursuit of honor played major roles in determining the choices available"

---

8. Ibid., 23.

9. Ibid., 33.

10. For instance, Asian, Latino, Euro-American, Midwestern, Coastal, Baptist, Anglican, etc. all approach conflict differently and each have different predetermined ideas on how to proceed in dealing with conflict.

to people in this world.[11] Honor and shame were the key pegs on which first century individuals hung their hats. People occupied varying levels social strata, which they maintained throughout their lives, and "status in the first-century Mediterranean world derived mainly from birth and was symbolled by the honor and prestige already accumulated and preserved by one's family."[12] It was paramount to a person living in the first century to defend their social status, maintaining honor and avoiding shame. Everyone knew both their own and other's social status, and so all public interactions in the first century Mediterranean society were conducted accordingly.

At the bottom of the social ladder were slaves. The status of a slave followed that of his or her owner, and thus the slave of a governor or other high-ranking citizen would have a much higher status than a slave serving on a rural farm in the far reaches of the Roman Empire. However, slaves existed outside of the honor/shame dynamic that characterized the interactions of the free. People with honor protected their honor by defending themselves from any kind of affront, physical or symbolic. However, slaves were routinely subjected to both insults and physical punishment and even random abuse from which they were not allowed to protect themselves and were expected to endure.[13] This plays itself out most especially in the fact that a slave's body was under the total control of his/her master, including sexual use of a slave (male or female) by the master or anyone the master permitted to use the slave in this way.[14] Because of this, "male slaves were considered to be without honor, and female slaves without shame."[15] Both slaves and slave-owners worshiped Jesus alongside one another, and therefore "problems emanating from the sexual . . . use of slaves are central to the understanding of slavery in the Christian era."[16] The people in our letter lived in this world in which the practice of slavery was merely a backdrop, "it was how things got done. It was the electricity of the ancient world."[17] The best evidence that we have indicates that the earliest Christians did not see owning slaves as incompatible with their Christian faith.[18]

11. Cohick, *Women in the World*, 22.
12. Malina, *New Testament World*, 90.
13. Glancy, *Slavery in Early Christianity*, 27.
14. Ibid., 9.
15. Ibid., 62.
16. Ibid., 9.
17. Wright, *Paul and the Faithfulness of God*, 32.
18. Glancy, *Slavery in Early Christianity*, 9.

Making Sense of the Letter to Philemon

If you were in Paul's shoes, and you were in this situation, and you were steeped in the history that he was steeped in, in which status, honor/shame, patronage, and slavery were all realities, you might write just this letter. Now, perhaps you are surprised that Paul didn't write another kind of letter, a letter that demanded that Philemon set Onesimus free. However, while Paul's letter to Philemon has been seen by some as a champion of slave rights, expecting that Paul was asking Philemon to free Onesimus and thus indicating an early Christian example of opposition to slavery in general;[19] a careful reading indicates that Paul stops short of telling Philemon to free Onesimus (even though this may in fact be what Paul wishes would happen). Indeed, Paul has asked Onesimus to return to the household of his enslavement, back to the one who owned him, rather than allow Onesimus to seek permanent refuge with the apostle himself. It can be difficult from where we sit in our modern world in which slavery is, while not eradicated, at least (for the most part) hidden from our view, to understand why Paul did not attack this issue head on. This, however, is something that is making twenty-first century demands of people in the first century; and this is an unfair burden to place upon Paul's shoulders. Modern-day mediators would do well to learn from Paul on this matter, and not demand more from the cultural context than it is able to give. In Paul's world, while "the demands of equality and love before God seem, in the modern perspective, to be fundamentally incompatible with the continuation of slavery . . . the two managed to continue to coexist, even flourish."[20] Paul worked with the situation in front of him, and only later considered larger, more systemic matters.

In addition, granting a slave his or her freedom in the ancient world, while being deeply desired by slaves, did not guarantee a resolution to the problem of their inequality in the world or in the body of Christ. For the value obviously placed on manumission by slaves is quite interesting in view of the incompleteness of the freedom actually granted to them, at least in the Greek and Roman worlds. By the last century BCE, Greek or Roman slaves manumitted in any of these ceremonies remained severely constrained by a host of obligations to their ex-master and the ex-master's family. A failure to fulfill these duties, as well as any others agreed upon as a condition of their release, could lead to punishment or re-enslavement under the charge of "ingratitude."[21]

---

19. Barclay, "Paul, Philemon and the Dilemma," 162.
20. Combes, *Metaphor of Slavery*, 62.
21. Ibid., 39–40.

The evidence shows that "manumission is not a softening but a tightening strategy for keeping slaves under control."[22] For this reason, modern readers must keep the question of manumission in perspective. If the church approved or even encouraged the manumission of slaves, it would have been doing nothing humane or radical for its time. Manumission was as much a part of the institution of slavery as the chain and the whip—simply another tool at the owner's disposal to motivate the slave to good service. To encourage legal manumission may seem a kindness to individual slaves, but it also confirms the owner's right to possess the slave in the first place.[23]

The manumission question presents other problems for the church as well. The fact is that Paul (and the church in general) depended on the spacious houses of the wealthy, like Philemon, in order to meet, and these large houses required slaves to maintain and run. There are questions concerning who would pay for the manumission of slaves, and if church funds could be used to free slaves (and if they were would there be spurious "conversions" of slaves simply to gain freedom)?[24]

However, if slaves were not to be manumitted but remain part of the household, it was also difficult to see how masters and slaves might erase all expressions of their status. How would a Christian master respond if a Christian slave refused an order, and "what would the brotherly relationship mean when the master stands ready with his whip"?[25] Would a master accept admonition from a slave, as Gal 6:1 says that Christians should be able to do for one another? How would a slave contribute to monetary collections for the church, when such money would come out of personal funds that were being saved for manumission (and technically belonged to the master in any case)?[26] And how would the Lord's Supper proceed, if the slaves who were to cook and serve the meal were to sit down and eat with their masters?[27] The "social realities of slavery would make it well neigh impossible to apply Paul's own understanding of 'brotherhood' to the relationship between master and slave. . . . Neither of these two main options—to manumit . . . or to retain . . . a slave—is really satisfactory."[28]

---

22. Marchal, "Usefulness of an Onesimus," 757.
23. Combes, *Metaphor of Slavery*, 62.
24. Barclay, "Paul, Philemon and the Dilemma," 176–77.
25. Ibid., 178.
26. Combes, *Metaphor of Slavery*, 41–42.
27. This problem indeed may not have been hypothetical at all, for it seems to be the situation that Paul addresses in 1 Cor 11.
28. Barclay, "Paul, Philemon and the Metaphor," 180.

If Paul were to require the freeing (manumission) of Onesimus, this would implicitly legitimate the institution of slavery. This makes it easier to understand Paul's letter to Philemon, in which he neither attacked slavery nor explicitly defended it. The most that can be said . . . is that he struggled with it, recognizing more or less consciously the tension between the realities of slavery and the demands of brotherhood. That struggle is, in historical terms, both explicable and understandable.[29] Paul was not about reforming this cultural institution, the immorality of which he may very well have been blind to, given his place in history. In any case, Paul showed "little concern with social questions beyond the boundaries of the church,"[30] and, it turns out that Paul has a much bigger prize in mind.

If you were in Paul's shoes, with the same knowledge of cultural background, and the same concern for unity among the communities of Jesus Christ, you would have to choose wisely the tools at your disposal in order to argue your point or navigate this ticklish situation. So, instead of demanding that Philemon free Onesimus, this little letter demonstrates Paul's very careful use of language and rhetoric, packing a powerful ask regarding a difficult and systemic social issue. Paul writes in somewhat cloaked language. He asks that Philemon would "welcome him as you would welcome me" (v. 17), and then expresses confidence that Philemon will "do even more than I ask" (v. 21). Watching Paul at work, we can see how he resolves the immediate problem between Philemon and Onesimus, rather than attempting to reform systemic and cultural problems. Modern-day mediators can learn from Paul, the master, in keeping these interpersonal issues at the forefront, before attempting to take on the systemic (and thus more difficult) problems.

This might surprise us, because we know that Paul, in his other writings, is no stranger to the use of power, and "was not naïve concerning it."[31] Paul believed that when he spoke, he carried God's authority. In 1 Thess 2:13 he tells the church, "When you received the word of God, which you heard from us, you accepted it not as a human word, but as it actually is, the word of God." Later in the same letter, Paul gave the church ethical instructions on proper behavior, he prefaced his instructions with, "it is God's will" (1 Thess 4:4). In addition, Paul is very concerned with, and takes responsibility for, how the churches he founded are faring. Paul "claims the position of the 'subject who knows' who is able and willing to give guidance" to these

---

29. Ibid., 186.
30. Ibid., 183.
31. Ehrensperger, *Paul and the Dynamics of Power*, 1.

communities.³² And Paul clearly has a view in this epistle of how he wishes for things to work out between Onesimus and Philemon, and "the alternatives are not equally good in Paul's eyes."³³ However, in his letter to Philemon, Paul shows much restraint, "using a less than normative force than that available to him, probably because he wants to preserve the person, 'father-son' character of the relationship with Philemon."³⁴

The family-laden language of this letter demonstrates Paul's unconventional use of authority. Paul refers to Philemon as his brother twice (in vv. 7 and 20) in this short letter. He refers to Onesimus as his son (v. 10), and obliquely he refers to Philemon in the same manner in v. 19 ("I say nothing about your owing me even your own self"). It is striking that in Philemon (as in all Paul's letters), he uses the term "father" sparingly. The *pater-familias* was one of the strongest examples of power that existed in the Greco-Roman world, with the *pater* retaining "absolute power . . . over property and family members, which included strict authority and sexual domination."³⁵ For Paul to have taken this mantle would have made a clear statement about his authority. But Paul most often uses the term father (coupled, interestingly, with the term "mother") in the Jewish notion of fatherhood/motherhood, which "resonate with an educational discourse in his letters."³⁶ In Philemon, "Paul's overt challenge to sibling solidarity"³⁷ leads to the climax of the letter in vv. 15b–16 "so that you might have him back forever, no longer as a slave but more than a slave, a beloved brother—especially to me but how much more to you, both in the flesh and in the Lord."

If you were in Paul's shoes, the one thing you were absolutely committed to would have been relationships within the churches you founded and cared for. In this, Paul demonstrates another quality a good mediator possesses. It is essential to be steeped in the community, having the concern and commitment to resolution Paul demonstrates in his care for this church, while still being able to keep perspective on the larger issues at hand. For Paul, his experience with Jesus Christ led him to believe Christians were to become a new community, transformed by the grace offered by Jesus Christ. The church was expanding beyond the areas surrounding Israel, and Paul was trying to foster "an emerging Christian movement with a vision of equality against the forces of the dominant patriarchal ethos of

---

32. Ehrensperger, *Paul and the Dynamics of Power*, 177.
33. Holmberg, *Paul and Power*, 82.
34. Ibid., 85.
35. Ehrensperger, *Paul and the Dynamics of Power*, 117.
36. Ibid., 128.
37. Hellerman, *Ancient Church as Family*, 119.

the Greco-Roman world."[38] And "where there is division among Messiah's people, their task, and Paul's longing, is that they may grow up 'into him' in terms of a powerful, loving unity. That is his prayer for Philemon and Onesimus."[39]

Paul was deeply concerned about the relationship between Philemon and Onesimus as brothers in Jesus Christ. For "Philemon to have responded angrily to Paul's letter by giving Onesimus his freedom but declaring that he never wanted to set eyes on him again would have meant defeat for Paul."[40] And, if Onesimus had waltzed into Philemon's household with his letter, triumphantly demanding his release (certified by the Apostle Paul) and leaving with a rude gesture, this similarly would have been a loss in Paul's view. While there were indeed many obstacles and practical concerns to work out, Paul's ultimate goal is to work out the implications of what it looks like that there is both slave-owners and slaves, free people, freed people (people who were formerly slaves but had become free), all worshipping alongside one another in the church. This larger vision is Paul's guiding principle and ultimate goal. Despite his close relationship with Onesimus, and his relationship with Philemon as a church leader, not to mention his beloved congregation in Colossae, Paul chooses this vision, rather than these relationships, to shape his resolution to this problem. Paul was clear about what he asked of Onesimus to make this situation right, and he is equally clear in his letter to Philemon and the rest of the church. Having been clear, however, he lets the situation play out, trusting the character of Philemon and Onesimus, as well as the watching and waiting church, to resolve this situation in accordance with his larger vision. Modern-day mediators can learn a lesson from Paul in this regard as well. Paul might not demand slaves be freed across the board (indeed, it is even possible that this is beyond his imagination given his place in history), but he does want slave-owners and slaves to worship Jesus Christ together, in unity, and on a level playing field in the places where they would meet (cf. Gal 3:28). Thus, clearly stating his goal for all the involved parties, Paul trusts these Christ-followers to work toward this solution together. In Paul's vision, "when the Christians gathered to worship, to fellowship, to meet and eat, the ruthless, divisive, and status-shaped backbone of the empire snapped."[41]

If you were Paul, living in Paul's world, you would approach this situation with caution, because the socially stratified nature of the world

38. Kitterage, *Community and Authority*, 6.
39. Wright, *Paul and the Faithfulness of God*, 18.
40. Ibid., 12.
41. McKnight, *Fellowship of Differents*, 93.

demanded it. By all indications, Philemon holds a higher social status than Paul. Scholars have traditionally assumed that if Philemon had a home big enough to host a gathering of the church, and was the owner of at least one slave (and probably more than one), he possessed enough material resources to have a house and a household of that size, and would command social respect in his community. Though scholars have argued that ownership of slaves was something that was present all throughout the social ladder[42] (for instance, there is records of slaves owning slaves[43]), Paul's approach to Philemon indicates that he possessed a respectable amount of honor in the community of Colossae. But, interestingly, not only does Paul approach Philemon very carefully in his letter, showing restraint and using less than the maximum amount of authority that was his to command, Paul in fact seems to lower in status. In v. 9 Paul refers to himself as "an old man and now also a prisoner of Jesus Christ," which would have downgraded his social standing.[44]

In addition to the difference in status between Philemon and Paul, the law is on Philemon's side here. As a fugitive slave, it is Paul's responsibility according to Roman law to return Onesimus to Philemon.[45] As a Jew who had a deep knowledge of Scripture, Paul likely had swirling in the back of his mind the instruction: "If a slave has taken refuge with you, do not hand them over to their master. Let them live among you wherever they like and in whatever town they choose. Do not oppress them" (Deut 23:15–16). However, Paul's vision for the church was more radical than even this command from the Hebrew Scriptures. Paul wants more than just a re-affirmation of Philemon and Onesimus in the status that they currently hold as slave-owner and slave; he wants for them to be brothers instead. Paul demonstrates for the modern-day mediator that relationship matters. A good mediated solution not only meets the needs and addresses the concerns of the people and parties involved in a way that is sustainable; it preserves and protects (at very least, doesn't damage) the relationships of the people involved.[46]

Instead of appealing to his authority in the strongest terms as an apostle to whom Philemon must listen (which would have made Paul an arbitrator, a role that is undesirable in conflict mediation)[47] in this letter, Paul

42. Friesen, "Poverty in Pauline Studies," 323–61.

43. Harrill, *Slaves in the New Testament*, Kindle e-book, location 2011.

44. Wright, *Paul and the Faithfulness of God*, 6, though he notes that Paul's degrading of his status in this instance is almost bragged about by Paul as if the case were the opposite.

45. Falx and Toner, *How to Manage Your Slaves*, 203.

46. Fisher, Ury, and Patton, *Getting to Yes*, 4.

47. Arbitration is when an outside party exercises authority to resolve conflict; for

demonstrates mediation in the first century by employing methods familiar to first century argumentation (technically called "deliberative rhetoric"), the object of which "is to exhort or dissuade."[48] So, "whether by training or observation, Paul used deliberative rhetoric when he appealed to Philemon, adapting the genre to his particular style and structure for letter writing."[49] In order to employ this method successfully, the writer must motivate the person that they wish to act by "establishing two primary motives for action, honor (*honestas*) and advantage (*utilitas*). These are supported by the skillful use of proofs, or appeals to the reason and emotions of one's hearer."[50] Since the purpose of using this type of argument "is to demonstrate love or friendship and to induce sympathy or goodwill, in order to dispose the hearer favorably to the merits of one's case,"[51] we can see why Paul might choose this method of persuasion to write to his social superior about the delicate matter of his broken relationship with Onesimus. Deliberative rhetoric has three parts with technical names, but which correspond nicely with Paul's letter to Philemon. The three parts include first of all setting the mood and gaining the ear of the listener;[52] secondly, the author advances the argument "with primary reference to motives of honor and utility";[53] finally, the author appeals to reason and emotion by "restating one's appeal; securing the hearer's favor; amplifying one's argument; and, setting the hearer in an emotional frame of mind."[54]

All three of these elements are at work throughout the letter of Philemon. After opening with his customary greetings (vv. 1–3), Paul launches into effusive praise of Philemon, heaping thanksgiving on him and detailing his prayer for Philemon (vv. 4–7), which corresponds nicely with the mood setting part of deliberative rhetoric.[55] Next follows Paul's appeal for Onesimus in vv. 8–16, which is the proof part of the letter, in which Paul presents "a perfectly balanced appeal to Philemon's character and feelings (vv. 8–10a)."[56] He continues in vv. 12–14 to offer Philemon an opportunity

---

instance, legal judges do this to determine assets in a divorce or disburse an estate.
48. Church, "Rhetorical Structure and Design," 18.
49. Bartchy, "Philemon," 306.
50. Church, "Rhetorical Structure and Design," 19.
51. Ibid., 20.
52. Technically referred to as "the Exordium." Ibid.
53 Technically called "the Proof." Ibid.
54. Technically called "the Peroration." Ibid.
55. Bartchy, "Philemon," 306.
56. Ibid., 307.

to maintain his honor, and to "express his true character, his 'goodness.'"[57] Paul goes above and beyond the rhetorical form in vv. 15–16, expressing that it may have been necessary for "Philemon to lose Onesimus as a slave in order to gain him as a "beloved brother."[58] And in vv. 17–22, Paul fulfills all the requirements of the final aspect of deliberative rhetoric,[59] in which Paul appeals to both reason and emotion to convince Philemon to act in a particular way toward Onesimus.

In using this particular method of writing, and keeping in mind that this was a very public performance, Paul, in a demonstration of masterful mediation, is putting an inordinate amount of pressure on Philemon to respond to his request favorably. Although a modern-day mediator must be careful to use his/her power carefully, so as not to abuse their position, Paul is not doing so here. Instead, by using this rhetorical ploy, Paul is essentially saying, "Far be it from me to force your hand—I wouldn't tell you want to do, now would I? No, of course not, think[s] . . . Philemon with a wry smile; you merely put me in an impossible position!"[60] And Philemon's reception of the letter, how he responds to Paul's request (shrouded in rhetoric as it is) will affect not just Onesimus, but also every other slave in the church, because the entire church, addressed in the letter (v.2), is also listening in as the letter is being read. So, while this letter is indeed very personal in nature, with the goal of restoring the broken relationships between Philemon and Onesimus (and perhaps Paul himself), it was never intended as a private letter. In writing this letter, Paul puts Philemon in a position where he will have to decide his relationship to Onesimus: would he deny his Christian identity by acting first of all with the prerogatives of an angry slave owner, or would he strengthen it by doing all in his power as Onesimus' patron to make him his "beloved brother"? His house church is watching, and Paul hoped to be there soon to see for himself.[61]

57. Ibid.
58. Ibid.
59. Called the Peroration (Ibid.).
60. Wright, *Paul and the Faithfulness of God*, 5.
61. Bartchy, "Philemon," 309.

Church Conflict Management and Paul's Letter to Philemon

What do we learn about conflict in the community as we read this little (but useful!) letter to the church that meets at Philemon's house? Let us take notes and watch as Paul handles this difficult situation masterfully.[62]

The first thing that we observe is that Paul is guided by the much larger vision that he sees at work in his community of Christ followers. While this is a personal situation that has arisen between two very real people, Paul's goal in writing this letter and sending Onesimus into the perilous situation he would find himself as he approached his master's house, was to help these two brothers in Christ "to *think within the biblical narrative*, to see themselves as actors within the ongoing scriptural drama: to allow their erstwhile pagan thought-forms to be transformed by a biblically based renewal of the mind."[63] Despite the complexities of their individual stories, and the way that their stories play out in the larger backdrop of the social realities of the first-century world, Paul doesn't lose sight of this larger prize—the church functioning in unity.

While from our vantage point, we would think that the issue would be crystal clear (for instance, that if Philemon were to free Onesimus, that would solve the problem of inequality between them), we have already seen how this situation is murky and complex. Onesimus may have our hearts as the one who is clearly the victim needing protection from his powerful master, but the fact is that he ran away from Philemon's household, and (if we are to take v. 18 at its face value) he also wronged Philemon somehow in the process. Even though we could come up with explanations for why he might have behaved in this way, the fact is that Onesimus is on the wrong side of the law and Philemon is on the right side of it to both own slaves and to exact punishment for Onesimus when he found him again. The New Testament is no stranger to difficult dilemmas and conflict-ridden situations, as the early believers struggled to work out the implications of their new status in Jesus Christ in relationship with one another. From Paul's perspective, "If anyone is in the Messiah, there is a new creation!" (2 Cor 5:17). And "Philemon himself is part of that new creation, and so is Onesimus, so

---

62. There is the beautiful little fact that there is, some sixty years later, a reference by Ignatius to a bishop of Ephesus by the name of Onesimus. It is certainly within the realm of our imagination to believe that this might refer to the one and the same Onesimus as is being addressed in the letter to Philemon. Although, Onesimus was a common name, so it is impossible to be certain (Wright, *Paul and the Faithfulness*, 15).

63. Ibid.

the question of their social status is radically outflanked."[64] So, work this out they must. There is no other option, from Paul's perspective, for Onesimus and Philemon were brothers in Jesus Christ. And "much as he valued freedom, the mutual reconciliation of those who belonged to the Messiah mattered more than anything else."[65]

The second thing that we see is Paul's masterful use of the rhetorical devices of his day. Instead of using the authority he could legitimately wield as an apostle as a stick to get Philemon to obey him, he makes multiple appeals to Philemon's character, allowing Philemon to appear to have taken the initiative when he does the right thing. Paul ascribes the best motives to Philemon and sites the great work that he has done "refreshing the heart of the saints" (v. 7). Paul doesn't demonize Philemon, nor use slurs or derogatory language when referring to him, or to the fact that he has owned a slave who has (presumably) run away from him. Paul allows the good parts of Philemon's character to shine throughout the letter, and he appeals to this character as the solution to the problem in which Onesimus, Philemon (and Paul) find themselves.

However, Paul also refuses to let this matter be a private matter between Philemon and himself (or Philemon and Onesimus). Paul gives both himself and Timothy as authors of the letter. In Philemon (and others of Paul's letters), when he lists himself alongside others as the author of the letter, the content of the letters can be perceived as the expression of a conversation of Paul and a group that is with him who negotiate the meaning of the Christ even in relation to the concrete concepts of everyday life in the communities, rather than the result of the thoughts of one man alone.[66]

Moreover, Paul writes to the church as a whole, not just to Philemon. Letter-writing in the ancient world was not conducted with sealed envelopes and private mailboxes, but with couriers who both carried and read the letter out loud (and even explained or clarified the contents of the letter)[67] and with the entire church listening in as it was read. And so, while the power of response rests with Philemon, an entire 'cloud of witnesses' is there to hear, see, and respond to what he was going to do. We can imagine that Paul's rhetorical flourishes could well have put Philemon in a spot where he could not truly respond in any other way than Paul wants him to respond and still retain his honor in the church. Still, the public aspect of this letter is powerful.

64. Ibid., 20.
65. Wright, *Paul and the Faithfulness of God*, 12.
66. Ehrensperger, *Paul and the Dynamics of Power*, 57.
67. Collins and Harlow, *Eerdmans Dictionary of Early Judaism*, 883.

This is an especially crucial point to keep in mind in modern-day conflict within our church communities. One of the criticisms of using a model of conflict management developed from Matt 18:15–17 is when we encounter a conflict that involves an imbalance of power in the church. This type of power imbalance is most readily seen in situations involving abuse. Victims have been further victimized, and those with power have been able to continue abusing that power by using techniques claiming that "Matthew 18 binds us to private confrontation of the abuser, or insisting that every issue be handled 'one-on-one' behind the closed doors of the pastor's office."[68] However, using this strategy works to promote secrecy, which works in favor of the abuser or the more powerful person in the situation.[69] Maintaining secrecy on this issue would have perhaps made Philemon more comfortable, but it would have been detrimental for Onesimus. And, while Paul deals with Philemon in a way that allows him to preserve his integrity, he does not allow Philemon to hide either. The entire community is witnessing this play out, which greatly elevates the position of the one who holds little (or no) power. By refusing to maintain secrecy, and involving the entire church in this interaction, Paul worked to even out the power imbalance between Philemon and Onesimus. The modern church has been complicit in covering up and/or enabling abusers, but "of any place or institution on earth, the people of Christ should prove to be the champions of the abuse victim, and victims as well as abusers should have no doubt about this."[70] Refusing to keep these types of conflicts private is one way to send this message.

Finally, Paul assumes a cross-shaped stance toward these two estranged brothers. Paul expects both Philemon and Onesimus to give something in order to make the situation between them right (Philemon has to give up his rights as a slave-owner, and Onesimus returns to his master, albeit with a powerful letter from Paul). But Paul is also willing to sacrifice something of himself as well. The clearest request in Paul's little letter is v. 17: "welcome him as you would welcome me." In the eloquent words of N. T. Wright:

> Paul's apostolic ministry reaches one of its high points as he stands there with arms outstretched, embracing Philemon with one and Onesimus with the other. That is what the ministry of reconciliation looks like. The cross itself, though not mentioned explicitly in Philemon, emerges here, embodied in the ministry

---

68. Crippen and Wood, *Cry for Justice*, 180.
69. Ibid., 177–81.
70. Ibid., 178.

of the imprisoned apostle, as the theological substructure of the pastoral appeal.[71]

We face difficult, complex, and troubling interpersonal situations in our everyday lives in the communities in which we live and minister as brothers and sisters in Jesus Christ. The wisdom and the posture of the Apostle Paul in his letter to Philemon may help us to imagine how we might also approach these situations of conflict within the churches of the people that we love and serve.

In observing all that is at work in this little letter of Philemon, we have seen Paul, the master mediator, at work; his example can serve modern conflict mediators well. Paul loved, cared for, and had a relationship with the church in Colossae, as well as both Onesimus and Philemon. He cares for the relationship between these two men, as well as their Christian life and witness, not to mention the healthy functioning of the church of which they are both a part. Similarly, a modern-day mediator cannot become detached from the people involved in the conflicts if they wish to strengthen and heal fractured relationships.

In addition to this, however, Paul also demonstrated his understanding of the world of this congregation and this conflict, with all of the background information involved. Using the tools available to him from this context, he outlines his case to resolve the conflict before him. In the same way, modern-day mediators must spend time discerning the cultural context in which they find themselves in order to provide long-lasting and effective resolutions to the conflicts before them.

In relinquishing his authority and refusing (in this case, at least) to act as an arbitrator, Paul demonstrates the ability of a good mediator to work on multiple levels. Paul's solution to this conflict works on many levels: he creates reconciliation between Philemon and Onesimus; he addresses issues of church health; and he works toward his grand vision for Christian fellowship. Paul was very clear in communicating the goal that he wanted to achieve, but he also relied upon Philemon, Onesimus, and the church community to play their respective parts to reach reconciliation in this case. Paul, in his letter to Philemon, demonstrates for us the characteristics and character of a masterful mediator.

Bibliography

Barclay, John M. G. "Paul, Philemon and the Dilemma of Christian Slave-Ownership." *New Testament Studies* 37 (1991) 161–86.

71. Wright, *Paul and the Faithfulness of God*, 20.

Bartchy, S. Scott. "Philemon." In *Anchor Bible Dictionary*, edited by D. N. Freedman, 306–9. New York: Doubleday, 1992.

Church, F. Forrester. "Rhetorical Structure and Design in Paul's Letter to Philemon." *The Harvard Theological Review* 71 (1978) 17–33.

Cohick, Lynn H. *Women in the World of the Earliest Christians: Illuminating Ancient Ways of Life*. Grand Rapids: Baker Academic, 2009.

Collins, John J., and Daniel C. Harlow, eds. *The Eerdmans Dictionary of Early Judaism*. Grand Rapids: Eerdmans, 2010.

Combes, I. A. H. *The Metaphor of Slavery in the Writings of the Early Church: From the New Testament to the Beginning of the Fifth Century*. Journal for the Study of the New Testament 156. Sheffield: Sheffield Academic, 1998.

Crippen, Jeff, and Anna Wood. *Cry for Justice: How the Evil of Domestic Abuse Hides in Your Church!* New York: Calvary, 2014.

Ehrensperger, Kathy. *Paul and the Dynamics of Power: Communication and Interaction in the Early Christ-Movement*. Library of New Testament Studies 325. London: T&T Clark, 2007.

Falx, Marcus Sidonius, and J. P. Toner. *How to Manage Your Slaves*. London: Profile Books, 2015.

Fisher, Roger, William Ury, and Bruce Patton. *Getting to Yes: Negotiating Agreement without Giving in*. 3rd ed. New York: Penguin, 2011.

Friesen, Steven J. "Poverty in Pauline Studies: Beyond the So-Called New Consensus," *Journal for the Study of the New Testament* 26 (2004): 323–61.

Glancy, Jennifer A. *Slavery in Early Christianity*. Minneapolis: Fortress, 2006.

Harrill, James Albert. *Slaves in the New Testament: Literary, Social, and Moral Dimensions*. Minneapolis: Fortress, 2006.

Hellerman, Joseph. *The Ancient Church as Family*. Minneapolis: Fortress, 2001.

Holmberg, Bengt. *Paul and Power: The Structure of Authority in the Primitive Church as Reflected in the Pauline Epistles*. Philadelphia: Fortress, 1980.

Keener, Craig S. *The IVP Bible Background Commentary: New Testament*. Downers Grove, IL: InterVarsity, 1993.

Kitterage, Cynthia Briggs. *Community and Authority: The Rhetoric of Obedience in the Pauline Tradition*. Pennsylvania: Trinity Press International, 1998.

Malina, Bruce J. *The New Testament World: Insights from Cultural Anthropology*. Louisville: Westminster John Knox, 2001.

Marchal, Joseph A. "The Usefulness of an Onesimus: The Sexual Use of Slaves and Paul's Letter to Philemon." *Journal of Biblical Literature* 130 (2011) 749–70.

McKnight, Scot. *A Fellowship of Differents: Showing the World God's Design for Life Together*. Grand Rapids: Zondervan, 2015.

Wright, N. T., ed. *The Kingdom New Testament: A Contemporary Translation of the New Testament*. 1st ed. New York: HarperOne, 2011.

———. *Paul and the Faithfulness of God*. Christian Origins and the Question of God 4. Minneapolis: Fortress, 2013.

3

Crucial Conversations at the Jerusalem Council

Paul Submits to Higher Authority

Acts 15:1–33

By Randy Johns and Ray Miller

How did the early church resolve issues when emotions were high and changes were happening too quickly to be comprehended? There were several conflicts that the early church faced but only one that forced a church-wide council to be consulted in Jerusalem. How were Gentiles to be received into the family of God? The covenant for so long had been only for Israel with some proselytes, and that came with certain markers such as circumcision, a sign that one was committed to the covenant of God. This became a crucial conversation for the early church to debate, discern, and decide. This crucial conversation could have evolved into a fractured church. Rather, because of the Spirit and the willingness to have this crucial conversation in a safe way, the church continued to flourish and expand to the utter most parts of the earth. In this chapter, we will explore the background and discussion of the Acts 15 Jerusalem Council through the lens of a "crucial conversation" as a complementary perspective on the conflict management theories of the opening chapter.

Crucial Conversations: Tools for Talking When Stakes Are High is a recent New York Times bestseller and is changing the way millions communicate. It has become an additional resource for conflict mediation and conflict management. The book seeks to equip its readers to navigate through difficult and challenging conversations skillfully. Authors Kerry Patterson, Joseph Grenny, Ron McMillan, and Al Switzler build their case from twenty-five years of involvement working among a variety of seventeen organizations. Through their experience, the authors have listened intently to a multiplicity of conversations, some healthy and productive, others harmful and unproductive. They conclude the ability to dialogue successfully boosts organizational performance and morale. What is true for organizations is also true for individuals, and churches.

What, then, is a "crucial conversation"? For these authors, a crucial conversation is "a discussion between two or more people where stakes are high, opinions vary, and emotions run strong." The temptation, often, is to steer clear of the difficult dialogue. The authors claim there are three routes to take when organizations or individuals encounter these situations. "We can avoid crucial conversations; we can face them and handle them poorly; we can face them and handle them well."[1]

Before suggesting skills to develop on how to conduct crucial conversations constructively, the authors ask why engaging in these conversations are avoided. They argue that often "when things matter most people are at their worst."[2] Our worst occurs because of an assortment of reasons. Most people are "wired" wrong. Their personalities are not conducive to confrontation. Pressure, stress, and anxiety overcome individuals. Confusion ensues. Perplexity strikes. People respond in self-defeating ways because they are unable to reach their intended goal. Frustration results. But, "when it comes to risky, controversial, and emotional conversations, skilled people find a way to get all the relevant information from everyone out in the open."[3] The authors begin to guide the reader down the path to become skilled conversationalists.

The journey commences with the understanding that "at the core of every successful conversation lies the free flow of relevant information."[4] This necessity of the sharing of information is discourse, discussion,

---

1. Patterson et al., ed., *Crucial Conversations*, 3.
2. Ibid., 4.
3. Ibid., 23.
4. Ibid.

even negotiation. This collection of pooled meaning is the "birthplace of synergy,"[5] of working together as a combined effort to reach a solution. Each player involved must start with their heart, that is, bear in mind their motivations and judge their intentions. Another important first step is refusing the "fool's choice," assuming the best resolution is an *either/or* option, rather than endeavoring to hunt and insist upon the all-important and ever-elusive *both/and*.[6]

Also necessary is providing a safe environment for the crucial conversation to take place. "As people begin to feel unsafe, they start down one of two unhealthy paths."[7] The first harmful path many take is silence. This silence may take different appearances. One is masking, "understating or selectively showing our true opinions."[8] Cynicism, patronizing, and speaking indirectly or obscurely would be examples. Another form silence takes is avoiding. "Avoiding involves steering completely away from sensitive subjects."[9] Conversation occurs but the actual issues are never discussed. Withdrawal is the final form of silence. An individual withdraws by exiting the conversation completely.

The second detrimental path many follow is violence. A violent approach attempts to convince, command, or coerce others to accept your point of view. Violence appears in diverse ways. Controlling is common. "Methods include cutting others off, overstating your facts, speaking in absolutes, changing subjects, and using directive questions to control the conversation."[10] Labeling is a second form of violence. Pigeonholing people dismisses them by categorizing or stereotyping unfairly. Violence also expresses itself through attacking. Making the opponent suffer becomes the goal. "Tactics include belittling and threatening."[11]

Again, these two unhealthy paths may be evaded by creating a safe environment for dialogue. Mutual purpose and mutual respect are the foundations of that safe setting. "When either of those two things are threatened, apologize when appropriate, fix the misunderstanding, or create a mutual purpose."[12] The authors suggest four skills to create a mutual purpose through the helpful acronym CRIB: commit to seek mutual purpose,

---

5. Ibid., 25.
6. Ibid., 46.
7. Ibid., 58.
8. Ibid., 59.
9. Ibid., 60.
10. Ibid.
11. Ibid., 61.
12. Ibid., 101.

recognize the purpose behind the strategy, invent a mutual purpose, and brainstorm new strategies.[13]

After suggesting ways to establish a safe environment, the authors begin teaching how to speak persuasively, not abrasively. This is done by wisely blending three ingredients—confidence, humility, and skill.[14] These fundamental ingredients create the perfect conditions for constructive dialogue. The authors then develop "five distinct skills that can help you talk about even the most sensitive topics."[15] These skills can be remembered through another acronym STATE. "It stands for *s*hare your facts, *t*ell your story, *a*sk for others' paths, *t*alk tentatively, and *e*ncourage testing. The first three skills describe *what* to do. The last two tell *how* to do it."[16] Important things to remember about facts: facts are the least controversial, facts are the most persuasive, and facts are the least insulting.[17] State your opinions through your story. Pursue the facts, stories, and emotions of others following them down their path and experience. Dialoguing tentatively implies talking carefully, cautiously, and thoughtfully. To encourage testing is to humbly and sincerely urge others to challenge and critique your views.

The authors expand on asking for the paths of others. To foster the free flow of meaning and help others leave silence or violence behind, be willing to delve into their paths for action. Begin with the attitudes of curiosity and patience. This supports the safe environment that has been created. The key is sincere and fine-tuned listening. Four components of proper listening skills are to ask appropriate questions, mirror to confirm the feelings of others, paraphrase to show not just that you understand but also that it is safe for them to share what they're thinking, and, finally, if the others continue to hold back, prime. Take your best guess at what they may be thinking and feeling. As you begin to share views, remember: agree with what you have in common, build upon those views, and compare when you disagree.[18]

Crucial Conversations concludes with a valuable reminder: "dialogue is not decision making."[19] A decision must be made. A resolution must result. Action must be activated. Don't be guilty of disregarded expectations and inaction. The key is deciding how to decide. The authors suggest four

---

13. Ibid., 102.
14. Ibid., 131–33.
15. Ibid., 136.
16. Ibid., 136.
17. Ibid., 138–39.
18. Ibid., 174–75.
19. Ibid., 178.

methods of decision-making.[20] The first method is "command," where decisions are made without involving others. The second method is "consult," where input is gathered from the group and then a subset decides. The third method is "voting," where an agreed-upon percentage swings the decision. And in the fourth method, there is "consensus," where everyone comes to an agreement and then supports the final decision. To help determine which method to use the authors advocate asking four questions: Who cares? Who knows? Who must agree? How many people is it worth involving?[21]

Once the decision is finally reached, the authors finish with several components of ending the process successfully. "Determine who does what by when. Make the deliverables crystal clear. Set a follow-up time. Record the commitments and then follow up. Hold people accountable to their promises."[22] Remember! "It's not about communication, it is about results."[23]

The Council at Jerusalem in Acts 15 certainly qualifies as a "crucial conversation." Stakes were high. The salvation of the converted Gentiles and the efficiency of Jesus' death for their salvation were at stake. Opinions varied. Christians from Judea who were Pharisees arrived in Antioch insisting that the Gentile Christians be circumcised and obey the Law of Moses in addition to their faith in Jesus. Paul and Barnabas reacted immediately and objected. Emotions ran strong. The sharp dispute and debate are proof.

Nature of Conflict

What was the nature of the conflict that led to the Jerusalem Council? The incident that created the need for the council was the group belonging to the circumcision who were teaching in Antioch that Gentiles had to be circumcised and follow all the Mosaic Law to be accepted into the family of God. What was behind this particular attitude? Why was the Holy Spirit falling on the Gentiles enough for this particular group? Embedded within Judaism was the idea that Gentiles were somehow morally "impure" unless they had fully converted to Judaism, which included circumcision for the men.[24]

Moral purity and religious or cultic purity are two separate discussions. One can be ritually unclean without being morally unclean. The common view during the Second Temple Period was that Gentiles themselves

20. Ibid., 180–82.
21. Ibid., 183.
22. Ibid., 187.
23. Ibid., 222.
24. Chilton and Evans, *Missions of James, Peter, and Paul*, 101.

were morally unclean, but not necessarily ritually impure. The ritual laws found in the Mosaic Law did not apply to Gentiles. E. P. Sanders gives a picture of this when he points to a rabbinic story about a Jew stepping on the menstrual blood of a Gentile woman who was not declared impure. Why? Sanders argues that most Jews believed that Leviticus 15 did not apply to Gentiles.[25]

Why then does Peter seem to equate impurity not only with the food associated with Gentiles, but Gentiles themselves? In Acts 10–11, Luke uses both the words "impure" and "profane" to describe the food and subsequently the Gentiles, and what common Jews would have thought of Gentiles in that day. Bauckham explains it well when he writes, "Since Gentiles are profane, these animals can be considered profane: the profane food of profane people."[26] Why was the food profane, and thereby the Gentiles themselves profane? Throughout the Old Testament the language of impurity is used almost synonymously with sin. However, one may categorize impurity offenses that are sins into three distinct categories: idolatry, sexual immorality of various kinds, and murder. These particular sins are what the Canaanites did to the land before Israel conquered and settled the land. Leviticus 18:2 states, "You are not to do what is done in the land of Egypt from where I brought you, nor do as the Canaanites have done in the land I am bringing you." Gentiles therefore are idolaters who defile the land of Israel. They are sexually immoral and are bringing sacrifices to false gods into the land of Israel. Therefore, they must be purged from the land.

Second Temple Literature seems to agree with this assessment. Ben Sirach calls upon God to hasten the day when he will destroy the Gentile nations, gather again all the tribes of Jacob, and establish the Israelite theocracy throughout the earth.[27] In Sirach 37:8, it says, "Pour out your furious, flaming anger, and let none of our enemies survive. Destroy those who have oppressed your people." A passage in the *Jubilees* also enlightens typical Israelite thought towards the Gentiles. In Jub 22:16, Abraham urges Jacob to:

> Separate thyself from the nations and eat not with them: and do not according to their works, and become not their associate; for their works are unclean, and all their ways are a pollution and an abomination and uncleanness.

This passage uses similar language that Peter uses in Acts 10–11 when talking about the Gentiles and table fellowship.

---

25. Sanders, *Judaism*, 73.
26. Bauckham, "James, Peter, and the Gentiles," 103.
27. Sanders, *Paul and Palestinian Judaism*, 331.

The Torah did not allow for Gentiles living in the land of Israel to worship YHWH as Jews did. For instance, Num 15:14–15 states:

> One who may be among you throughout your generations, and he wishes to make an offering by fire, as a soothing aroma to the Lord, just as you do so he shall do. As for the assembly, there shall be one statute for you and for the alien who sojourns with you, a perpetual statute throughout your generations; as you are, so shall the alien be before the Lord. There is to be one law and one ordinance for you and for the alien who sojourns with you.

That passage and others like it include Gentiles in the people of God, as long as they act as Israel does and follow the law. Obviously, most Gentiles did not. However, some Gentiles were interested in YHWH worship, especially in the Diaspora. Sometimes, these Gentiles were called "God-fearers," which Cornelius seems to be in Acts 10. There were also some Gentiles who were proselytes, or as Sanders calls them, "righteous Gentiles."[28] A righteous Gentile is one who accepted fully the covenant including all the commandments. Failure to follow the commandments would also mean failure to accept the covenant. While we do not fully know the exact process of how Gentiles became part of the covenant, from the literature we do have we know that males were circumcised, there were reports on the sincerity of the conversion, and then most likely a ritual bath.[29] The party of the Pharisees at the Jerusalem Council seems to be coming from this perspective when they say during the debate in Acts 15:5, "It is necessary to circumcise them and to direct them to observe the law of Moses." It is certainly not that they are against the Gentiles coming into the family of God. It is a question of identity within God's covenant family.

Crucial Conversationalists at the Jerusalem Council

When it mattered most, were these first century Christians at their worst? Did they ignore the disagreement? Did they address the situation only to handle it poorly? Or, did they engage in the crucial conversation and handle it effectively? Were they skilled conversationalists? One of the first steps for any conflict mediator is to identify the parties involved and to identify their key interests. First, let's do some background on all the parties involved before heading into the crucial conversation.

28. Ibid., 206.
29. Ibid.

Peter

In the first half of the book of Acts, Peter is a major player. In chapter one, Peter organizes the search for a replacement for Judas. In chapter 2, Peter is the one who gives the Pentecost sermon that saw thousands of people come to faith in Jerusalem. Then in chapters four and five, Peter takes a lead role as a spokesman for the Jerusalem church, giving witness to the work of the Spirit. Later on in a letter to the Galatian churches, Paul calls Peter a "pillar" of the Jerusalem church in Gal 2:9. At this point in the narrative, Peter had not gone to the Gentiles, nor does it seem that he had any plan to bring the Gospel to the Gentiles, despite the Lord telling the disciples that they will be His witnesses to the ends of the earth. Then in chapter ten, Peter has a vision of eating unclean animals, and then an interaction with the Gentile Cornelius where he witnessed the Holy Spirit coming down on Gentiles! At this point, Peter took place in two conversions—Cornelius's and his household's conversion to faith in Jesus as Messiah, and Peter's own conversion to viewing Gentiles as declared clean by God through faith in the Messiah. Peter struggled with God but was converted to a "gospel that crosses all boundaries and leaves no one out."[30] This came as a startling, but exciting pronouncement from the Jerusalem church when Peter witnessed to what the Spirit had done. The Jerusalem church at that time concluded in Acts 11:18 that "God has granted to the Gentiles also the repentance that leads to life." After the church continues to expand to Gentiles, and some Jews were uncomfortable with the Gentiles not following the full Mosaic Law, Peter acts as the spokesperson for the Gentiles at the Jerusalem council.

Paul and Barnabas

Barnabas appears early in Acts and is described as an encourager in Acts 4:36. The first time we meet his partner Paul, he is described as a persecutor of the early church. After the risen Jesus appears to him, Barnabas becomes a mentor in the faith for Paul. The two of them wind up in Antioch, and beginning in chapter thirteen they are sent out among the Gentiles proclaiming the Gospel of Jesus. They see many place their faith in the Messiah. They triumphed over sorcerers. They heal the lame, and when Paul and Barnabas return to Antioch in Acts 14:27, they report on the work God has done through them among the cities they visited, especially how God had "opened the door of faith to the Gentiles." While Peter carried the argument for the Gentile mission, Paul and Barnabas gave a full report of the

---

30. Guder, *Continuing Conversion of the Church*, 166.

works they had seen the Spirit do to the apostles and elders gathered at the Jerusalem Council.

Party of Pharisees

The incident of Peter and Cornelius, and now the report of Paul and Barnabas gave rise to the universal church's first major conflict. Acts 15 introduces "certain individuals that came down from Judea to Antioch and were teaching believers: 'Unless you are circumcised according to the custom taught by Moses, you cannot be saved.'" This caused a sharp "dispute and debate" with Paul and Barnabas, who saw the Spirit moving among the Gentiles without having to be circumcised. The conflict caused the church in Antioch to consult with the Jerusalem Church in order to come to a resolution to the conflict of how Gentiles become part of God's church. It was at the conference that Luke introduces us to the party of the Pharisee who said in Acts 15:5, "It is necessary to circumcise them and to direct them to observe the Law of Moses." It is important to note that in Luke's narrative the Pharisees are not always portrayed as negative, though certainly some of them did stand as enemies of Jesus and the church. This particular group of Pharisees were obviously believers in the Messiah, and were a vital part of the Jerusalem church. The group of Pharisees and the original group that sparked the debate with Paul and Barnabas in Antioch were related in some way.

James

The last key player in this debate was James the Just, the leader of the Jerusalem church. Technically, it is James and the elders, but as Bauckham points out, "Acts names no single leader but where leadership is clearly described, James is so described."[31] James is the half-brother of Jesus and is mentioned by Paul in Galatians as one of the pillars of the Jerusalem church. In Acts 12:17, Peter instructs the gathered believers at Mary the mother of John Mark to tell "James and the brethren" about Peter's miraculous escape from prison. Early church tradition has James as the leader of the Jerusalem church. For instance, the Gospel of Thomas 12 states, "The disciples said to Jesus, 'We know that you will depart from us. Who is to be our leader?' Jesus said to them, 'Wherever you are, you are to go to James the Just, for whose sake heaven and earth came into being.'" Eusebius, the famed Christian

---

31. Bauckham, "James, Peter, and the Gentiles," 154.

historian, quotes a Palestinian Christian historian named Hegesippus who explained James's nickname came about "because of his excessive righteousness." James spent so much time in prayer for his people that his knees were like camels. Eusebius explains,

> And he was in the habit of entering alone into the temple, and was frequently found upon his knees begging forgiveness for the people, so that his knees became hard like those of a camel, in consequence of his constantly bending them in his worship of God, and asking forgiveness for the people.[32]

James's character was such that he "was remembered for his righteousness and his stalwart defense of the Christians in Jerusalem during the difficult days leading up to the destruction of the temple in AD 70."[33] James stayed in Jerusalem for over thirty years until his death shortly before the Roman invasion of the city. In Acts 15, James seems to be the one overseeing the council. The council is made up of key players such as Paul and Barnabas, Peter, the apostles, and elders. James is the one though that gave his "judgment." The Jerusalem Council pretty much assents to what James says. Through his wisdom and leadership, a consensus is reached.

The Crucial Conversation Itself

The process of solving this controversy begins with the believers in Antioch choosing the method of "consulting" to help settle this dispute. Input was gathered from the church in Antioch and then a subset, the apostles and elders in Jerusalem, would settle the matter. Paul and Barnabas were appointed along with some other Christians from Antioch to go meet with the leaders in Jerusalem to discuss this issue (Acts 15:2). That a safe environment was created is indicated by the warm welcome the entourage from Antioch received in Jerusalem (15:4). The free flow of relevant information is ascertained by the full report of what God was doing among the Gentiles and the permitting of the Christian Pharisees to voice their opinion (15:4–5). Luke does not seem to suggest any hesitation of all involved to voice their opinion, nor the display of any violence. After the Christian Pharisees state their case, Peter witnesses to his experience of ministry to the Gentiles (15:7–11). The entire assembly maintained the safe environment by peacefully listening (15:12a) as Barnabas and Paul were allowed to speak. Just

---

32. Maier, *Eusebius*.
33. Just, "Apostolic Councils of Galatians and Acts," 264.

like the Christian Pharisees and Peter, they shared their facts and told their story (15:12b).

James then took the stand (15:13). He has listened well. He affirms what Peter has reported (15:14). He applies prophetic literature to agree (15:15–18). He concludes that the Gentile Christians do not have to be circumcised and do not have to obey the Law of Moses (15:19). James sustains a sensitivity for Jewish Christians by requiring the Gentile Christians to be sensitive as well through abstaining from food polluted by idols, from sexual immorality, from meat of strangled animals and from blood (15:20–21). It is James's opinion that the Gentiles should be asked to "abstain" from these four things. This verb, *apechesthai*, means "to avoid contact with or use of something," "to keep on avoiding doing something," or "to restrain from and keep from doing" and can be translated as "keep away, abstain, refrain from."[34] The first requirement prohibits purchasing meat that may have been used in an idol offering. Most scholars opine that the expression "pollutions of idols" has a specific reference to food that is unclean because it has been offered to idols. This could mean that they could no longer purchase meat from the public markets, since much of the meat sold in these markets had come from idol temples. The second prohibition concerns "sexual immorality," a term that refers to any kind of unsanctioned sexual immorality. The third item is "what has been strangled," an infrequent term understood generally to mean "meat of strangled animals," i.e., meat from animals that were improperly butchered, with the result that the blood has not been drained from them. The Mosaic Law prohibits eating such meat (Lev 17:14; cf. Gen 9:4; Exod 22:31).[35] The fourth prohibition concerns "blood," a term that could refer to murder, i.e., the spilling of blood, but refers more plausibly to eating food made from the blood of animals, which the Mosaic Law prohibits (Lev 17:10–11; cf. Lev 3:17; 7:26–27). The first two demands relate to sins for which Gentiles were notorious, that is, idolatry and sexual immorality; while the other two relate to matters that would endanger table fellowship between the Gentiles and Jewish Christians, that is, eating animals that had been strangled and eating blood.

Schnabel offers six main interpretations that have been suggested, the last two being the most likely:[36]

1. The four stipulations are practical measures meant to facilitate the (table) fellowship between Jewish Christians and Gentile Christians as "ad hoc advice on how not to offend certain Jews."

34. Schnabel, *Acts*, 642.
35. Ibid., 643–44.
36. Ibid., 644–45.

2. The stipulations correspond to the Noahide commandments that the Jews regarded as normative for humanity.

3. The stipulations correspond to the cardinal sins that a Jew was not supposed to commit under any circumstances—idolatry, fornication, and murder (blood).

4. The stipulations come from the catalogues of vices and virtues that Jews used in teaching Gentiles when they became proselytes.

5. The stipulations should be interpreted in the context of the Jewish diaspora on the background of the Old Testament polemic against idolatry; they direct the Gentile believers to refrain from participating in pagan cultic and other practices.

6. The four stipulations should be interpreted in terms of the regulations that Lev 17–18 formulates for Gentiles who live in Israel as resident aliens.

The final statement of James's decision recorded by Luke is the rationale for the stipulations in v. 20. It is difficult to perceive its primary relationship with the four stipulations, but certainly suggests a Gentile knowledge and sensitivity to Jewish scruples.

Though the method of consulting was used to resolve the issue, consensus also occurs as it appears everyone agrees and supports the decision (15:22, 30–31). It would also seem from Luke's account, the Jerusalem council avoided the "fool's choice" by not settling for an either/or choice. Luke does not chronicle any requirements or constraints on the Jewish Christians. It is safe to assume they continued to circumcise their infant boys and obey the Law of Moses as their heritage invited. Both the Jewish Christians and the Gentiles Christians lived out their faith in Jesus and obedience to God as their consciences demanded.

Luke's report finally suggests once the decision was reached that what was decided was delivered responsibly (15:30), follow up occurred (15:32–33), and the Gentile Christians were held accountable to the requirements (21:25).

To illustrate and review, observe the demonstration of the two *Crucial Conversations'* acronyms by the Jerusalem Council. The CRIB acronym: all involved were *c*ommitted to seeking the mutual purpose of the salvation of the Gentiles (15:2), *r*ecognized the purpose behind the strategy (15:4–5), *i*nvented a mutual purpose (15:11), and *b*rainstormed new strategies (15:20). The STATE acronym: again, the opposing sides *s*hared their facts and *t*old *t*heir stories and *a*sked for others' paths (15:4–21), *t*alked tentatively (15:22–29), and *e*ncouraged testing (15:30–33).

For the modern church, conflicts can sometimes be brought before a higher authority. Denominational leaders, associations, and other judicatory officials often have training and experience to help congregations resolve conflict. It is always better for these sorts of bodies to be proactive by initiating the mediation rather than waiting for the conflict to be brought to them. Your local church polity will determine who serves as a higher authority and how much power they possess in conflict resolution. Some bodies can serve as arbitrators who resolve the conflict by issuing a ruling to be followed. Other bodies possess limited power, so they exercise their skill as crucial conversationalists to help those in conflict resolve their difference and find a peaceful resolution. Whatever your local church polity may be, bringing people skilled in crucial conversations helps congregations resolve their conflicts more quickly than if they try to resolve them alone.

Conflict is unavoidable and inevitable; combat is avoidable and optional. Conflict is often seen as wrong and dangerous, rather than being an opportunity for growth. Conflict is often "spiritualized" by making every battle between right and wrong. Learn to invite, appreciate, and work through disagreement in constructive ways through the power of the difficult task of having a crucial conversation. Remember! It is not just about communication; it is about results. The first century church avoided division. They were skilled conversationalists! Will today's church be the same?

Bibliography

Bauckham, Richard. "James, Peter, and the Gentiles." In *The Missions of James, Peter, and Paul: Tensions in Early Christianity*, edited by Bruce Chilton and Craig A Evans, 91–142. Novum Testamentum Supplements 115. Boston: Brill, 2005.

Chilton, Bruce D., and Craig A. Evans. *The Missions of James, Peter, and Paul: Tensions in Early Christianity*. Novum Testamentum Supplements 115. Boston: Brill, 2005.

Guder, Darrel. *The Continuing Conversion of the Church*. Grand Rapids: Eerdmans, 2000.

Just, Arthur. "The Apostolic Councils of Galatians and Acts: How the First-Century Christians Walked Together." *Concordia Theological Quarterly* 74 (2010) 261–88.

Maier, Paul L. *Eusebius, the Church History: A New Translation with Commentary*. Grand Rapids: Kregel, 1999.

Patterson, Kerry, et al. *Crucial Conversations: Tools for Talking When Stakes Are High*. 2nd ed. New York: McGraw-Hill, 2012.

Sanders, E. P. *Judaism Practice and Belief 63 BCE–66 CE*. Eugene, OR: Wipf & Stock, 1992.

———. *Paul and Palestinian Judaism*. Philadelphia: Fortress, 1977.

Schnabel, Eckhard J. *Acts: Zondervan Exegetical Commentary on the New Testament*. Grand Rapids: Zondervan, 2012.

4

Learning to Love in Faith, Rather than Fight with Power

Paul as Mediation Teacher

1 Corinthians 8–11 and Romans 14–15

By Doug McPherson and Ben Tertin

When a local pastor, let's call him Pastor Dave, built a new church ministry around a Fantasy Football league, he had no idea how successful—and controversial—it would become. On one hand, his previously struggling church was now on the mend, finally opening its heart to the reality of a changing world and the need for fresh engagement with real neighbors. In Pastor Dave's part of the country, Fantasy Football is a big deal, and this ministry quickly became something far more than a chat group for football nerds. It was a true Christian fellowship, a growing community clearly adding to the health and well-being of the overall church, and after having watched the church experience a long period of decline and difficulty, Pastor Dave was feeling rejuvenated and hopeful.

But Pastor Dave's excitement gets quashed when Byron, a 30-something single whom Dave baptized around Easter, confronts him about this ministry. Prior to joining the church, Byron had been obsessed with daily fantasy sports gambling. Through his addiction, Byron had racked up over $20,000 in debt. The hopelessness he felt as he sank deeper into financial ruin had ultimately driven him to Redemption Church in the first place. In the months since, Byron had put his faith in Christ, joined a small group for accountability, and begun the slow process of freeing himself from the shackles of his old habits.

Upon hearing of Redemption Church's fantasy football league, Byron was distraught. Knowing the grip of addiction, he feared the allure of competition and camaraderie that came with the league might ensnare him once again, becoming a virtual gateway back into his old routine. He also felt betrayed by the very community to whom he had turned for rescue. With tears in his eyes, Byron asked Pastor Dave, "Would you please cancel the league? I can't stay here if you don't."

Free but Conflicted

When conflicts arise between fellow Christians, we often assume that one party is in the wrong, or perhaps some hidden sin is to blame. But that is not always the case. The scenario above illustrates the surprising truth that many conflicts between devoted followers of Christ can be traced to expressions of the faith they share. Different interpretations of the freedom granted to believers in the New Testament have led to arguments, church divisions, and even the dissolution of some organizational partnerships. Yet, if our shared devotion to Christ and his Kingdom binds us together, uniting us as the one people of God, how can anything drive us apart? Is it too much to think that God's people can learn to get along?

Our goal in this chapter is to examine how the Apostle Paul wrestled with this freedom-conflict tension: first, at Corinth, where believers disagreed over eating idolatrous meats, and second, in Rome, with the union of different kinds of lives into the one freeing life of Christ. While some resources focus primarily on managing conflict, we believe the New Testament leads us toward a principled way of life that moves beyond mere management. Paul calls us to a fellowship with Jesus and one another that not only erodes the desire for power and correctness, desires which often spark and fuel conflict, but that also clarifies what we mean by "freedom" in the first place. We will see how a movement into Jesus' economy of grace and reliance on *his* power and *his* correctness is a movement away from conflict, beyond conflict management, and into the expansive divine love at the heart of conflict resolution.

Where and What to Eat in First-Century Corinth

Many conflicts of freedom are rooted in contextual elements that change over time. For instance, in my (Doug's) own church tradition, the hotly debated issues of past generations included playing billiards, dancing, viewing R-rated movies, and drinking alcohol. During my formational years, however, a pool table had become a staple of student ministry, we went across the street to the dances held by the Methodist church, and *The Passion of the Christ* proved that certain R-rated movies were acceptable. Some are still holding out hope for the discovery of a textual variant that proves Jesus turned the wine into water. While the issues may change, the basic challenge of living as a unified community of believers apart from uniformity on personal convictions remains.

In the Greek city of Corinth, the conflict surrounded the issue of eating meat. This became controversial for the Corinthian believers because of the connection between meat and pagan worship. Temples dedicated to the gods dotted the landscape in the Greco-Roman world, and animal sacrifices were a standard part of temple life. Whether offered as a part of the regular cultic liturgy, or in conjunction with a special feast or a local festival, most of the meat available to the masses had been offered in idol worship.[1] This created a problem for many of the Corinthian Christians. Should a follower of Jesus eat meat associated with idolatry or not?

The question required more than just a simple answer. While the Jewish people had long been known for avoiding food offered to idols, for the vast majority of the population in the Greco-Roman world, temple sacrifices and festivals were embedded in the fabric of everyday life.[2] Participation in these observances was both normal and expected, regardless of whatever one may believe about the gods.[3] Abstaining from the sacrifices likely meant being labeled by neighbors as socially disruptive, as many believed that every resident had a duty to keep the community in the gods' good graces through regular offerings. At the very least, withdrawing from cultic ceremonies would deprive believers of key socializing opportunities.

Some in the Corinthian church wanted to participate in the temple festivities while maintaining their devotion to Jesus. Though unnamed by Paul, scholars have commonly referred to them simply as "the Strong." Clues found in 1 Corinthians suggest that this group justified their ongoing

---

1. Willis, *Idol Meat in Corinth*, 13–15.
2. Harrison and Yamauchi, "Food Consumption," 321–22.
3. Wright, *Paul and the Faithfulness of God*, 252–75.

involvement in the cultic ceremonies.[4] By arguing that idols were not actual gods, but simply inanimate blocks of wood or rock that were powerless before the one true God, the Strong group defended their right to eat idol meat freely and without any compromise in their exclusive commitment to the Christ.

At the same time, others within the Corinthian church held the conviction that eating meat offered to idols violated true devotion to Jesus.[5] This group is called the Weak, a derogatory name that probably came from the Strong group, and which Paul employed for clarity as he addressed the issue.[6] According to Paul, the Weak resisted eating idol meat because some members of the group were recent converts from the pagan Roman religion (1 Cor 8:7). Eating idol meat was a return to their former way of life, a life they had left upon conversion to Christianity.[7] For them, idols still represented gods that stood in opposition to the gospel of Jesus. The Weak viewed idols not as harmless blocks of wood or rock, but as symbols of their previous allegiance.

This was a complex issue, and great care had to be taken to offer a solution that fostered unity within the Corinthian church while still maintaining Christian freedom. In 1 Cor 8–11:1, Paul offered a thoughtful, nuanced response that was both principled and practical. To fully grasp his counsel, we need to understand the religious context that he addressed.

Wise Principles for Different Contexts

In ancient Corinth, like any other Greco-Roman community, one could expect to find meat in three places: temples, meat markets, or at dinners in private homes.[8] Paul addressed all three settings in his letter, beginning with idol temples. Recent archaeological discoveries have given vital insights into the temple practices that contributed to the idol meat controversy.[9]

Most animal sacrifices would be slaughtered at the temple and then, after being inspected for any blemishes or discernible omens, they were

---

4. Fotopoulos, *Food Offered to Idols*, 260–61. See especially 1 Cor 8:4–6, 8.
5. Willis, *Idol Meat in Corinth*, 105.
6. Ibid., 94–95.
7. This means that many in this group were not Jewish, though one expects that the Jewish believers within the church would have sided with the Weak against the Strong. It seems likely that this disagreement was between two groups of gentile Christians. Ibid., 93.
8. Fotopoulos, *Food Offered to Idols*, 258.
9. See Murphy-O'Connor, "Corinth That Saint Paul Saw," 147–59.

divided into three parts. One part was burned on the altar, the second part was consumed by the worshiper and his guests, and the third part was placed on the god's special table.[10] This embodied the belief that the god shared in the sacrificial meal with the worshipers, creating fellowship between the participants and the deity. Cult officials probably ate from the portion on the god's table once it had served its symbolic purpose. Whatever meat exceeded their needs was sold in the meat market.[11]

In addition to the regular offerings, special sacrifices were given in conjunction with cultic observances or state-sponsored festivals. Even local associations or guilds might host a temple feast in tribute to their patron deity.[12] These festivities could be compared to our modern holidays, being times of community-wide celebration, relief from the ordinary routine of life, and excessive indulgence.

Some temples were also used to accommodate private dinner parties. Archaeologists have identified three dining rooms in the temple of Asklepios, the Greek god of healing, which housed such dinners.[13] Several papyrus invitations have been discovered which summoned the recipient to dine at the temple of Sarapis, an Egyptian god highly esteemed in Corinth.[14] As New Testament scholar John Fotopoulos points out, declining such an invitation could result in social or economic harm.[15] The occasion of these meals could range from a birthday or a wedding, to a thanksgiving meal for healing or an appointment to a new post.

Paul began his response to the Corinthians by addressing the defense apparently offered by the Strong (1 Cor 8:1b, 4–5a, 6, 8).[16] While affirming that idols possess no innate power, Paul pointed out that the idols still posed a real threat to the Weak. Past participation in cultic worship had a powerful and lasting influence on members of the Weak group, forming their perceptions and vulnerabilities. We can imagine that the sounds and smells of the temple festivities triggered many memories for them, including some dark and traumatic experiences.

Several years ago, I (Doug) led a mission trip to Cambodia, where the dominant religion is a very animistic form of Buddhism. The people there tend to give a lot of attention to the spirit world, especially to appeasing

---

10. Willis, *Idol Meat in Corinth*, 16–17.
11. Ibid., 17.
12. Ibid., 13–15.
13. Fotopoulos, *Food Offered to Idols*, 49.
14. Ibid., 102–10.
15. Ibid., 69–70.
16. Ibid., 260–61.

the spirits through offerings and other observances. One member of my team was a first generation Cambodian-American who had converted to Christianity in her late teens. Though a decade had passed since she had left her old religion, every time she caught a whiff of burning incense or heard the ritualistic chanting, she was gripped by fear. She possessed a deep faith in Jesus, yet even after so many years she remained quite sensitive to the influence of her former way of life.

Some in Corinth had learned to fear the gods' wrath since childhood, and fear drove their religious observances. Fear can be a difficult thing to unlearn. Imagine the fear felt by Corinthian Christians who faced their first sailing trip since they had quit offering sacrifices to Poseidon, the keeper of the seas. Observing their Christian brothers and sisters eating at an idol temple might be just enough for them to justify presenting a small offering of their own "just in case."

Also, we must not forget the significant social pressure on the Corinthian believers to participate in the sacrifices. Seeing a fellow Christian participating in a cultic meal might encourage those from the Weak group to seek relief from such pressure by returning to temple festivities (1 Cor 8:9–12). Though the Strong group viewed such involvement as harmless, for the Weak this meant nothing short of syncretism, a violation of their exclusive devotion to Jesus.

Paul's Principles

Having shown how the actions of the Strong could damage the Weak, Paul introduced the first of two principles that were to guide the Corinthian believers to unity when navigating questions of freedom: *Do no harm to the fellowship of believers* (1 Cor 8:13; restated 10:24, 32). Notice that avoiding controversy or hurt feelings was not his primary motivation. Paul did not implore the believers to refrain from anything that would raise eyebrows in the fellowship. Rather, what troubled Paul was anything that caused legitimate damage or "woundedness" to a fellow Christian.[17] He did not fear the Weak taking offense at those participating in the temple feasts; he feared the Weak being harmed by the example of the Strong. Paul called the Corinthian believers to eschew anything that damaged the community of believers, pointing to his own ministry as an example of limited freedom for the benefit of others (9:1–27).

The second principle underlying Paul's advice to the Corinthians is this: *Do nothing to compromise unrivaled allegiance to Jesus* (10:21; implied

---

17. Thiselton, *First Epistle to the Corinthians*, 654–55.

in 8:7). The Lord Jesus, the Messiah to whom Paul bore witness, demanded and deserved undivided devotion. Anything that encroached on a believer's commitment to Jesus was a violation. While the Strong justified their behavior, declaring that the lifeless idols posed no threat to them, Paul warned them that idolatry was nothing to take lightly. Gleaning from Israel's history, he reminded them of other times when God's people had betrayed their devotion to Him (1 Cor 10:1–13).

Allegiance, Allegiance, Allegiance

With this principled foundation firmly in place, Paul offered a few practical guidelines for the Corinthian Christians to follow as they managed the tension between individual freedom and the unity of the Body. First, Paul banned all believers from participation in the temple sacrifices and feasts (1 Cor 10:14–22). Comparing the temple meals to the Lord's Supper, he argued that both are instrumental in drawing the participants together as a worshiping community (1 Cor 10:16–21). The idol is just a block of wood or rock, but the idol meal is an act of allegiance with the powers that oppose Christ and his people. This is a clear violation of principle two. Followers of Jesus have no business engaging in such behavior.

Second, Paul declared all the believers free to eat from the meat market (1 Cor 10:25). This may have shocked a few of the Corinthians. After all, most of the meat that came through the market had been sacrificed to idols.[18] Some was left over from the temple worship, having been symbolically placed on the gods' tables. Once it had fulfilled its cultic purpose, it was sold in the market. We also know that some meat markets, like the one at Pompeii, had a shrine dedicated to the Imperial cult within the market building.[19] Animals butchered at the meat market were probably sacrificed in conjunction with the Imperial cult. Yet, Paul encouraged the believers to purchase meat from the market and to eat it freely. Why did he not perceive this as inconsistent with his earlier call to "flee from idolatry" (1 Cor 10:14)?

The brief explanation given is a quotation from Ps 24:1, "The earth is the Lord's, and everything in it." Appealing to a favored Jewish text, Paul reminds the Corinthians of God's sovereignty over all, including the very meat in question. The meat was not contaminated by its history; it carried no lasting consequence for those who ate it. When Christians purchased and ate meat from the meat market, they did so as an act of commerce under the sovereign rule of God, not an act of worship in fellowship with

---

18. Branch, "Butchers & Meat," 226–32.
19. Gill, "Meat-Market at Corinth," 392–93.

the idol cult. For Paul, this made a world of difference. Christians did not compromise their exclusive devotion to Jesus by consuming market meat, because doing so was not an act of allegiance to a false god.

Finally, Paul gives detailed instructions for dining at an unbeliever's home (1 Cor 27–30). Formal dinners held a special place in Greco-Roman society, and the Corinthians probably loved receiving dinner invitations.[20] Dinners, however, also included sacrificial food. Frequently, the host presented his sacrifice at the temple, and then brought back a portion to eat with friends and associates. At other times, the host might sacrifice the animal within the home.[21]

Paul encouraged the Corinthian believers to freely attend dinners, eating the food offered without question. If, however, the believers were informed that the meat had been sacrificed, then they must abstain. While it may seem that Paul is splitting hairs at this point, this direction is completely consistent with the two principles laid out earlier.

Imagine that Phillip is a Christian from the Weak group who was invited to an unbeliever's home for dinner. On the way there, he sees his pagan host carrying several cuts of meat out of a temple toward his home. When Phillip follows his host into the house, he finds Erastus, a fellow Christian, has also been invited to this dinner. Phillip anxiously tells Erastus that the meat has been sacrificed. Erastus, following Paul's counsel, does not eat the meat, because he does not want to harm Phillip. He exercises his freedom, not for his own rights or interests, but for the benefit of his Christian brother.

Or, let's imagine that the pagan host tells Erastus that the meat has been offered in a sacrifice. If Erastus eats, his host will consider him to have shared in the sacrificial meal. This time Erastus abstains because he does not want to compromise his allegiance to Jesus in the eyes of his host. By exercising his freedom in Christ to abstain from eating, Erastus is demonstrating his singular devotion to Jesus before his unbelieving host. With these conditions in place, Paul provided clear direction for how the Corinthian Christians could participate in private dinners without harming their brothers and sisters or violating their allegiance to Jesus.

The apostle's counsel is just as relevant to the struggles of contemporary churches as it was to the Corinthian believers of his own day. Living within a Spirit-guided fellowship is not for the faint of heart. Paul's letter to the Corinthians shows that resolving conflicts of personal freedom can be challenging and, at times, even a bit messy. As churches follow the Spirit into this messy realm, though, they can plan for and engage each attendant

---

20. Fotopoulos, *Food Offered to Idols*, 158.
21. Ibid., 258.

challenge with Paul's principles, now seen more through a lens of modern mediation principles. For example, writing conflict mediation procedures into church bylaws and teaching them in membership classes could be a way to communicate not only the process for mediation but also the heart behind it. Teaching members how to handle conflict more skillfully prevents the potential for larger conflicts to grow, which allows the church community to get past conflict mediation into healthy interpersonal fellowship. In the end, the apostle's counsel not only serves as sound teaching for mediation, but it also helps culture creators learn to set strong foundations that diminish the potential for conflict in the first place.

We should expect questions and conflicts over personal freedom to arise, especially as the gospel leads us beyond cultural and geographic boundaries. Several years ago, I (Doug) began taking yoga classes at the local fitness center. Not one of my Christian brothers or sisters questioned me, because in Texas yoga is viewed simply as a form of exercise. A few months later, I traveled to rural India to encourage and teach local pastors. While there, I learned that a few believers were teaching yoga in connection with the ministry. This was of grave concern to my new friends, because in India, yoga is inextricably tied to Hinduism. For my Indian brothers and sisters, practicing yoga is comparable to the Corinthian practice of sharing in an idol sacrifice; it is a clear violation of one's allegiance to Jesus and it raises a big conflict for Christians with differing perspectives. Living so as *not to harm the fellowship of believers* and *to do nothing that would compromise unrivalled allegiance to Christ*, I may very well practice yoga in my Texan context and, for the sake of my friends living in a culture still deeply enmeshed with Hinduism, I avoid yoga. By following Paul's principles, and understanding that all exists under God's rule (rather than mine), I can live faithfully for Jesus without instigating conflicts that damage fellowship or introduce rival allegiances.

Freedom From or Freedom To?

So far, this Pauline trajectory looks pretty good, as it takes us out of ourselves and requires us to acknowledge significant differences woven into the hearts and minds and beliefs of our brothers, sisters, and neighbors in different contexts. But we will miss the deeper truth if we stop there to merely conclude that contextual realities either grant or restrain the Christian's freedom; in other words, to say that our context governs what a Christian can and cannot do is equivalent to saying, "Your 'freedom' is actually subject to the law of context." How could we rightly call this "freedom" when we still feel significant restraint? That's a good question, but here is an even better one that must be answered first: Does Paul see Jesus setting the Christian free *from* something or set free *to* something?

To many people in our world today concepts of liberation, autonomy, and independence are to freedom what flour is to bread. The term "freedom" denotes a certain untethering, suggesting that the freest human being in our declaration-of-independence culture is the one who has figured out how to live with zero restraint and nary a care in the world. From this angle, contemporary interpretations of Rom 14:5b—"Each of them should be fully convinced in their own mind"—can easily run amok. But when Paul is writing to his friends in first-century Rome (and elsewhere), his talk about freedom does not sound quite like freedom *from* something, as it reveals a sense of the Christian now being free *to* live within Christ-created parameters, whereas he or she was not previously able to do so. Paul simply had no sense that freedom in Christ resulted in anything like ethical independence.

What would interpreters in Paul's own day have thought about all of this? There was much common ethical talk about the "two ways" of living, one way toward the natural law in which freedom would be found, and the other toward one's own destruction through diversion from that natural law.[22] Hellenistic readers, even with the most bare-bones philosophical sophistication found something of value in Paul's writing, but what? More importantly, what did he intend for them to find?

J. Louis Martyn suggests that "the two ways" ethical construct of common pagan philosophy in Paul's Hellenistic world had long since become a properly basic way of understanding human power and its relationship to right and wrong. The individual had an independent power to exercise and, therefore, a choice to make, as if facing a fork in the road, between this way or that. But instead of speaking of the orthodox "two ways"—either of which an essentially autonomous human agent could choose—Paul refers to not one but two active powers, namely the flesh and the Spirit of the crucified Christ.[23] The great news, to Paul, was that moral agency was no longer found in something that a human being had accomplished, "achieving autonomous, moral progress, for example, by strenuous philosophical endeavor."[24] Morality was found in something done to the human being by God through the liberating death and resurrection of Christ, but this does not mean that people are God's miniature puppets who passively find goodness in themselves placed there by another. "On the contrary," writes

---

22. Martyn, "Gospel Invades Philosophy," 27.
23. Ibid.
24. Ibid., 29.

Martyn, "it is *radically free*, liberated from the nefarious and lethal power of Sin, liberated *to* love, *to* rejoice, *to* be patient, *to* have faith, *to* be gentle, *to* have self-control, and *to* bear the other's burdens, thus *fulfilling* the Law of Christ."[25] Indeed, we see a sense of being freed from sin, but the trajectory set by Christ is not toward freedom from everything in autonomy; by avoiding the "two ways" language of his day, Paul reorients the Christian mind away from personal power, toward the power of God who is pure righteousness, through his inbreaking action in the Spirit of Jesus. "Freedom" for the human being, from this framework, is tightly bound *to* the life of another, namely Christ alone.

When Paul says we are "free" to live according to our conscience, and should therefore not judge another's,[26] he does so in the context of understanding "freedom" as a movement not from tethering to untethering, as it were, but from bondage to sin and death to becoming bond slaves of Christ.

Trust in Christ and in his gospel means that a person can genuinely act in thankfulness toward God and in faith placed in God alone. Rather than faith or trust in oneself, which is trust in something bound to the limits of mere human potential, faith in Christ breaks all shackles that would otherwise prevent one from living in his freedom, according to his way. Freedom is Christ-defined, not autonomously defined. Similarly, the Stoic contemporaries of Paul would suggest that saying "I can do whatever I want" is only a statement about human potential, not a statement about an ethical good or true freedom. In this arena, along with others, Paul seems unafraid to borrow some from the Stoics. Freedom for the Stoics was found in the "law of nature," and the person most able to live according to this natural law was the freest being. The Jewish philosopher Philo operates the same basic way, in terms of freedom for God's people, but replaces the Stoic "law of nature" with divinely revealed Torah. In other words, there is no sense in *any* of these thinkers that all actions are essentially neutral, and their right-ness or wrong-ness finds its basis in the autonomous human will. Instead, the Stoics would say that actions adhering to the law of nature are inherently good and free, while Philo would say the same but would replace "law of nature" with Torah.[27] In sum, actions that work against God's intended way of life for human beings exemplify a return to slavery. Paul can easily be heard using similar categories when he speaks of freedom.

The Christ-follower embracing his or her graciously given freedom therefore lives by the natural law of God—the gospel of Jesus

---

25. Ibid., *emphases* added.
26. Cf. Rom 14:3–5.
27. See Horsley, "Law of Nature in Philo and Cicero."

Christ—knowing from God's own revealed word that all is the Lord's and that partaking of anything with the virtue of thankfulness and allegiance to Christ, or faith, is an exercise of the purest freedom in the history of humankind. With this as a backdrop, we now turn to one final passage from Paul.

The Strong and Weak: Romans 14–15

The Roman church experienced conflicts similar to those in Corinth in terms of disputes between the strong and the weak about moral superiority. It is important to see that he uses "strong in faith" and "weak in faith" categories, as opposed to those who have faith versus those who do not. In Rome, as in Corinth, questions about food and acceptable dinner guests are prominent, but here the groups are not so much former idolaters who are now Christians versus other Christians as much as they are Jewish versus non-Jewish Christians. And other questions are being debated in Rome, as well, such as who gets to determine which day is the correct day to worship. Paul's emphasis here seems to be more focused on the divisions between Jewish Christians who wanted to keep a kosher kitchen or Sabbath-grounded worship structure and Gentile Christians who felt no such desire in either category. "Both groups are given the freedom to follow their own scruples," writes New Testament scholar Craig Blomberg, "but neither has the right to disparage the other."[28] Paul's instruction dissolves human-only foundations of moral superiority, suggesting varying degrees to which one understands and experiences life in the gospel. "Weak" does not mean wrong, nor does "strong" mean correct. Jesus determines ontological correctness, whereas the human being's motive reveals where he or she stands in terms of God's righteousness, and Paul urges believers to act in thankfulness to God and faith in him.

Even with the best intentions, when a stronger person tries to exercise power over the other in order to strengthen them, conflict arises. As C. S. Lewis put it, "Of all tyrannies, a tyranny sincerely exercised for the good of its victims may be the most oppressive. It would be better to live under robber barons than under omnipotent busybodies."[29] But when one follows Paul's instruction to "receive" rather than dominate or attempt to control the weaker person (Rom 14:1) he or she can rest confidently in the fact that God remains the true sovereign, that Jesus judges correctly and accordingly, and that the only true master with any real power in this picture is Christ himself: "Who are you to pass judgment on another's servant [implying that

---

28. Blomberg, *From Pentecost to Patmos*, 261.
29. Lewis, *God in the Dock*, 292.

the other is a servant not of man or law, but of Christ]? Before his own master [that is, Christ] he stands or falls. And he will stand, for the Lord is able to make him stand" (Rom 14:4, NRSV).

In sum, *when you embrace your freedom to live in faith, you will end conflict; when you embrace pursuits for power and your own correctness, you will create conflict.* To be sure, such a thesis is easier to write about than it is to comprehensively live by, but the truth of it remains. Try to overpower your brother or sister, and however much you believe it to be for his or her good, you will actually be submitting yourself to the flesh-driven law of sin and death by believing that their transformation is ultimately your responsibility. Such betrays a distrust in God's wisdom and power coupled with an unhealthy trust in self. And by attempting to forcibly change other people's behaviors and consciences, unlike Jesus who constantly sought the Father's will rather than his own, you will become the usurper foisting yourself into the role reserved for the true Master, a Master who—unlike you and me—is able to make even the weakest Christian stand up in righteousness and divine glory.

Faith as Ridiculous, Thankful Allegiance

Finally, we cannot underestimate the sheer insanity of Paul's words, according to the zeitgeist of his world, not to mention our own; by taking him seriously, we are able to see how living with this kind of radical freedom will likely sound ridiculous to our modern mindset. Clambering for moral superiority has been a fashionable hobby throughout history, and the heart of this struggle beats with faith in humanity rather than faith in God, whom Paul sees as morally superior to all. By pledging allegiance to certain governments or systems of law, we do say, "I submit my life to you, which means that I trust you for ultimate well-being." So, in Jewish-Christian context in Rome, moral superiority has already been codified in the Law for centuries; correctness was clearly spelled out. If one's allegiance was placed in the Law or nation or genetic ties to Abraham, it was necessarily not placed in God. Paul wants to reorient trust beyond such things and toward God alone, but some see his move as morally digressive. When Paul says, "I know and am convinced in the Lord Jesus that there is nothing unclean in itself," he is transforming and expanding a foundational narrative in the Jewish identity and reorienting his people away from misplaced trust.[30]

For the Shema-grounded Jewish way of life, symbolic practice mattered deeply. And for a Jewish Christian, like Paul, the significance of

30. Rom 4:14.

symbolic practice did not diminish on the freeing road to Damascus; instead, it was totally reworked. And because food—what you could eat and who you could eat it with—was "the most important, and tricky" symbol,[31] eyebrows raise when Paul essentially dismantles the notion that some food is unclean as he follows in the footsteps of Jesus.[32] Instead, he strikes to the heart and suggests that any food received in thankfulness and devotion to God is indeed good. The physical substance is of little importance. And as N. T. Wright suggests, "To say that something previously forbidden has now become something 'indifferent,' so that it is up to the individual whether they go this way or that, is a move of earth-shattering importance."[33] Remember that Saul of Tarsus was about as rigid as it gets in terms of rules like this, and so this new direction is less an upgrade and more an upheaval. Paul was making a conscious ethical decision that resulted from a total gospel transformation of his thinking from a focus on the things of goodness to the heart of goodness.

"For the Kingdom of God does not consist of food and drink, but righteousness, peace, and joy in the Holy Spirit," says Paul. The most important and tricky symbols of his people, of his identity in God and Israel, were not destroyed as much as they were expanded and enhanced to now transcend the material and law, aiming at the nature of true humanity in Christ and its maturation. "Let us then pursue what makes for peace and for mutual upbuilding" (Rom 14:19).

Symbolically speaking, to Saul of Tarsus, the truths about life with God were previously embodied and displayed through inflexible food laws and regulations on who meals could be shared with. So, if you wanted to say "I love God" and "I eat pork," he was going to engage you in a conflict, even a severe conflict. To do so would not be malicious but would zealously and symbolically demonstrate a truth that he believed God genuinely wanted to reveal. Now, in these new days, God is expanding his revelation not to abrogate previously revealed truths but to bolster, support, and radically expand beyond our comprehension the idea of belonging to God.

Paul sees Jesus' gospel now planted and germinating in this world, and as it grows in the lives of God's people, it is normal and reasonable to expect that it will transform the way God's people live symbolically. Some of the biggest truths that this breaking news would offer revolved around unprecedented and widespread inclusion of people previously deemed unclean,

---

31. Wright, *Paul and the Faithfulness of God*, 358.

32. See, for example, Jesus' radical expansion of clean versus unclean in Mark 7:1–23.

33. Wright, *Paul and the Faithfulness of God*, 359.

deeper personal engagement with motives that govern behavior, and an exponentially clearer vision of the Kingdom of God drawing near in the first stages of a long-awaited eschaton. In other words, Paul was opening God's people to a new freedom, one that now allowed them to more fully embody God's expansive love.

"OK!" an overzealous believer might say at such news. "I pledge allegiance to the God of creation. I have strong faith in him. And because of this, I approve of all meats, all substances, and even yoga and fantasy football! I am very holy and righteous, indeed." But this attitude betrays something other than the principles we have already set out, even though it would be lauded in our day as much as it was in Paul's. The Roman imperial cult revolved around public demonstrations and displays of devotion. To show others your religious practice was a properly basic, and good, thing to do. But Paul sees an inherent divisiveness in this that will cause the breakdown of Christian fellowship and create conflict. So he says, "So whatever you believe about these things keep between yourself and God. Blessed is the one who does not condemn himself by what he approves" (Rom 14:22). "The inward freedom does not have to be expressed outwardly in order to be enjoyed: One may enjoy it in one's own inner life—a secret known only to oneself and God," writes C. E. B. Cranfield. "And, if a weak brother is going to be hurt by one's giving outward expression to one's freedom, then one should be content with the inward experience of it, of which God is the only witness."[34]

To miss the latter point could lend toward a fundamental mistake in resolving real conflicts with real people in our contemporary context. As we noted up front, conflict is almost always sparked by desires for *power* and *rightness*. One says this, the other says that, and both work different angles to win. Power. But from Paul's perspective, the "win" was not in diminishing the enemy or getting the final word or passing the proposal by a simple majority vote at your elder-board meeting; the win was to love, forgive, and accept another brother or sister, however weak they might be, and by doing so you display the precise nature of gospel and Jesus himself, who forgives and loves men and women while they are yet sinners.

What Would Jesus Smoke?

Just before Washington State legalized marijuana in 2014, pastors in the Pacific Northwest were floundering. When it used to be that a simple dance with Mary Jane could land you a hefty fine or jail time, the Christian

---

34. Cranfield, *Romans 9–16*, 726.

pot-smoking ethic relied heavily on state and federal law: "Whatever your opinion is about the reefer, the laws of the land forbid it, and God seems interested in us obeying the authorities that he himself established." It was truly a no-brainer, which might be why we didn't think about it much. But now weed is legal, and the current legislative trajectory suggests a massive social upheaval in terms of this drug's place in our culture. Pastors have no reason to fear, but they do have much reason to pray for wisdom and guidance from the Spirit on these matters. If you suppose that legalization won't make it to your state anytime soon, you might be assuming too much. And if you think it's not already in your church, naïveté may be infiltrating your bookshelves.

How will you respond when a Life Group or Bible Study in your church starts to include some THC-saturated tinctures, pot brownies, or sativa-enhanced breath mints next to the brewskis and chilled chardonnays at the summertime rendezvous? When you and the believers in your fellowship begin to discover faithful, loving members who use marijuana, will a dramatic conflict ensue? How about when your son or daughter opts out of the mainstream US alcohol culture altogether, abstaining from the pilsners and pinots of culturally acceptable celebration to instead spark a spliff? Talk about a complex issue of Christian freedom that drives us to Jesus as the ultimate judge, perfect sanctifier, and only source of true life!

Remember, most of the arguments you might muster up against the negative health impacts of marijuana use can likewise be argued about alcohol, but such is nearly impossible to see when you have grown up in a culture that criminalizes the substance. And if you throw raw idolatry into the mix, it gets even more complex.

During my undergraduate studies, I (Ben) wrote for my school newspaper and ended up researching a group of local Rastafarians in north Portland, Oregon, called the "Newborn Tribe." Rastafarian culture views alcohol the way mainland US citizens see marijuana. Rastafarianism forbids all alcohol use, no matter what, but it celebrates marijuana as a gift from God used in worship and celebration. So when a Rasta finds Jesus and enters your church, do you hand him or her communion wine and appeal to the traditional proof texts? I think we have learned from Paul that to do so would be to set a significantly destructive stumbling block before that person. Will you embrace faith and step into the freedom of Christ, refusing to *harm the fellowship of believers* and refusing to *compromise unrivalled allegiance to Christ*?

And what about the opposite angle? What happens when a group of Christian Rastas, or just average American Christians, start using marijuana in the exact same way Christian Protestants use pints at the pub? If both receive their buds or their brews with thankfulness to God, can they exist in loving, respectful fellowship and allegiance to Christ, in faith? No doubt this might be possible, even if it seems ridiculous from our currently familiar angle. Yet, many Rastafarian worship practices actually employ marijuana use as a way to receive communal revelation from the great "I-n-I" and the incarnate Christ, whom they believe to be Haile Selassie III, a former emperor of Ethiopia from 1930–1974. Paralleling the situation Paul addresses in Corinth, like believers refusing to eat meat sacrificed to idols, men and women stepping out of pot-laced idolatry and into the grace of Jesus' gospel may view pot smoking as too closely related to their former idolatrous ways, therefore opting out of any further consumption is how they love and honor God. While others will see it as nothing more than a skunky, sticky substance that grows naturally and is useful for human remedies or is profitable for the same reasons my Grandpa Virgil viewed his cold Pabst as profitable on a summer day after lawn mowing.

And you can bet that as soon as marijuana finds widespread acceptance, when subsequent generations chuckle about how it was once deemed unclean, some other potentially volatile clash of opinions, powers, and judgments will bid believers to come and fight rather than to come and die to themselves. In that moment, remember the gospel and the unfathomable love of Jesus, who graciously loves all and trusts the Father as sovereign. And we can recall the words of Paul, as he drives us to an unbreakable fellowship and insurmountable allegiance to Christ alone as the one who created all things, who is redeeming all things, and who will rightly make weak and strong alike stand in his beautiful kingdom of peace.

Conclusion

In the end, are we saying that efforts to keep the Christian fellowship solid will preclude any changes that may offend the weaker brothers or sisters to the degree that they become behind-the-scenes usurpers of leadership? "Surely not!" we cry out, fighting for justice and rights and the power to lay claim to ultimate correctness. And then we might remember how we pulled over on the way to church that morning to let our five-year-old boy use the bathroom. The *truth* is that he should have known better than to leave without remembering to take one last potty; we've told him a thousand times! And then he started whining and crying, never admitting his fault in it. He was simply not seeing the error; he failed to recognize the true sovereign (me). So why did I pull over, get the nasty key with a giant flip-flop for a keychain, and gently help my boy get that business taken care of?

Because the profound love of God breaks my status as father, leader, pastor, elder, scholar, and all-around man on a mission status and instinctively moves me to simply understand that little Wesley is young, and he is weak. With ease he is crushed. With a glance, or a word, or an impatience of any kind I can devastate him. But none of that status or mission matters if one of the siblings is freaking out about everything constantly. The moral compass and comprehension of the mature, or strong, are far more developed; yet, because of love and a desire for fruitful fellowship with my child, I do not count my authority as something to be grasped too tightly, but instead give leeway to my weaker brother. To stay unwavering on the mission of travelling from A to B on time, in this specific case, would have brought a level of discord to the relationship that just wasn't worth it. Hitting pause on the mission was OK; greater goals were worth the cost in patience, convenience, and personal goals.

It strikes us that all we have discussed in this chapter leads to an unsettlingly beautiful conclusion. At times—perhaps many, many times—the stronger, wiser, rightful and proven leaders of the community will find themselves being collectively wagged *and* will be at utter peace about it. Do we let the weaker, more foolish, endlessly distracted, and overly emotional sibling call the shots sometimes, even at great cost to our own reputations and missional plans? What about all of the other people in the car? Must they suffer, as well, just for the well-being of the family unit and ongoing bonded relationship with a weak sibling, who, nonetheless should have known better? The messengers of God, his apostles, appear to be saying, "Yes."

After all, wasn't Jesus a person who suffered under the utter insanity of foolish, weak, easily distracted—throw in "murderous"—people? Yet "Father forgive them, for they know not what they do" is where his heart is.

The strongest leaders, the most morally astute and theologically robust believers in the group must let the tail wag the dog sometimes, and as they watch budgets bleed and plans fall through, they don't bat an eyebrow because they trust. *Truly,* all fear buckles under love and faith in God alone. Loving that weaker brother or sister, in Paul's eyes, means gently restoring, forgiving, going to great lengths for them, taking financial hits, taking public reputation hits, thwarting missional progress, all while you press on in faith. But there's more . . .

This is the same Paul who put all relational ties on the line when he stood up in Peter's face in Antioch, blasting him in front of everyone for twisting the gospel. There are times when the weaker sibling is just going to have to pee his pants.

We conclude, then, that no simple code exists for these scenarios where freedom sparks conflict, no how-to that works the same in New Zealand and New Jersey. Our longing for that sort of simplicity may be harming our sensitivity to the leading of the Spirit, in the end, moving us back toward slavery while we think we're moving toward rightful freedom. How we crave law, the universal standard. If you're late, according to the world that is bad, no matter what. But in God's economy, if you're late because of your love toward his people, your patience and perseverance and putting up with others' burdens in the effort to build one another up into a divinely fruitful fellowship, then being late is recreated into a truly good thing. The allure of law pales alongside love.

And inseparably bound to Christian love is wisdom, moving differently in different congregations and individuals and times and places. How long should the stronger put up with nonsense? Is it ever right to allow yourself or others suffer simply because of the weakness and immaturity of another? We have surely been suggesting that the answer is *yes*, and *constantly*, but what about cases of oppression and injustice? Where's the line?

Again, we want law to solve something that only love can remedy. The way of the Christian is a way of wisdom. The stronger siblings let the tail wag the dog and do so joyfully and filled with trust in God's ultimate justice, and they do so with wisdom. No pastor wants to shoulder such a burden, and yet, this is way of the cross that so grounds all of Paul's teaching. Endurance and perseverance are the keys for Paul's way of life. He calls us to a level of patience with others that will probably only rarely makes sense. Ask yourself: Does it make sense that God saved me? But he also calls us into impossibly complex situations where literally zero action can sufficiently respect all parties involved with endless patience and endurance. Consider a 100-year-old church that has never swayed from its convictions on complementarian leadership structures. For a pastor or leader to risk distressing the fellowship, or worse to fracture bonds, for the purpose of ensuring rightful respect for Christian freedom is wrong. But it is not always wrong, as Peter would tell you while recollecting on that suppertime moment with Paul in Antioch.

The wise leader will lean heavily on God for more wisdom, direction, and aid. He or she will see Paul's great principles of fellowship and allegiance to Christ as desperately worth pursuing, even at huge costs. And he or she will also know that there are times for in-your-face public rebukes. And the kind of wisdom that can unravel such knots comes from Jesus himself, through his word and his people.

Bibliography

Blomberg, Craig L. *From Pentecost to Patmos: An Introduction to Acts through Revelation.* Nashville: B&H Academic, 2006.

Branch, Robin Gallaher. "Butchers & Meat." In *Dictionary of Daily Life in Biblical and Post-Biblical Antiquity*, edited by Edwin M. Yamauchi and Marvin R. Wilson, 226–32. Peabody, MA: Hendrickson, 2014.

Cranfield, C. E. B. *Romans 9–16.* International Critical Commentary. London: T&T Clark, 1979.

Fotopoulos, John. *Food Offered to Idols in Roman Corinth.* Wissenschaftliche Untersuchungen zum Neuen Testament 2. Reihe 151. Tübingen: Mohr Siebeck, 2003.

Gill, David W. J. "The Meat-Market at Corinth (1 Corinthians 10:25)." *Tyndale Bulletin* 43 (1992) 389–93.

Harrison, Roland K., and Edwin M. Yamauchi. "Food Consumption." In *Dictionary of Daily Life in Biblical and Post-Biblical Antiquity*, edited by Edwin M. Yamauchi and Marvin R. Wilson, 321–22. Peabody, MA: Hendrickson, 2015.

Horsley, Richard A. "The Law of Nature in Philo and Cicero." *Harvard Theological Review* 71 (1978) 35–59.

Lewis, C. S. *God in the Dock: Essays on Theology and Ethics.* Grand Rapids: Eerdmans, 1970.

Martyn, J. Louis. "The Gospel Invades Philosophy." In *Paul, Philosophy and the Theopolitical Vision*, edited by Douglas Harink, 13–36. Eugene, OR: Wipf & Stock, 2010.

Murphy-O'Connor, Jerome. "The Corinth That Saint Paul Saw." *The Biblical Archaeologist* 47 (1984) 147–59.

Sanders, E. P. *Paul: The Apostle's Life, Letters, and Thought.* Minneapolis: Fortress, 2015.

Thiselton, Anthony C. *The First Epistle to the Corinthians.* The New International Greek Testament Commentary. Grand Rapids: Eerdmans, 2000.

Willis, Wendell. *Idol Meat in Corinth: The Pauline Argument in 1 Corinthians 8 and 10.* Eugene, OR: Wipf & Stock, 2004.

Wright, N. T. *Paul and the Faithfulness of God.* Christian Origins and the Question of God 4. Minneapolis: Fortress, 2013.

5

All Too Human

Leader Loyalties and Spiritual Unity
Paul as Arbiter

1 Corinthians 1–3

By Michael C. Thompson and Greg Mamula

Introduction

She stood at the end of one of the long hallways of the church that morning, waiting to have one last word with the pastor. In her life, she had experienced much success as a businesswoman who had built her own company. She was well known and respected by many. She had become frustrated at what was an apparent lack of good leadership in the church, especially since her many suggestions never seemed to be taken seriously enough. It was no secret that the congregation was struggling and that the church had become a shell of its former self. There seemed to be too much noise, with everyone offering their own advice to get out of this present mess. Most of them meant well but clearly didn't have the organizational insight that she possessed. So, she stood there, with her years of business acumen at the ready, waiting to share her wisdom with the all-too-young-and-inexperienced pastor.

As she waited she wondered if her words would make an impact this time, or if they would be ignored as they had been before. Still, she had to try. Her heart was with this church, and it had been for years. She had to try on behalf of those who had come to her, asking for her leadership to step forward and get things back on track. This had become a calling, and everyone was well aware that the situation was becoming quite drastic. Thinking about these things increased her sense of determination. She wasn't about to be derailed by some drawn-out theological nonsense that could not focus on pragmatic challenges of declining attendance, diminishing equity, decreased cash flow, or a defunct church leadership.

Having built a successful business had allowed her to contribute a lot of money to the church over the years, which she did gladly. But those who are able to invest so much into the church ought to have some guarantee of influence on how those resources were used. This seemed like simple common sense to her mind. This is why so many had come around her to face this difficult season, and why she knew it was time to be firm. *If the church leadership was not going to listen to her, then she would simply take her money to a church that would.*

And that is the first thing that she said when the pastor came around the corner.

Division

As you have probably guessed already, the story you have just read is true, and the absence of names is quite intentional. Unfortunately, a good amount of church conflict emerges from those who choose to do the wrong things for all the right reasons. So often it all begins with a genuine desire for the church to do well, but only through a narrow vision of what makes a healthy congregation. In our culture, the quest for building better churches is often driven by comparison with either other well-known ministries or some version of what our congregation used to be. Those who choose to stand up out of this genuine concern can quickly gain support from others who share in the hope of a thriving ministry (although for many groups the details of this achievement are left undefined). And yet, even from a collective gathering of genuine believers who have a passion for the ministry of the local church, situations like this can become ripe for division. In a moment, shared visions can become group divisions, and the edification of believers can turn into party lines.

Those at the helm of such emerging divisions in the church can become what Marshall Shelley described as "well-intentioned dragons,"[1] and they can wreak havoc on congregations, leaving a path of destruction in their wake. Once there are competing visions in the church there is the potential for division. Although rarely occurring over issues of doctrine, these battles often occur within the daily life and work of the church—budgets, music style, outreach strategy, etc. The pastoral challenges are great in such situations, especially when leader loyalties find their way to the fore of the conflict.

Corinth Background

When Paul wrote to the Corinthian believers he addressed a congregation divided by differing visions of how to live according to the gospel in everyday life.[2] This community of believers represented a variety of social, economic, religious, and ethnic backgrounds.[3] Coming together into this new assembly created a number of differing expectations and visions regarding the social impact of the gospel. Theirs was a world of social prominence, and those who could demonstrate advancement among spiritual gifts would certainly expect notability within the church.[4] To become an influencer in the emerging assemblies of Christianity as it took hold within the Roman world was to help establish the church's place and status. The realities of the Romanized culture had a definite impact on the dynamics of Corinthian Christianity, and at the time of Paul's writing to them, this church had become increasingly divided around differing visions of the gospel in a way that was heading toward certain disaster.

The city of Corinth was of no small significance in the ancient world, noted for its cosmopolitan nature, major construction projects, prominent temples and shrines, and the popular Isthmian games.[5] Perhaps unsurprisingly, the Corinthian church had also become well known and successful, both in numerical growth and outward spiritual experience.[6] And yet, the cultural realities had produced an assembly that was lacking unity, whose

---

1. Shelley, *Well-Intentioned Dragons*.
2. Cf. Mitchell, *Paul and the Rhetoric*, 1.
3. Witherington, *Conflict and Community in Corinth*, 1–35.
4. Meeks, *First Urban Christians*, 119–20.
5. Background information for Corinth can be found in various commentaries and introductions. A topical review of such information is found in Ferguson, *Backgrounds of Early Christianity*.
6. Barclay, *Pauline Churches*, 201.

experience of the Spirit was not producing a faithful obedience to the gospel. Too much influence was being given to individual personalities, perhaps being shaped by the realities of worship within various households, where distinct loyalties could be reinforced.[7] At any rate, the Corinthian believers were quick to participate in the church as but "one segment of their lives,"[8] rather than embracing the message of the gospel as a total transformation into a new way of living.[9]

Although Paul had founded the church in Corinth, his first letter is written several years later, while the apostle was staying in Ephesus (16:5–9). He writes having recently received news from Chloe that the community is caught up in quarrels and division (1:11). We cannot say to what degree the church was unified before these issues were brought to the attention of the apostle, but he responds with the hope of correcting the thoughts and behavior of the Corinthian believers so that they might live and work together in the truth of the gospel.

Disunity

In order to hear Paul's remedy to the disunity among the Corinthian church, we must first identify the nature of the division. To this, Barclay makes an important observation, "One of the most significant, but least noticed, features of Corinthian church life is the absence of conflict in the relationship between Christians and 'outsiders.'"[10] In other words, Paul writes this letter to focus on the *internal dynamics* of the community, not to any opposing force from the pagan world of Romanized Corinth. In recognizing this, it becomes clear that the apostle instructs the church that the definition of the church is drawn from the message of the cross and that cultural behavior, for both individual and community life, ought to be transformed as a result. One of the themes of this book is the potency of the cross for dealing with conflict in a church, so much is this the case that one can say the cross is the Pauline solution to church conflict. How that cross resolves conflict and how the principal parties will embrace that cross are factors as well, but the basic point remains: in church conflict Paul offers the cross.

The Corinthian divisions have brought this community to the brink of disaster, and Paul wastes no time in addressing the problems of misguided

---

7. Meeks, *First Urban Christians*, 76.
8. Barclay, *Pauline Churches*, 200–201.
9. Interestingly, on this point Barclay includes a footnote: "This could help explain how the church survived despite its many divisions," in ibid., 201 n.36.
10. Ibid., 188.

leader loyalties that have taken hold in the church (1:10–17). Though many attempts have been made to identify these divisions as various parties among the Corinthian congregation,[11] it is wisest to use caution in drawing such conclusions. As Dunn suggests, "The divisions in Corinth should not be exaggerated."[12] Paul's language here probably does not refer to any official "party" in our modern sense, and so we need not imagine any fixed membership among those who are aligning themselves with Paul, Apollos, Cephas, or Christ.[13] In such designation we see the realities of Roman culture and the language of benefaction, whereby individuals would ally themselves to those of good standing and reputation in the city-community.[14] For Paul, therefore, despite many asserting the contrary view, the divisions among the Corinthians are not so much defined by ideological or theological positions, but rather by the overshadowing of large personalities and influences that were connected to the church community.[15] This is about personality cults.

It is also important to recognize Paul's own surprise at hearing the news that his name is being used in a way that is bringing about division within the church. His strong disapproval demonstrates that these party lines were not official designations within the community, and there is no reason to suppose that either Apollos or Cephas were approving (or even aware) that their names were being used as well.[16] Although Paul expresses a degree of shock and anger at learning about these leader loyalties—*Was Paul crucified for you?* (1:13)—he rather quickly moves forward in addressing the situation, as though he is familiar with such cultural dynamics that work in the Roman world. The divisions in Corinth is, in large part, a product of these believers being unable to overcome their cultural worldview of benefaction and social rank for the sake of embracing the gospel.[17]

The context of Paul's argument against division is found in the assertion that the gospel has a difficult task in drawing individuals out of a worldly way of thinking and living, and into a cross-centered life—a way that appears foolish to the world's ears.[18] Every believer comes to faith hav-

---

11. For a review of these positions, see Thiselton, *First Epistle to the Corinthians*, 123–36.

12. Dunn, *Beginning from Jerusalem*, 791.

13. Mitchell, *Paul and the Rhetoric*, 71.

14. Clarke, *Secular and Christian Leadership*, 93.

15. Even the language employed throughout 1 Corinthians helps our understanding, as Paul uses the type of political rhetoric that is most often reserved for political-type factionalism. See Mitchell, *Paul and the Rhetoric*, 67ff.

16. Hays, *1 Corinthians*, 22.

17. Clarke, *Secular and Christian Leadership*, 23–29.

18. Schnabel, *Early Christian Mission*, 2:1582.

ing to reconcile their own cultural identity with the message of the gospel. For those who lived in Romanized Corinth, social advancement for the sake of cultural prominence was a real possibility.[19] This is where the emphasis of Paul's position takes shape: when any person takes precedence in the church over the primacy of Christ—that which he is claiming to be happening within the Corinthian church—the message of the gospel is subverted. Paul's words in 1:13–17 can thus be understood as a discussion within the cultural language of benefaction, whereby what Christ has done for the believer to be of greater significance than any of the work by other leaders within the community. As a result, it is Christ who deserves total allegiance, taking precedence even over the apostles.[20]

Having said all of this, it is important now to turn to the slogan, "I follow Christ" (1:12). There have been numerous attempts to make sense of this phrase, without a clear consensus among scholars. A surface-level reading might assume that this is a group who are trying to ignore the divisiveness of these competing leader loyalties, and so these are the community members who have the right perspective. However, that Paul would include this phrase among the other caricatured positions indicates there is probably more going on. The weight of the evidence seems to point toward two possibilities: that this is a group wanting to act independently of the community leadership altogether,[21] or that this is a rhetorical strategy by Paul to point to what he believes to be a rather ridiculous division.[22] Both options seem to fit Paul's overall language, and it might not be possible to make any further determination to the precise meaning of this phrase. Yet, Paul's use of these four slogans in setting the tone of his letter shows his level of concern and the seriousness of the situation. The adherence to individual leaders in the church is harmful to the gospel because it diminishes the role of Christ. By placing Christ in a list that reflects cultural benefaction, Paul is able to emphasize the absurdity of elevating *any* human leader to a status that could cause division within the church.[23]

Understanding the disunity of the Corinthian church is the interpretive key to Paul's message, but attempting to do so through the identification of these groups is not the correct approach. First, as we have mentioned above, the slogans that Paul uses are most likely caricatures of the attitude

---

19. Carter, "'Big Men' in Corinth," 53.

20. For an introduction to the perfections of grace in a culture of benefaction, see Barclay, *Paul and the Gift*.

21. Thiselton, *First Epistle to the Corinthians*, 133–34.

22. Garland, *1 Corinthians*, 49.

23. Cf. Hays, *1 Corinthians*, 23.

that lies beneath the division in the community. Trying to read 1 Cor 1–3 from the basis of these four designations is most likely going to produce an erroneous picture of the situation. Second, it is best to understand this opening section of Paul's argument as it relates to the remainder of the letter. There are many issues that require the apostle's attention in 1 Corinthians, and the presence of community division is constant. Hence, when Paul begins with the broad identification of groups that follow himself, or Apollos, or Cephas, or Christ, he is pointing to the reality of a disunity that is running deep within the community, and failed attempts (if any) to reconcile in the gospel.[24] When we examine 1 Corinthians from the perspective of the many debated issues in the church, we are given a better understanding of what these caricatured groups represent in Paul's mind.[25]

So, Paul's concern is that the disunity of the Corinthian church are rising from differing perspectives on issues pertaining to how believers ought to live faithfully to the gospel in the midst of a pagan culture. In trying to answer these questions and concerns, it had become commonplace for these believers to attach themselves to one of the prominent voices in the early church. But more than choosing one answer over another, these leader loyalties had begun to look more like the Romanized culture than the gospel; the Corinthian allegiances had become tools for division rather than tools for edification within the body of believers.[26] Perhaps we can imagine that there was genuine concern for faithfulness to the gospel underneath this harsh reality, and it is quite possible that most individuals did not see themselves as doing harm to the work of the church. But Paul sees the movement of division at work in the church, as increasingly these groups were becoming entrenched in the community and worked against the unity of the Spirit (2:10–16). And to those who make the claim, "I follow Christ" (1:12), Paul's response shows that even such noble-sounding language can be little more than a cover-up for divisive behavior in the church, and that those who take this line have essentially reduced Christ to one voice among others.[27] All of this behavior together has contributed to the fracturing of the church, and so Paul will look to reestablish a genuine unity among these believers.

---

24. Mitchell, *Paul and the Rhetoric*, 67.
25. Carter, "'Big Men' in Corinth," 53.
26. Barclay, *Pauline Churches*, 18.
27. Hays, *1 Corinthians*, 23.

Unity

In order to combat the division running rampant in Corinth, Paul urges these believers to a renewed appreciation for the cross of Christ and its implications for the church (1:18—2:16). He speaks of the cross in absolute terms: there is no human wisdom that can be added to it.[28] In his evangelistic experiences Paul has watched the cross of Christ become a stumbling block to Jews and foolishness to Gentiles (1:23), while at the same time seeing the cross of Christ as the power and wisdom of God (1:24).[29] Paul proclaims the cross precisely because it is the reversal of worldly wisdom and power—a turning point in the story of salvation—that stands in direct opposition to the culture of benefaction that is presently corrupting the Corinthian church.[30] Through Christ a new way of living has broken into the world, one that enables believers to live in unity and harmony. The reality of this message ought to have a humbling effect on every believer, for, in Stott's words, "Christ crucified is both God's wisdom and ours."[31]

Paul directs the Corinthians to the cross as a way to challenge the prevailing social culture in which persons sought to gain status and position by aligning themselves with prominent figures in the community, a behavior he saw as destructive to the church. Paul thus challenges the cultural wisdom with the foolishness of the gospel message: a crucified Messiah. If the believers in Corinth can grasp the centrality of the crucifixion to the gospel, then the power of the cross can give shape to the community of faith. Those who choose to be defined by the cross of Christ are therefore called to live in such a way as to demonstrate this revealed wisdom and power of God. In sharing this foolishness of the cross there is unity for the church, for here is the fundamental truth that establishes a new social structure through which the work of the Spirit can reveal God's wisdom to every believer (2:10–13). At first blush, it may appear that Paul's words are little more than an attempt to outdo the already-present boasting and social positioning of those in the Corinthian community, though at closer examination it is clear that he constructs his argument on the completely different foundation of the cross: "But we have the mind of Christ" (2:16).[32]

Having laid out his foundation for unity in the cross of Christ, Paul returns to the divisive situation in the Corinthian church in a direct effort to

---

28. Fee, *First Epistle to the Corinthians*, 66.
29. Cf. Bird, *Anomalous Jew*, 96.
30. Thiselton, *First Epistle to the Corinthians*, 173.
31. Stott, *Cross of Christ*, 221.
32. Hays, *1 Corinthians*, 47.

diffuse the allegiance to church leaders for the sake of the gospel (3:1–4). Although the Corinthians see themselves as being spiritually advanced, Paul points out that their behavior keeps him from being able to address them as anything but worldly people (3:1). The divisions around certain voices and teachings are revealing a community that is more devoted to a worldly way of living than to living out the gospel.[33] Taking into account all that he has established up to this point in the letter, Paul now turns to the work of the Spirit in achieving the unity of the church (3:5–23). Moving outward from the cross, the apostle now emphasizes the true nature of the church community: it belongs to God, who created it and who will judge it.[34] Never afraid of mixing metaphors, Paul's description of a unified church community rapidly utilizes three images to describe the nature of the kingdom of God and work among his people.[35]

Whereas those in Corinth have become divided over the work of Paul and Apollos (at this point he leaves off the references to following Cephas and Christ), here the two are declared to be *fellow workers* (3:9) who accomplish their assigned tasks in cooperation with one another and with God.[36] The ministry of the church thus becomes focused on that which God accomplishes through his people, without focus being drawn to his people themselves.[37] For Paul, it is God who assigns the work of the gospel, God who grows that work, and God who rewards his people for their gospel laboring.[38] From this foundation, the church can flourish in the unity of Christ and share together in a diversity of spiritual giftedness and accomplishment as the presence of the kingdom of God is realized (3:8).[39] It is thus God alone who is responsible for the life of the church, and so he is the one who assigns the tasks of planting and building a holy community (3:5–15).

Although it is impossible for us to determine just how the divisions around certain leaders in the Corinthian church began, at the point of Paul's writing the situation has become counter-productive to the gospel. It is likely that it was "natural" for Roman Corinth than that one or two key leaders provoked the disunity. Throughout his argument Paul asserts that this

---

33. On this, cf. Thiselton, *First Epistle to the Corinthians*, 295: "It seems almost impossible here to improve on the force of the REB: 'are you not all too human?'"
34. Hays, *1 Corinthians*, 51.
35. Ibid.
36. Mitchell, *Paul and the Rhetoric*, 98.
37. Cf. Schnabel, *Early Christian Mission*, 947.
38. Garland, *1 Corinthians*, 111.
39. Cf. Fee, *First Epistle to the Corinthians*, 133.

was not the intended outcome of any of these leadership figures. It would not be a stretch to say that the community's division was not the intended outcome of any of the believers who have become caught up in the conflict. To answer this situation Paul reminds the Corinthians that they are God's field and God's building and that those who have worked among them are nothing more than servants doing the assigned work of their master (3:9). All of the boasting that was taking place in this church has not been the result of spiritual maturity and advancement, but rather a failure to grab hold of the central meaning of the cross of Christ. The Corinthian believers had a high evaluation of themselves, which Paul considers erroneous, for "they are leaving God out of their assessment."[40]

In 3:10–15 Paul uses the metaphor of a building's construction to describe the church, and highlights the judgment of the work. Since God is the owner, he will have the final word on the quality of work done by his servants. Consistent with his earlier argument, Paul asserts that Christ is the one foundation for the structure and that this has been laid down for the Corinthians, by Paul himself, so that others may do their work in building up the church (3:12–13). The warning that is included here has to do with the quality of that which is placed on the church's foundation, and it is a statement made in direct opposition to those whose work fosters division.[41] Although Paul explicitly denies that individual salvation is in question (3:15), the reference to fire reminds the reader of the eschatological judgment that will determine which kingdom labors have an eternal value.[42] The movement of these first three chapters presents an important understanding of the gospel's ministry, protecting the community of faith from developing a lofty view of those who work as servants of the church, while also reminding every believer to value the work of the church as part of God's kingdom.[43]

Faithfulness

If the Corinthian church is God's building, then they are a temple—a place where the divine presence is experienced and mediated to the world (3:16–17). The gathered community is identified as a sacred space that is not to be corrupted by worldly behavior. For Paul, this is quite serious, for "those who damage the unity of the community are interfering with God's chosen mode

---

40. Hays, *1 Corinthians*, 61.
41. Fee, *First Epistle to the Corinthians*, 136.
42. Schnabel, *Early Christian Mission*, 952–53.
43. Davies, *Studies*, 42.

of presence, and they will certainly incur judgment."[44] It is imperative that these believers listen to the words of the apostle, and be deceived by the world's standards no more (3:18). The same can be said to the church in any culture when any person or any goal takes primacy over the cross of Christ. This is a bedrock affirmation for those who come to the Christian faith, as every believer holds to the supremacy of Christ in his church.

Problematic situations, such as the one Paul addresses in Corinth, arise not because members of the community change their *confession* of Jesus's supremacy over the church, but when they change their *behavior* of submitting to his authority. In many cases, those who are causing division and conflict in the church are not doing so because they want to do damage to the church body (though sometimes they may single out an individual or small group on which to inflict harm). These *well-intentioned dragons* often "see themselves as godly people, adequately gracious and kind, who hold another viewpoint they honestly believe is right."[45] And so, depending on the issues that come to the surface in a church's area of conflict, those who become leaders within the factions and division could be any member in the life of the congregation.[46] Often those who find themselves in this position are key leaders in some area of the church, though not always in an official capacity. But for those who feel their voice is not being heard, gathering around a more charismatic personality becomes a key remedy to their struggle.

Conflict within the church becomes more complex when we consider that so often the initial intentions of those who have an influential voice or presence is to see the church do well in its mission. Men and women who want to do their part in serving the church can quickly find themselves in a place of division, which is why it is important to be on constant guard regarding such matters. There is no evidence that Peter or Apollos

---

44. Hays, 1 *Corinthians*, 58.

45. Shelley, *Well-Intentioned Dragons*, 47.

46. This does not limit the scope of influence to those who regularly attend or participate in the life of the congregation, as there have been instances where those who hold this type of influence are former attenders, some who have relocated to another congregation, and others who now refrain from church attendance altogether. Depending on the specifics of the community, such figures might still hold considerable influence over the thoughts and decisions of the congregation. One pastor who had recently moved into a new community had discovered that absolutely no decisions regarding building and grounds could be made without the approval of Fred. He then learned that Fred lived in a neighboring property to the church building, but had not been to any function or event of the church for more than thirty years! Nobody could explain how this situation had come about, but this was one of the challenges this pastor now faced in ministering to this community.

were doing anything to intentionally undermine Paul's ministry among the Corinthians. And yet, the divisions that had occurred as a result of men and women aligning themselves with these dynamic figures in the church had made their well-intentioned ministry of partnership of the gospel into a reality of fragmentation. This is why Paul "reverses the pattern of seniority" in Corinth, by reminding the believers that they do not belong to any of the apostles, but rather it is the apostles who belong to the work of the church— all under the authority and unity of Christ Jesus (3:21–23).[47]

It is clear that Paul had a significant amount of authority among the Corinthian community, and so he addresses this division head on. For many situations, especially in the modern church, it may be better to have an outside voice to help identify the situation and help move everyone toward reconciliation. When working with people in conflict, especially those whose fundamental desire is to see the church do well, the goal of reconciliation is to identify areas of agreement, strengthen and maintain these agreements, while strengthening the relationships of those involved, whether leader or those who have circled around them in support.[48] Paul's first step in confronting the Corinthians is to remind them of their identity in relationship to Christ Jesus (1:10). It is through the Cross of Christ and the work of the Spirit that believers can have relationships maintained in unity.

In his writing, Paul addresses the church as a real-life community at work in the ministry of the gospel. He does not speak in abstract terms, but instead engages these believers from within the cultural dynamics in which they live and work. It is the community as a whole that is the center of his focus here, over and above any single personality. When he looks ahead to the coming evaluation and judgment of the work that is being done through the church, he speaks of the community as a whole, not the merits of the individual spiritual life (3:12–14).[49] Yet again, the importance of corporate unity comes to the fore of the Christian community, revealing the disruptive nature that comes from more individualistic approaches to faith.

---

47. Clarke, *Secular and Christian Leadership*, 125.

48. Taken from the Harvard Negotiation Project, "Any method of negotiation may be fairly judged by three criteria: It should produce a wise agreement if possible; it should be efficient; and it should improve or at least not damage the relationship between the parties." Fisher, Ury, and Patton, *Getting to Yes*, 4.

49. Hays, *1 Corinthians*, 51.

Paterfamilias

One final aspect to consider when reading Paul's instructions to the divided community in Corinth is that of *paterfamilias* (head of the family). The setting of the house-church was the most common existence for Christians in the first century, and there are many ways in which this gives shape to the writings in the New Testament.[50] As we have already discussed, the dynamics of this context have contributed to the situation in Corinth. It was in the model of the household that the earliest Christian communities began to emerge, which then helped define their relationship to the larger society.[51] Often, this language is overlooked in studying Paul, yet "the comparison of the Christian community with a 'family' must be regarded as the most significant metaphorical usage of all."[52] In addressing the Corinthian church Paul consistently leans on the language of kinship to remind the believers of their strong familial bond in the church.

In the Greco-Roman world of the first century a person's social status, honor, and identity were closely connected to the family unit to which one belonged.[53] Such would have created a sense in which the individual would rely on other family members to help shape and define one's identity.[54] That is to say, a person's social image would have been tied to their family, in some ways indistinguishable from their household, and rooting their sense of worth on the reputation of their kin. Understood within the boundaries of an honor-and-shame society, it would have been expected for each member of the family to live in such a way as to build up and enhance the overall reputation of the household.[55] And, although family units tended to be small in terms of living arrangements, the family authority could have an extended reach beyond individual households.[56]

If we consider the nature of a family as a fundamental aspect of Roman society; if we acknowledge the development of the early Christian communities around the model of the Roman household; if we understand the nature of *paterfamilias* in the operation of these households; if we take into account that nature of familial reputation as a distinguishing factor in Roman society, and if we understand the extended reach of the *paterfamilias*

---

50. Clarke, *Pauline Theology of Church Leadership*, 147.
51. Meeks, *First Urban Christians*, 76–77.
52. Banks, *Paul's Idea of Community*, 49.
53. Sandnes, *New Family*, 56.
54. Malina, *New Testament World*, 58–59.
55. Ibid., 32–33.
56. Jeffers, *Greco-Roman World*, 83.

to include smaller households in the same family, then the manner in which Paul addresses the Corinthians takes on the distinctiveness of a family *of faith*, under the singular head of the family, demonstrating a particular way of life that reflects on the family as a whole—most importantly the *paterfamilias*—to establish an honorable reputation in the larger society.

As such, the language of Paul in 1 Cor 1–3 is, first of all, a call to obedience. From within this perspective of a familial setting, the apostle reminds the believers of the cross of Christ in order to correct their behavior as members of the church. The division that is occurring is nothing short of a breakdown in this household of faith, working to usurp the *paterfamilias* of Christ with other, unqualified, family members. Further, the unity to which Paul summons the Corinthians demands a cruciform behavior—living in a way that demonstrates the sacrificial love of Christ Jesus rather than the self-serving actions of social power and advancement. No matter how these divisions began, they are now fracturing the church, and Paul instructs them to unity in the context of family reputation and relationships. It is Christ crucified that provides believers with this kinship, which ought to be demonstrated in the unified nature of the church rather than the divisions that have been created.

The Goal Is Love

The Apostle Paul writes to a divided community of believers in Corinth, and the entirety of 1 Corinthians is set within that context. The leader loyalties that are pointed out in the opening chapters mostly likely did not give rise to the multitude of issues that are contained in the letter. Rather, as is common in most modern church conflict, it is disagreement on issues of how best to live out the implications of the gospel that has given rise to the factionalism that comes from aligning with certain voices in the church. For the Corinthians, this meant aligning yourself with big names like Paul, Apollos, or Cephas—those who had prominence and influence throughout the whole early church. And then there were those who claimed simply to follow Christ, but who probably did not rise above the fray of real-life disagreement any more than the rest. Their words may have sounded noble but, in Paul's critique, they have simply diminished the significance of Christ in the community by making him one voice among many (perhaps using the phrase "I follow Christ" as a mask to hide their own agenda).[57] Certainly, the modern church has its fair share of popular personalities that are invoked into debates and divisions of which they never intended to be a part.

---

57. Hays, *1 Corinthians*, 23.

In addressing the issues that Chloe's people have brought to his attention, Paul begins to deal with the division by working through those issues that are causing the disagreement. In doing so he becomes a mediating voice that has listened to the issue, provided wise counsel, and then moves the believers forward to unity. From this division he makes a summons for unity, and in working through these issues he continually points to *love* as the means by which the Corinthian's factionalism can be overcome.[58] Paul's emphasis on love reaches its climax in the famous testimonial to love in 1 Cor 13. While the most immediate context of this description of love is the proper use of spiritual gifts (12:1–11), it is important to also remember that Paul remains within the larger discussion of unity among believers (12:12–31). A congregation that has given in to the divisions of social power and prominence become nothing more than a resounding gong and clanging cymbal of confusion and disunity in an already disharmonized world (13:1).[59] For those living in a Roman world that prized accomplished speech and rhetoric, those who exercised the spiritual gifts of the church—in this specific reference, the use of tongues—the crashing and clamoring of noise is disruptive and reflects poorly on the family of faith.[60]

And so, Paul has the goal of love in mind from the beginning, as an appropriate response to the crucified Christ as a means of bearing witness to his sovereignty and reign to the world. Spiritual words and actions without love are meaningless, leaving room for human pride and achievement to break down the community of faith.[61] In this family of faith, especially in light of the crucified Christ, believers are called to minister in humility, serving the church with the knowledge that God will judge the work that is accomplished by his people (3:10–15).[62]

In order to accomplish this, the church will always need to be about the work of reconciliation, especially in times of conflict. It is important to remember that many of the *dragons* that are encountered in the ministry of the church are, in fact, *well-intentioned*. That is, at some point each believer desires to have a community that lives by kingdom values. Unfortunately, it is when these ideas and perspectives of how to achieve this reality differ that the seeds of conflict are so quickly sown. If we can hear the Apostle Paul's words still today, returning to the crucified Christ, then we will find the unity of the Spirit above all things in the church. Every church conflict has

---

58. Mitchell, *Paul and the Rhetoric*, 168–69.
59. Cf. Davies, *Studies*, 37–38.
60. Cf. Thiselton, *First Epistle to the Corinthians*, 1038–39.
61. Hays, *1 Corinthians*, 222.
62. Davies, *Studies*, 44.

its own complexities, and it is a mistake to think that any one-size-fits-all approach to resolution is attainable. This is visible even within the Pauline letters, for with each letter he sends out, he speaks to the unique details of that particular congregation. Although he works on the same foundation of the gospel, his approach demonstrates the importance of speaking to each community on their own terms.[63]

Based on our study of Paul's writing to the Corinthians and elsewhere in the New Testament, Paul's call to live united under the cross of Christ is lived out pragmatically by loving Christ and our fellow church member. Faithfulness to Jesus as Lord, sacrificial love for others, and a healthy emphasis on church unity and peace work together to create the type of Christian community Paul wanted the Corinthians, and our modern churches, to be. Modern church conflict mediation seeks to adopt the most basic elements of modern mediation practices as it seeks to create peace through right relationships. Christian conflict mediators add to these basic ideas a complete submission of the church community and peace-making process to the cross of the resurrected Jesus. Not every congregation will struggle with leader loyalties getting in the way of church unity. But for those who must face this reality, Paul teaches us to remember that we are all servants of the crucified Christ, who has shown us the way of sacrificial service in the kingdom of God. Further, Paul reminds us of the seriousness of such division within the church, as it tears apart the work that God is doing through his people. The follower of Christ is summoned to live in love toward one another, resulting in a unified family of faith that can be a dynamic presence of the kingdom in this world. Paul's instructions are appropriately captured by Bonhoeffer, "Those who love their dream of a Christian community more than the Christian community itself become destroyers of that Christian community even though their personal intentions may be ever so honest, earnest, and sacrificial."[64]

Bibliography

Banks, Robert J. *Paul's Idea of Community: The Early House Churches in Their Cultural Setting.* Grand Rapids: Baker Academic, 2012.
Barclay, John M. G. *Paul and the Gift.* Grand Rapids: Eerdmans, 2015.
———. *Pauline Churches and Diaspora Jews.* Grand Rapids: Eerdmans, 2016.
Bird, Michael F. *The Anomalous Jew: Paul among Jews, Greeks, and Romans.* Grand Rapids: Eerdmans, 2016.
Bonhoeffer, Dietrich. *Life Together.* New York: Harper and Row, 1954.

63. Christensen and Johnson, *Healing Church Strife*, xii.
64. Bonhoeffer, *Life Together*, 27.

Carter, Timothy L. "'Big Men' in Corinth." *Journal for the Study of the New Testament* 66 (1997) 45–71.
Christensen, James, and Thomas F. Johnson. *Healing Church Strife in the New Testament and Today: Beyond Matthew 18:15–17*. Eugene, OR: Wipf & Stock, 2016.
Clarke, Andrew D. *A Pauline Theology of Church Leadership*. London: T&T Clark, 2008.
———. *Secular and Christian Leadership in Corinth: A Socio-Historical and Exegetical Study of 1 Corinthians 1–6*. Eugene, OR: Wipf & Stock, 2006.
Davies, Rupert E. *Studies in 1 Corinthians*. London: Epworth, 1962.
Dunn, James D. G. *Beginning from Jerusalem*. Grand Rapids: Eerdmans, 2008.
Fee, Gordon D. *The First Epistle to the Corinthians*. Grand Rapids: Eerdmans, 1987.
Ferguson, Everett. *Backgrounds of Early Christianity*. 3rd ed. Grand Rapids: Eerdmans, 2003.
Fisher, Roger, William Ury, and Bruce Patton. *Getting to Yes: Negotiating Agreement without Giving In*. 3rd ed. New York: Penguin, 2011.
Garland, David E. *1 Corinthians*. Grand Rapids: Baker Academic, 2003.
Hays, Richard B. *1 Corinthians*. Louisville: John Knox, 1997.
Jeffers, James S. *The Greco-Roman World of the New Testament Era: Exploring the Background of Early Christianity*. Downers Grove, IL: InterVarsity, 1999.
Malina, Bruce J. *The New Testament World: Insights from Cultural Anthropology*. 3rd ed. Louisville: Westminster John Knox, 2001.
Meeks, Wayne. *The First Urban Christians*. 2nd ed. New Haven: Yale University Press, 2003.
Mitchell, Margaret. *Paul and the Rhetoric of Reconciliation: An Exegetical Investigation of the Language and Composition of 1 Corinthians*. Louisville: Westminster John Knox, 1993.
Sandnes, Karl Olav. *A New Family: Conversion and Ecclesiology in the Early Church with Cross-Cultural Comparisons*. Berlin: Peter Lang, 1994.
Schnabel, Eckhard J. *Early Christian Mission*. 3 vols. Downers Grove, IL: InterVarsity, 2004.
Shelley, Marshall. *Well-Intentioned Dragons: Ministering to Problem People in the Church*. Minneapolis: Bethany House, 1994.
Stott, John R. W. *The Cross of Christ*. Downers Grove, IL: InterVarsity, 2006.
Thiselton, Anthony C. *The First Epistle to the Corinthians*. Grand Rapids: Eerdmans, 2000.
Witherington, Ben, III. *Conflict and Community in Corinth: A Socio-Rhetorical Commentary on 1 and 2 Corinthians*. Grand Rapids: Eerdmans, 1995.

6

The Corinthian Conflict and the Collection

Paul Builds Relationships through Wise Agreements

2 CORINTHIANS 8–9

By Andrew Gleddiesmith and Ric Strangway

Introduction

In Roger Fisher and William Ury's seminal book on negotiation, *Getting to Yes: Negotiating Agreement without Giving In*, they suggest that three criteria be used in evaluating progress toward the end-goal of a negotiation: producing wise agreement, efficient process, and improved (or at least not damaged) relationship. They suggest that growth in these three criteria is achieved by separating people from the problem, focusing on interests not positions, creating multiple options for mutual gain, and using objective measurements. When Paul tackles the issue of the collection with the Corinthian believers he is attempting to achieve a wise agreement while improving their fragile relationship. The efficient process aspect of the negotiation is already set out and the question is whether they will follow the process of setting aside a weekly amount to then be gathered together for the total collection. Paul will attempt to negotiate the Corinthian believers' involvement by focusing on their shared interests and by separating the problem from the people. The aspect of separating the problem from the people is difficult because the problem is the Corinthians' evaluation of Paul; it's a question of whether or not they trust him. As we will see, Paul will attempt to reduce his presence in the negotiation by not being too demanding. We will begin by outlining Paul's relationship with the Corinthians before assessing his argument to the Corinthians in 2 Cor 8–9 and then evaluating the argument as an example of Fisher and Ury's negotiation principles.

Paul's Relationship with the Corinthian Believers

Reconstructing Paul's relationship with the Corinthians is difficult, but it appears to develop as follows: Paul's first visit to Corinth is recorded in Acts 18. He spends eighteen months (likely 50–early 52 CE.) there establishing a church community before leaving for Ephesus en route to Jerusalem. Paul's next contact with the church in Corinth occurs through a letter mentioned in 1 Cor 5:9–13. After this Chloe gives an oral report to Paul about the situation in Corinth (1 Cor 1:11) and then Stephanus brings a letter and provides a report (1 Cor 16:17–18). In response, Paul writes a letter (1 Corinthians) and sends it with Timothy (1 Cor 16:10–11) to Corinth. Paul then visits Corinth in what is known as the "painful" visit (2 Cor 2:5–11; 7:11–12) before sending another letter, called the "tearful" letter, with Titus (2 Cor 1:8–9). Titus returns with a hopeful report. Paul then sends a fourth letter (all or part of 2 Corinthians) with Titus in preparation for his third visit.[1]

Paul's Conflict with the Corinthian Believers

After Paul's first visit, what he describes as "divisions" and "quarrels" (1 Cor 1:10–11) develop. These divisions appear to focus on the various Christian teachers the Corinthians encountered. Comparison between teachers led to different factions, each supporting their favorite teacher. Paul refers to this problem in relation to Apollos and himself in 1 Cor 4:6. These divisions increased as the various householders who hosted the Christian community sought to increase their own prestige through supporting the better speaker.

---

1. DeSilva, *Introduction to the New Testament*, 560.

This reflected the city of Corinth's general ethos of social competition, with this pursuit of social prestige flowing over into other areas of church life as well. A discussion about eating meat sacrificed to idols is framed as between the "strong" and the "weak" (1 Cor 8). The community's shared meal (Lord's Table) begins to be divided according to social status (1 Cor 11). The gifts of the Spirit also became a cause of division in the church, with the more dramatic gifts being prized as superior (1 Cor 12–14). With the core relationships of the church so divided, conflict began to overflow into many other areas: taking each other to court, extra-marital sexual pursuits (1 Cor 6), and response to the immoral brother (1 Cor 5).[2]

In the midst of all this conflict, Paul's behavior while in Corinth was also under scrutiny. Paul was specifically criticized for failing to take support (1 Cor 9), for his inferior rhetorical skill and presentation (1 Cor 1:17; 2:1–5), and because his teaching was considered unspiritual and insufficiently lofty (1 Cor 2:6—3:3).[3] These doubts about Paul brought into question his integrity in regard to the collection for the poor in Judea (1 Cor 16). After Titus's visit, Titus reports to Paul that there has been a response of repentance by the Corinthians and that the "offender" who attacked Paul has been excluded from the community. The bad news is that the "offender" was acting on behalf of outsiders who are attempting to undermine Paul's authority by questioning his legitimacy as an apostle and arguing that others are superior bearers of revelation.[4] Paul, in response, writes 2 Corinthians, in which he hopes to reinforce the improved relationship that is developing. He is also very aware that there is still conflict, tension, and opposition that he needs to be careful *not* to strengthen. Second Corinthians is written to prepare the way for Paul's future visit by reducing the potential for conflict relating to the collection for the poor in Jerusalem.[5]

When examining 2 Corinthians, our focus will be the section dealing with the collection itself (2 Cor 8–9). Paul desires to encourage the church in Corinth to give generously, while simultaneously removing doubt about his intentions and not enflaming the conflict further by pressing his authority. To do this, he chooses to use a three strand strategy: Paul will call upon the cultural value of honor and shame to set the scene for generous giving; he will place generosity in a theological frame as an essential part of the gospel; and he will provide details about the security of the gift to allay fears that he will misappropriate it. These three strands will be woven together

2. Ibid., 564–65.
3. Ibid., 565.
4. Ibid., 586.
5. Marshall, *New Testament Theology*, 282.

to make a persuasive argument that will overcome the barriers the conflict has created. He will also continually and consistently avoid any *demand* that they give and any statement of an expected *size* for the gift. Instead, Paul will use the rhetorical strategies of the first century in order to achieve the maximum influence upon the Corinthians within their conflicted relationship.

Paul's Argument for the Collection in the Midst of Conflict

Paul begins his argument for the Corinthian church to contribute generously to the collection by describing the experience of the Macedonians. The Macedonians provide Paul with an ideal model with whom the Corinthians can compare themselves and from whom they can begin to learn about the theology of grace (gift), which compels generosity as part of the necessary response to the gospel.[6] Verse one of chapter eight begins by introducing the Macedonians, explaining that God first gave them grace (gift). Paul's theological frame for generosity acknowledges first that the origin of all gifts is God.[7] There is a flow from God to the Macedonians, in which the Macedonians are expected to see themselves as conduits of grace to others. The important aspect of this inflow of grace from God with regards generosity is that Paul expects there to be an excess, an abundance beyond the Macedonians' needs, this surplus will then be passed on to others.[8]

Verses 2–5 expand how the Macedonians demonstrated this gift that God had given to them in relation to the collection. Verse 2 highlights how they gave despite the severe trial and resulting poverty in which they found themselves. There is an unusual expectation here that generosity can flow from a combination of joy and poverty.[9] Somehow the confidence in God's giving transforms the Macedonians' ability to give. By v. 4 we see that they are so captured by God's generosity to them that they urgently plead for the privilege of sharing in the service to the Lord's people. Verse 5 reiterates Paul's theological conviction about giving: The Macedonians first gave themselves to the Lord; it was this giving that enabled the Macedonians to give themselves to Paul and his collection.[10] The model the Macedonians provide is more personal than a good moral example or even imitation of God. The Macedonians participate in God, receiving his transforming gift

---

6. Cf. Barclay, *Paul and the Gift*.
7. Gorman, *Apostle of the Crucified Lord*, 372.
8. Barclay, *Paul and the Gift*.
9. Gorman, *Apostle of the Crucified Lord*, 372.
10. Ibid.

of Christ Jesus, and due to their incorporation in God give generously—even when it seems unlikely or impossible for them. What this means is that the flow of the gift is not exterior to them but interior. Their inner life is reshaped by the flow of the gift from God through them to those in need.[11]

Verses 6 and seven move the focus of the argument to the Corinthians. Now the question is, are the Corinthians as incorporated into God's life as the Macedonians? Notice how the cultural desire for honor and the theological argument for generosity combine to influence the Corinthians. The instruction to Titus raises the question of whether the Corinthians are going to complete the particular act of grace expressed in the collection. Will they demonstrate that they have been transformed by God's gift to become people who are generous even in their poverty?[12] Verse 7 flatters the Corinthians by listing areas in which they excel, in order to encourage them to grasp hold of this opportunity to demonstrate just how great they are. While Paul flatters, a methodology we would probably consider negative, it is important to recognize the way in which Paul is offering an opportunity to the Corinthians to enter more fully into the will of God. Paul wants the Corinthians to *choose* to become generous.[13] Paul's invitational manner corresponds well with Stone, Patton, and Heen's key insight in *Difficult Conversations: How to Discuss What Matters Most* that "one cannot change other people, but one can change the way they converse with them."[14]

Verse 8 continues Paul's invitation to the Corinthians, by shifting the comparison from the Macedonians to Christ Jesus. Paul affirms that he is not commanding them in how they should act. There is no explicit compulsion for them to be generous. Instead, the Corinthians will be evaluated in relation to both the Macedonians and to Christ Jesus in terms of how willing they are to be transformed by the gift of God. Verse 9 expresses Jesus' journey from riches to poverty so that the Corinthians might become rich. Jesus represents the way of life of those filled with God. Verse 9 is slightly confusing, as it seems to suggest that Christ Jesus ends up in poverty. Instead of understanding verse nine this way, we should instead understand Christ Jesus as being rich, and that knowing he was rich he joined the Corinthians in their poverty in order that they might become like him in richness.[15] The dynamic of grace, of gift-giving, expresses true wealth as a generosity in which the person gives themselves for others. The dynamic of God's life

---

11. Barclay, "Lectures on *Paul and the Gift*."
12. DeSilva, *Introduction to the New Testament*, 590.
13. Gorman, *Apostle of the Crucified Lord*, 372.
14. See Introduction, [x-ref].
15. Gorman, *Apostle of the Crucified Lord*, 373.

into which the Corinthians are being drawn is to give of themselves so that others may be as rich as they are.[16]

Paul's major argument is set up by 8:1–9. These verses argue that generous giving to the collection is important for two reasons: so that the Corinthians will be honored among the people of God; and as a sign of their transformation in Christ as self-giving people who pass on what God has given them. Paul has invited them to participate in what God is doing in the collection and so demonstrate their agreement with his theological explanation of who God is and how he has transformed them. The rational argument is strengthened by an appeal to the desire to be honored in relation to the Macedonians and out of loyalty to Christ Jesus. They are to demonstrate their greatness with regards to the gift they have received.

Paul then continues to build his argument by going into further detail regarding the Corinthians' history and specific issues of concern regarding gift giving and the collection. Paul starts out in verses ten to twelve by encouraging the Corinthians to complete the process they have begun. He praises them for their initial eagerness while emphasizing that completing the giving is where true honor lies for the Corinthians. If the Corinthians act now, they will be honored both for their eagerness and for their successful completion. Once again, we get a glimpse of Paul's underlying theology of generosity and its rootedness in the gospel. The Corinthians' willingness makes their gift acceptable, not the size of the gift. The Corinthians are not being measured by what they do not have—it is their attitude that is of foremost interest to Paul. Hence, Paul will not *compel* them to give.[17]

Paul then aims to remove one of the minor arguments that is, presumably, being made against the collection: that it impoverishes one group to the benefit of another group. He explains in verses thirteen to fifteen that the aim is not that the Corinthian church becomes hard pressed but that there might be equality between the various church communities. Those with plenty in one area will supply the needs of others. For Paul, the equality goes beyond an equal distribution of resources and extends into the area of equal partners who contribute to each other.

In vv. 16–24, Paul undermines any suggestion that the collection is to benefit himself by referencing Titus's support for the collection and by introducing the two brothers who will act as safeguards against any attempt by Paul to misuse the collection. Paul begins by declaring Titus's enthusiasm for the collection. The Corinthians have a more positive relationship with Titus, and Paul hopes to use their trust in Titus to bolster their trust in him.

---

16. Barclay, "Lectures on *Paul and the Gift*."
17. Gorman, *Apostle of the Crucified Lord*, 373.

Paul introduces the brothers who will safeguard the collection with high praise. Their repute is above contradiction in all the churches. Paul explicitly acknowledges that this safeguard is being put in place so that the right thing will be done in the eyes of men. Paul ends the demonstration of the collection's security by calling once again for them to show their honorable status when they meet these men.[18]

Chapter 9 begins with a reversal of perspective from the beginning of chapter eight. Now, instead of holding up the Macedonians as the model of generosity with regards to the collection, Paul tells the Corinthians how he boasted about them to encourage the Macedonians to give. The Corinthians were honored by Paul to the Macedonians, but the honor they received for their initial enthusiasm is now threatened because of their failure to follow through. Paul worries that he will be embarrassed and notes that they will be embarrassed too.[19] It is as if Paul uses their initial honor in the eyes of the Macedonians to increase the pressure on the Corinthians to finalize the collection. Paul presents the sending of "the brothers" to Corinth not as a threat, to whip the Corinthians into shape, but as insurance that the Corinthians will maintain their honor with the Macedonians. He is careful in verse five to declare that the aim is to encourage a generous gift, not a gift that is begrudged. While exerting maximum pressure on the Corinthians, Paul wants to emphasize that the attitude of the gift is what is important to his theological perspective. This is an interesting line that Paul is walking: influencing without coercing.

From v. 6 onward Paul plunges back into the theological framework for generosity in order to provide further encouragement to the Corinthians. The earlier theological argument was developed in a manner that placed full participation in God's life as the reason for generosity. The argument was invitational in nature. This theological argument, by contrast, carries an increased element of warning: if the Corinthian church does not participate generously, they will be left outside the fullness of God's life. The warning is layered: as one sows, one also reaps; God loves a cheerful giver; generosity allows one to abound in good works and righteousness; and only generosity allows one to participate fully in thanksgiving to God. All of these arguments are based on the idea that if generosity really takes us to the heart of God's character, to reject generosity is to remove yourself (at least somewhat) from God's presence. Because of the weight of these warnings, Paul has inserted in verse seven the importance of each person deciding in

18. Ibid.
19. Ibid.

their heart what they will give. Paul desires that believers in Corinth take on the attitude of God, of Christ, and therefore the narrative of the gospel.[20]

Paul then sums up his entire argument in vv. 12–15 by expressing how the Corinthian church's service, presumably as priests, supplies the needs of God's people and results in thanksgiving. For Paul, the gift believers in Christ Jesus were given continues to overflow in generosity, causing others to receive and offer gifts in turn, which continues the cycle. As part of this cycle, the Corinthians will be honored for their obedience and benefit from whatever the return gift is. In Paul's view, the highest honor (the biggest gift) is God's indescribable gift that first began the ongoing flow of gifts that now underpins the generosity of the Corinthians.[21]

A Challenge in Evaluating Paul's Argument

One of the challenges of evaluating Paul's argument in 2 Corinthians 8–9 is the question of how we should think about the rhetorical manner in which Paul uses the cultural context of honor-shame to motivate giving. Part of the problem is that it is easy to assign pejorative words, such as manipulation, to these parts of Paul's argument—as they seem abrasive to those of us brought up in an individualistic context. For some, Paul seems to be urging competition in a manner that is very disconcerting in our world today. It will help us deal fairly with Paul if we remember two things.

First, while today we rarely use honor-shame as a motivating factor for giving at the personal level, we do use other techniques to set the scene. One of these techniques is the well-crafted video (with powerful images, emotive music, and passionate voice-over) that stirs the viewer to compassion for the disadvantaged and turns them toward the value to be found in making the world a better place. Another technique frequently used today is use of personal story-telling to draw the listener into the story of someone who saw the world changed through generosity, or someone whose own world was changed by the generosity of someone similar to the listener. The important aspect we need to remember with regards to Paul's technique is that we ourselves do not encourage people toward generosity from a position of complete disinterest. Even on the world stage, we still use honor-shame to encourage national giving. The frequent use of percentage of GDP (and other similar measurements) as a way to encourage nations to give more relies on the power of honor-shame to cause a nation to manage their image.[22]

20. Ibid., 374.
21. DeSilva, *Introduction to the New Testament*, 590.
22. Barclay, "Lectures on *Paul and the Gift*."

Second, we often have a very simplistic understanding of the position from which people make decisions. Often we view the decision-making process as binary, with one option being spontaneous internal decision-making on the part of the individual, and the other option being coercion by an outside party. Deeper reflection would suggest that these two poles instead mark a continuum within which the internal and the external affect us in varying measures. With regards to people influencing us, we can easily imagine a situation in which someone's explanation of the correct response could be offered as a suggestion with the person also *choosing* to follow that advice. There is a range of ways in which people can influence us without manipulating us, though the boundary between the two is difficult to discern.[23]

When reading this section of 2 Corinthians, it may feel like Paul applies extreme pressure to the Corinthian church. We suspect that the rhetorical nature of the culture and the normalcy of the honor-shame manner of speaking mean that the Corinthians would not have experienced the pressure as significantly as we do in our context. This does not mean, however, that Paul is not crafty with the way he constructs his argument. He wants to exert influence, but perhaps he does slip in manipulation. The crossover point is a grey area, after all. We just need to be careful not to *discount* Paul's argument as *simply* manipulation. In light of his refusal to state an amount or demand a gift, we would suggest that his primary intention is to influence the Corinthians rather than manipulate.

Paul's Strategy for Dealing with the Corinthians in Relation to the Collection

In 2 Corinthians 8–9, Paul aims to encourage the Corinthians to give generously to the collection despite the residual effects of the conflict. The conflict between Paul and the Corinthians is not primarily about the collection, but the Corinthians are very unlikely to give generously to someone they don't trust. Therefore, Paul needs to encourage the Corinthians to give generously without offending them and thereby enflaming the conflict. The goal of getting the Corinthians to give to the collection clearly impacts Paul's strategy with regards his argument. In order to reduce the possibility of the previous conflict impacting future generosity, Paul provides three people (Titus and the two brothers) who will ensure that the collection will benefit the poor and not Paul. The Corinthians distrust Paul's motives due to their conflict about and with him. They dishonor Paul's integrity by suggesting that he

23. Ibid.

is lying to them about the purpose of the collection. Paul could respond angrily, defending his honor. This, however, would make his conflict with the Corinthians a more central element of the relationship and thereby would probably impede the collection. Instead, Paul chooses to accept the dishonor and to provide the Corinthians with reassurance about the purpose of the collection. By doing this, he ensures that the collection remains the focus of the relationship, rather than allowing focus to be pulled back to their opinion of him. This would seem to be an important role for us to consider when we enter into conflict. Does arguing for our own honor simply enflame the conflict further and impede other good results that might come from the relationship?

The details of Paul's strategy have been outlined above, but the substantial argument is a combination of a call upon their honor, relative to the Macedonians, and a theological argument that invites them to see the world as a great cycle of gift giving. With regard the Corinthians honor, Paul compares them with others, he flatters them, he truthfully affirms their good qualities, and he threatens them with being left out of God's gift-giving cycle. Paul draws significantly on their desire to better themselves (both in ways that we would consider positive, and in ways we might consider negative). The use of the social framework of honor does reveal to us that Paul understands who the Corinthians are and what motivates them. Paul has engaged them well in conversation and has learned who they are. He shows the ability to understand their perceptions, interpretations, and values—all important aspects of any conflict process. Paul has engaged in learning with the Corinthians as his focus, and he puts his knowledge to good use.

Paul also uses the conflict to clearly express his theology of giving and its rootedness in the gospel. He expresses his interpretation of reality and the values that flow from that. This helps the Corinthians to understand Paul's intention in gathering the collection. Paul works hard to explain why the Corinthians need to join him in his understanding of the gift-giving God who selflessly gives in order to express love. This provides an opportunity for the Corinthians to set aside their critique of Paul (as inadequate with regards to public speaking and spiritual gifts) and join with him in working together on the task of the collection. Paul's theological explanation invites the Corinthians to consider their own identity and potentially give a positive response to Paul by drawing alongside him.

Paul is also very careful not to *compel* the Corinthians to give. Initially for the reason that he lacks the ability to do so, but also because the very process of overcoming their conflict requires that he invites them to consider who they are and how they want to respond. He engages with them in a manner that honors their concerns. The Corinthian's identity, values, perceptions, and interpretation of the situation are not simply to be written off as foolish; instead, Paul seeks to change these things through persuasion and the presentation of a better way of engaging.

The final note on Paul, the Corinthians, and the collection is that Paul appears to have been successful. Second Corinthians 8–9 appears to have worked. In his letter to the Romans, Paul comments that he has collected funds from Macedonia and Achaia (Rom 15:26); Corinth was the major city in Achaia. Paul's mixture of appeal to the Corinthian's social values, his theological explanation, his provision for the security of the funds, and his unwillingness to compel them to give resulted in a successful collection. However we evaluate Paul's technique in arguing for the collection, we should remember that he succeeded.

Learning from Paul

Reading and understanding Paul's approach to the Corinthians in regards to the collection is certainly valuable in and of itself. What can we apply to our life and leadership in the church today? When faced with opposition and mistrust how do we act? When compelled to move forward in the face of conflict what can we learn from Paul? We offer three suggestions.

Paul's central appeal is to the gospel. The greatest motivation for Paul in his teaching to the churches is his understanding of grace and its affect on behavior. Becoming part of God's life requires that the individual and the community take on the character of the God they worship. This is Paul's central concern. The collection is an important sign that the Corinthians have grasped the gospel. Paul engages with the Corinthians with the primary aim that the Corinthians will commit fully to the way of life made possible by the gospel.

Paul's willingness to set aside his own reputation and the perceived dishonor the Corinthians show him is based on his understanding of the gospel as requiring a cruciform life. Paul is living out, in his own life, Christ's movement from riches to poverty—in order that others may share in Christ's richness. The cruciform shape of Paul's life means that he takes on disgrace in order to create the opportunity for the power of the gospel to work in people's lives. This is an important lesson for us as we live, and as we lead. How do we prioritize the gospel above our sense of self-importance as we engage in conflict? Our desire should be that people enter more fully into the gospel, not that our own position is respected and expanded.

Paul's awareness of the cultural and social dynamics that impact the Corinthians allows him to express his call to action in a manner that resonates with the Corinthians. Our task is to become wise readers of cultural and social dynamics that influence people's behavior. This will allow us to call upon supporting cultural and social resources as we engage with people in a situation of conflict, further strengthening our appeal.

Bibliography

Barclay, John M. G. "Lectures on *Paul and the Gift: Explorations in Paul's Theology of Grace.*" Vancouver: Regent Audio, 2009.

———. *Paul and the Gift.* Grand Rapids: Eerdmans, 2015.

DeSilva, David A. *An Introduction to the New Testament: Context, Methods and Ministry Formation.* Downers Grove, IL: IVP Academic, 2004.

Gorman, Michael J. *Apostle of the Crucified Lord: A Theological Introduction to Paul and His Letters.* Grand Rapids: Eerdmans, 2017.

Marshall, I. Howard. *New Testament Theology: Many Witnesses, One Gospel.* Downers Grove, IL: IVP, 1993.

7

The Table and the Cross
Paul Calls for Unity Around the Table

1 Corinthians 11

By Jeff Blair and Derwin Gray

A few years ago, my (Jeff) family went on vacation to Disney World. One afternoon as we were waiting in a mile-long line to board one of the children's attractions, my two rambunctious boys, Keith and Jack, were provoking and poking at one another. Finally, following numerous exhortations from me to cut it out, I separated them from each other, Keith in front of me and Jack behind Jennie. This brought immediate peace. One of the reasons I remember this incident is that a dad standing behind us commented on our sagacious tactic. "Divide and conquer," he chuckled. The enchanted joy of Disney World returned by a simple act of separation. Often, the way to make peace is to create space between quarrelling parties, and the study of Paul and Barnabas (chapter 1) illustrated such a strategy. Sometimes, however, *separation is not an option.*

The early church was a family, and like our own families today, sometimes they didn't get along. When the Apostle Paul's children were living in discord with their brothers and sisters in Christ, how did he respond? For Paul, in some circumstances *separation is not an option because division would be a subversion of the gospel.* The Lord gave Paul the message and ministry of reconciliation in Christ Jesus (2 Cor 5:18–19). In fact, for Paul both justification and *reconciliation* are at the center of his message of salvation. In Rom 5 Paul states that we are "justified by faith," then advances his argument beyond justification to reconciliation. Justification is the means to reconciliation, first of humans to God (Rom 5; 2 Cor 5), then of humans to one another (Eph 2–3; Rom 15). Reconciliation is the heart of the message and ministry of Paul. So, splitting up is off the table because separation would undermine the gospel.

My (Jeff) co-author for this chapter is my brother, Derwin Gray. I am white; Derwin is black. It is inconceivable that Paul—who "opposed Cephas to his face" over refusing to eat with the Gentiles—were he here today, could possibly endorse any circumstances under which Derwin or I might exclude the other from the Lord's table based on racial, ethnic, or socioeconomic differences. Paul parted ways with Barnabas with respect to his *missionary work*; but the same Barnabas "stood condemned" with Cephas (Gal 2:11, 13) when he refused to eat with Gentiles. Can we imagine Paul returning to Antioch, perhaps finding himself in a church service with Barnabas, refusing to share the table with his brother Barnabas? Such a scenario is unthinkable. *Separation, in this circumstance, was not an option because it would be a subversion of the gospel of reconciliation.* Derwin will discuss his personal experience with pastoring a multi-ethnic congregation in South Carolina later in the chapter as a concrete example of Paul's ministry model.

In the opening chapter, Visser and Mamula point out that the Chinese word for "conflict" is a combination of two characters, "danger" and "opportunity." I will discuss the opportunity in this situation in a moment, but the danger here is a grave one, literally a matter of life and death. Paul says to them, "Many of you are weak and ill, and some have died" (1 Cor 11:30) because of their divisions at the table. The Lord's Supper, which should have brought life to the Corinthians, had become like a medicine meant to heal but taken wrongly, poisoning them to death; their sin of separation was an *abomination.*[1]

In Luke 22 and 1 Cor 11, followers of Jesus are fighting around the Table of the Lord. Luke 22:24 says that while at the Lord's Table a "dispute" arose among the disciples concerning who was the greatest. In 1 Cor 11:18 Paul says he has heard that there are "divisions" among the Corinthians when they gather around the Lord's Table.[2] The aim of this chapter is to

1. Thiselton, *First Epistle to the Corinthians*, 895–96.

2. The rationale for linking these two texts is not only their similar conflict dynamics, but they also share similar language. They are the only Lord's Supper institution texts in which Jesus says, "Do this in remembrance of Me." There is no consensus on

consider the nature of these quarrels and discover the strategies revealed in these texts to bring about reconciliation.

What we will see is that *the conflict in Corinth is caused by the "haves," those of high social standing, separating themselves from the "have-nots," those of low social status.* The well-to-do are physically eating in separate spaces, likely eating better foods, possibly even before the poor arrive, thus undermining the point of "communion." What is happening is not unlike the days of segregation in the United States where one might find a sign reading, "Colored Served in Rear." *Paul's goal in the letter is to create unity where division is the present reality.*

We will see that in order to address this travesty, Paul's approach employs a number of the strategies laid out by and Visser and Mamula in the introduction to this book. For instance, Paul *focuses on the issue* by *identifying* with the Corinthians and the Corinthians with one another. As Visser and Mamula explain, it is a wise strategy to get the parties on the "same side of the table" and look at the issue together. Paul also uses *affirmation* to build trust between him and the wealthy, and the parties with one another. Paul utilizes brilliant rhetoric in 1 Cor 1–2 to persuade them to dramatically change their thinking. Finally, Paul issues what amounts to a dictum "from the Lord" to show that there is no room for separation, negotiation, or arbitration.

Guess Who's Coming to Dinner? The Table in the Ancient Mediterranean World

One of humanity's greatest achievements was the invention of food, not just fodder. All animals eat fodder. Humans invented food. Food is not merely something that you put in your stomach and digest. *Food is an occasion for a social act.* It's an occasion for meeting. It's an occasion for conversation. Food is something that stirs the senses.[3]

It is important to understand the cultural background of shared meals if we hope to discover the dynamics of discord around the Lord's Table among the first followers of Jesus. It will be helpful to think about the New

---

the relationship of the institution texts. It seems likely that Nolland is correct that the similarity of language is due to the early church's liturgical practice rather than some sort of common literary source. Nolland comments, "For vv 19–20 Luke clearly draws on a tradition that has a family likeness to that which we find in 1 Cor 11:23–26." Nolland, *Luke 18:35—24:53*, 1044.

3. Mumford, "Closing Statement," 96.

Testament context of table fellowship under two headings, boundaries and bonding, and one would be hard-pressed to find two more salient categories.

Boundaries

Well-known social historian of the New Testament period, S. S. Bartchy, stresses the significance of shared meals in the world of the New Testament, stating that

> It would be difficult to overestimate the importance of table fellowship for the cultures of the Mediterranean basin in the first century of our era. Mealtimes were far more than occasions for individuals to consume nourishment. Being welcomed at a table for the purpose of eating food with another person had become a ceremony richly symbolic of friendship, intimacy and unity.[4]

New Testament scholar Eugene Boring claims that in first-century Judaism to "eat with" someone signified a level of intimacy akin to "sleeping with" someone today.[5] To share a meal with another meant to accept them and to be accepted by them. "Meals," in the ancient world, according to Dennis Smith, another scholar of ancient meals, delineate "social boundaries in terms of who is excluded and who is included."[6]

The creation and maintenance of social boundaries was the raison d'être for the Jewish dietary laws (*kashruth*). There is a surprising severity of language associated with the dietary laws. In the Torah, transgression of food law, sexual impurity, and pagan worship are all placed in the category of *to'evah*, "abomination." The pagan practice of burning children in the fire as an act of worship is *to'evah* (Deut 12:31); the sexual perversions that caused the land to "vomit out" the inhabitants of Canaan are *to'evah* (Lev 18:24–30); so also the foods forbidden in *kashruth* are *to'evah* (Deut 14:3). Baruch Levine, expert on the Ancient Near East, comments, "A triad of religious sins emerges—dietary, cultic, and sexual—all associated with impurity and all linked to the destiny of the Israelites as a people distinguished from other nations" and that "underlying all the dietary regulations is a *broad social objective: maintaining a distance between the Israelites and their neighbors*, so that the former do not go astray after pagan religions."[7] Because the sort of food placed upon the table is determined by the sort of

---

4. Bartchy, "Table Fellowship," 796.
5. Boring, *Mark*, 389.
6. Smith, "Table Fellowship," 303.
7. Levine, *Leviticus*, 242–44, emphasis added.

people sitting around the table, food laws have been a powerful means of creating social boundaries between the Jewish people and those outside. The reason these boundaries are so important to maintain is that the children of Israel are the children of YHWH, His unique covenant people,

> You are children of the Lord your God. . . . For you are a people holy to the Lord your God; it is you the Lord has chosen out of all the peoples on earth to be his people, his treasured possession. You shall not eat anything *to'evah*. . . . For you are a people holy to the Lord your God. (Deut 14:1–3, 21)

Boundary and identity are bound together; the faithfulness of the Jews to the food laws testifies to their identity as God's chosen people. *Kashruth* is not about what Jews eat; it is about who Jews are. Even under threat of death, many Jews have refused to transgress these identity-bearing statutes.[8]

The rest of the Mediterranean world did not have the sort of boundary-marking dietary customs as in Judaism, but their table fellowship did reflect group boundaries. By their very nature, shared meals must include some and exclude others. Associations, ubiquitous in the Mediterranean world, were a primary context for fellowship meals. In his oft-cited entry on associations in the Mediterranean world, Frederick Danker notes that associations were formed based on common interests such as devotion to gods or local heroes, the promotion of the arts, and "an almost endless variety of guilds that shared a common trade or practice."[9] Common interests created a division between the association and the outside world. Another type of boundary was also typical of these social gatherings—most of the time societies were "socially homogenous," that is, they drew people from the same side of the tracks.[10] Shared meals not only created boundaries, but also reflected them. This tendency of meals to be shared by social equals held true not only for associations, but for all contexts of table fellowship.

---

8. For instance, 1 Macc 1:62–63, "But many in Israel stood firm and were resolved in their hearts not to eat unclean food. They chose to die rather than to be defiled by food or to profane the holy covenant; and they did die." See also the ghastly accounts of the martyrdom of Eleazar in 2 Macc 6 and of the seven brothers in 2 Macc 7. In each case, they were tortured to death due to their refusal to eat "swine's flesh." Bradley Blue notes how Greco-Roman authors write with disdain on the Jews' fastidiousness with respect to the food laws, "Diodorus Siculus is the earliest (extant) pagan author to mention the Jewish reluctance to engage in table fellowship with a Gentile. In his *Bibliotheca Historica* he comments that the Jews 'had made their hatred of humankind into a tradition, and on this account had introduced utterly outlandish laws: not to break bread with any other race, nor to show them any good will at all' (Diodorus Siculus *Bib. Hist.* 63.2)." Blue, "Food, Food Laws, Table Fellowship," 377–78.

9. Danker, "Associations, Clubs, Thiasoi," 501.

10. Meeks, *First Urban Christians*, 79.

There were a myriad of reasons a group of people might gather together for a meal (e.g., Jesus at the wedding in Cana in John 2, or at the house of Zacchaeus the tax collector in Luke 19). Invitations to the table would be sent out,[11] and the rest of the world would be left out.

Bonding

In the formation of an association, the creation of boundaries was coupled with an intentional process of social bonding. Boundaries are about *identity* vis-à-vis the outside world; bonding is about *unity* and *intimacy* within the society. Aristotle maintained that "the essence of association (*koinōnia*) is friendship (*Eth.Nic.* 8.9.1 [1159b])."[12] Dennis Smith explains the significance of the Table for the forging of human social bonds:

> To the ancients, sharing a meal was embued (*sic*) with ritual meaning and *often signified the most solemn and intimate of social relationships*. . . . The formal meal or banquet was *the primary social event* for the ancients and one which carried a great deal of meaning. Dining together *created a tie or bond among the diners*, which in turn created an ethical obligation toward them.[13]

The fellowship meal was the primary activity of associations in the ancient Mediterranean world. Unity and intimacy were fostered by the sharing of food, drink, talk, life. The association banquet met an essential need in human life, for, as Aristotle said, "Man is by nature a social animal" (*Politics*, 1253a). Everybody needs a place where "everybody knows your name." Ramsay MacMullen's description of the purpose of the funerary associations has broad application to ancient societies: "Their objects were simple, summed up in the phrase 'social security': to have a refuge from loneliness in a very big world, to meet once a month for dinner. . . and at the end of life. . . to be remembered in a really respectable funeral."[14]

---

11. See Luke 14:7-24.

12. Danker, "Associations, Clubs, Thiasoi," 501. C. S. Lewis's chapter titled "Friendship" in *The Four Loves* is a brilliant treatment of the kind of friendship to which Aristotle referred. Lewis claimed, "To the Ancients, Friendship seemed the happiest and most fully human of all loves; the crown of life and the school of virtue" (87). Lewis, *Four Loves*, 87–127. Jesus is a "friend" of sinners, Matt 11:19.

13. Smith, "Table Fellowship."

14. MacMullen, *Enemies of the Roman Order*, 174, as cited in Smith, *Symposium*, 124.

Cultivating and maintaining unity among those who gathered around the table could, however, be challenging. This is a critical point: *the relative status of each guest was an especially sensitive matter.* There was a sort of pecking order that revealed who was the high and who was the "low man on the totem pole." The typical Greco-Roman banquet was held in a room with couches arranged along the walls. The Greek dining hall of the wealthy normally had seven to eleven couches, each holding one, sometimes two, guests. The Roman dining room was called a *triclinium*, a "three-couch room," with each of the couches accommodating three people. Although this arrangement allowed for intimacy,[15] it could also foster division. The placement of guests around the room by the host revealed the status of the guests.[16] It is no surprise that this often caused conflict. While it was true that "the meal was an occasion when the outside world was to be set aside and a new community of equals to be established," it was also the case that the seating of guests according to status was a deeply embedded custom of that world. Therefore, "there was a constant debate between the two opposite values of social stratification and social equality."[17] In order to facilitate unity, associations laid down rules and codes of ethics. Dennis Smith lists some of the most common rules:

> 1) injunctions against quarreling and fighting, 2) injunctions against taking the assigned place of another, 3) injunctions against speaking out of turn or without permission, 4) injunctions against fomenting factions, 5) injunctions against accusing a fellow member before a public court, 6) specifications for trials within the club for inter-club disputes, 7) specifications for worship activities.[18]

Jesus Ben Sira weighs in on what constitutes wise behavior at banquets. In 31:14–15 he offers what may be called the "Golden Rule" of the Table:

> Do not reach out your hand for everything you see,
> and do not crowd your neighbor at the dish.

---

15. Plutarch argued that "people who bring together too many guests to one place do prevent general conversation; they allow only a few to enjoy each other's society, for the guests separate into groups of two or three in order to meet and converse, completely unconscious of those whose place on the couches is remote and not looking their way because they are separated from them by practically the length of a race course.... So it is a mistake for the wealthy to build showy dining rooms that hold thirty couches or more. Such magnificence makes for unsociable and unfriendly banquets where the manager of a fair is needed more than a toastmaster. Quoted in Smith, *Symposium*, 25.

16. Appendix A is taken from Smith, *Symposium*, 16–17.

17. Smith, *Symposium*, 283.

18. Smith, "Meals and Morality," 323.

Judge your neighbor's feelings by your own,
and in every matter be thoughtful.

We are beginning to see some of the deep social dynamics that led to conflict around the table at Corinth. Paul is dealing not merely with bad manners as in Ben Sira 31. The lower-class Corinthians could not "crowd their neighbor at the dish," because they were not in the same room! Not only did they not have the *best* place at the table, they had *no* place.

For years, the slogan for the Olive Garden Italian restaurant was, "When you're here, you're family." Relatively recently they changed their slogan to, "Go Olive Garden" (emphasis on *Go*) "to cater to a more modern lifestyle," reports Candice Choi of CBS.[19] The chain had been "more about this traditional family meal—that long, lingering meal, with lots of laughter, lots of joy," but "the chain decided the image no longer reflected today's hectic lives." So, they decided that "when you're here, you're family" no longer accurately reflected who they were. The wealthy Corinthians had forgotten who they were in Christ, and therefore had forgotten the vision of Jesus and carried forward by Paul, that "when you're in Christ, you're family." No custom in the ancient world said, "When you're here, you're family" more loudly or clearly than eating together around the table. In order for Paul to resolve this conflict, Paul will have to *remind* them of this vision. He will do this in 1 Cor 11:23ff. when he reminds them of the authoritative word of the Lord.

Of Mussels And Magpies: The Nature of the Division, the Vision

S. S. Bartchy states, "One distinctive feature of Jesus' ministry was his practice of a *radically inclusive and non-hierarchical table fellowship* as a central strategy in his announcement and redefinition of the inbreaking rule of God."[20] Table fellowship is a major theme in the Gospel of Luke. Jesus is often at the table, and much of Jesus' teaching is done while at a shared meal. Bartchy describes the ministry of Jesus as portrayed in Luke as a "roving banquet hall."[21]

The community to which Luke writes is significantly stratified socially. Luke-Acts scholar F. Scott Spencer maintains that Luke's audience is similar

---

19. "Olive Garden to Ax Famous Slogan, Freshen Up Image," CBS news, October 5, 2012. https://www.cbsnews.com/news/olive-garden-to-ax-famous-slogan-freshen-up-image/

20. Bartchy, "Table Fellowship," 796. Emphasis added.

21. Ibid., 800.

to that of the church in Corinth. 1 Corinthians 1:26 is a key verse in understanding the social makeup of these communities, "Consider your own call, brothers and sisters: *not many* of you were wise by human standards, *not many* were powerful, *not many* were of noble birth."[22] A majority of the community was from the lower end of the social register, but a few were of higher status. For instance, Gaius, in whose house the "whole church" gathered, and Erastus, the "city treasurer," (Rom 16:23) enjoyed a reputable status, as did Theophilus in Luke 1:1–4.[23] Philip Esler offers a summary of the likely makeup of the Lucan community:

> [T]he community encompassed individuals both from the highest strata in the city—Roman officers, for example, and possibly even decurions—and also from the lowest levels, the beggars and the impoverished day-labourers. The presence within the same group of representatives from the glittering elite and from the squalid urban poor was very unusual in this society and created severe internal problems.[24]

It is into this social setting that Luke sends his gospel advocating for "radically inclusive and non-hierarchical table fellowship." Throughout the gospel, we can see Luke pressing this point. For instance, in Luke 14, while Jesus is at a fellowship meal, He instructs His fellow guests to choose the lowest seat when they are invited to a banquet (v. 10). He then turns to the one who had invited Him and says that when sending out invitations to a banquet one should not invite "friends or your brothers or your relatives or rich neighbors," but instead invite those who could never return the honor, "the poor, the crippled, the lame, and the blind" (v. 12–13). In his gospel,[25] particularly in his table texts, Luke wants his readers to envision a world in which Jew and Gentile, slave and free, rich and poor, men and women are

---

22. 1 Cor 1:26. Emphasis added. All Bible citations are from the NRSV unless otherwise noted.
23. Spencer, *Gospel of Luke and Acts of the Apostles*, 78.
24. Esler, *Community and Gospel in Luke-Acts*, 221.
25. This theme of radical table fellowship continues in Acts. The story of the two travelers on the road to Emmaus (Luke 24) serves as a bridge from the gospel to the Acts (Talbert, *Reading Luke*, 230). It is around the table in the breaking of bread, especially as one has welcomed a "stranger" (v. 18), that the presence of the risen Lord is experienced. In Acts, it is first the Jews in the Jerusalem environs who experience joyful life around the table (2:46–47). Later, Peter stays with a Gentile God-fearer (Acts 10–11). Paul stays in the home of Lydia the Gentile God-fearer in Philippi; and while in Philippi at the home of the jailor, Paul stays and eats at the table of this Gentile. Such is the pattern in Luke-Acts.

joyously gathered around one table as one family of the Messiah, then to become an incarnation of this vision.

As Jesus in Luke, Paul's vision of radical reconciliation was not only between Jew and Gentile. In Gal 3:28–29 Paul declares:

> There is no longer Jew or Greek,
> there is no longer slave or free,
> there is no longer male and female;
> for all of you are one in Christ Jesus.
> And if you belong to Christ,
> then you are Abraham's offspring,
> heirs according to the promise.

Paul's vision is of the obliteration of all boundaries in Christ. In Christ Jesus, all barriers to unity—ethnicity, status, gender—are demolished. Those who are Christ's possession are all equally children of Abraham and heirs of the covenant promises. All of these are freed to gather around the Lord's Table in joy and peace. This vision of unity in Christ is crystal clear in 1 Corinthians as well.[26] The evidence shows that this vision became reality, at least in part. The gospel had brought Jew and Greek, slave and free, male and female together into the same group. In many ways, however, when the group gathered, the real work had just begun.

The Division

Luke 22:24 says, "A dispute[27] also arose among them as to which one of them was to be regarded as the greatest." In 1 Corinthians 11, Paul says,

> For, to begin with, when you come together as a church, I hear that there are divisions among you; and to some extent I believe it. When you come together, it is not really to eat *the Lord's Supper*. For when the time comes to eat, each of you goes ahead with *your own supper*, and one goes hungry and another becomes drunk. What! Do you not have homes to eat and drink in? Or do you show contempt for the church of God and humiliate those who have nothing? What should I say to you? Should I commend you? In this matter I do not commend you! . . . So then, my brothers and sisters, when you come together to eat, wait for

---

26. See 1 Cor 1:1–2; 3:9, 16–17; 12:27.

27. *Philoneikia*, only here in the NT, but the adjective, *philoneikos* occurs in 1 Cor 11:16. The word derives from *philo-* and *nikē* = *loving victory,* the idea of desiring to argue for the sake of winning the argument rather than discovering the truth. Thiselton, *First Epistle to the Corinthians*, 847.

one another. If you are hungry, eat at home, so that when you come together, it will not be for your condemnation.[28]

When the Corinthian Christians come together to worship as a church, they are not truly together because there are divisions (*schismata*) among them. Some go away from the worship service hungry and humiliated, others drunk and proud. The directive to correct this offense is that they "wait for one another," which means everyone—Jews and Greeks and slaves and citizens and men and women, that is to say, *brothers and sisters*—get around the table and eat the meal together, fellowshipping as a family!

We are not able to reconstruct all of the details of what was happening at the Corinthian assembly. What is clear is that in the church of Corinth there were haves and have-nots.[29] The "not many" of 1:26 who enjoyed the social currency so important in Corinthian culture—worldly wisdom, power, noble birth—were, through their behavior at the Lord's Supper, magnifying the status differences between them and their brothers and sisters of low rank who made up the majority of the church. What did this look like?

Gerd Theissen asks four questions regarding the nature of the transgression at the Corinthian assembly that caused Paul to oppose it so stridently.[30] For the details, I direct the reader to Gerd Theissen's groundbreaking book on this. Following is a summary of his questions and findings. First, *Did the groups gather in separate rooms at the Lord's Supper*? Theissen finds that they did, dividing along socioeconomic lines.[31] Second, *Was there a division in the time of their dining*? The answer again is, yes. The details of the text support the reconstruction that the rich would have eaten their fill of the fine food they provided for themselves, and the poor would arrive only in time to eat the little fare they could afford.[32] This would make good sense

---

28. 1 Cor 11:18–22, 33–34. Emphasis added.

29. 11:22, the "have-nots" are exactly that, literally: *tous mē echontas* = "those who have nothing." Paul literally asks the "haves," *mē gar oikias ouk echete?* = "For *you have houses* in which to eat and drink, don't you?"

30. Theissen, *Social Setting of Pauline Christianity*, 147.

31. Jerome Murphy-O'Conner describes the scenario that likely unfolded as the Corinthians gathered: The mere fact that all could not be accommodated in the triclinium (main dining hall) meant that there had to be an overflow into the atrium. It became imperative for the host to divide his guests into two categories: the first class believers were invited into the triclinium while the rest stayed outside. Even a slight knowledge of human nature indicates the criterion used. The host must have been a wealthy member of the community and so he invited into the triclinium his closest friends among the believers, who would have been of the same social class. The rest could take their places in the atrium, where conditions were greatly inferior. Murphy-O'Connor, *St. Paul's Corinth*, 181–82.

32. Marshall, "Lord's Supper," 571.

of Paul's admonition in v. 33, "wait for one another." We will take Theissen's third and fourth questions together: *Did some get more food than others?* and *Did some get better fare than others?* Once again, sadly, Theissen finds these to be true. Notice that Paul makes a sharp distinction between two descriptions of the Supper; in v. 21 he says that they are not truly eating "the Lord's Supper" (*kuriakon deipnon*), but they are eating "their own supper" (*idiom deipnon*). These two contrast the ownership of the meal; does the meal belong to the Lord or to the rich? A likely reconstruction, therefore, is that the rich brought their "own" food, refused to share with their brothers and sisters as the "Lord's Supper," but instead "devoured their own" copious dinner in the presence of the poor.[33] The affluent would have enjoyed not only more food, but richer fare. Dennis Smith provides an analogy from the Roman world, quoting Martial:

> Since I am asked to dinner, no longer, as before, a purchased guest [i.e., client], why is not the same dinner served to me as to you? You take oysters fattened in the Lucrine lake, I suck a mussel through a hole in the shell; you get mushrooms, I take hog funguses; you tackle turbot, but I brill. Golden with fat, a turtledove gorges you with its bloated rump; there is set before me a magpie that has died in its cage. Why do I dine without you, although, Ponticus, I am dining with you? The dole has gone: let us have the benefit of that; let us eat the same fare.[34]

The nature of the division, then, centers around the question of status.[35] The disciples argued about who was the greatest (Luke 22). The prosperous Corinthians flaunted their advantages in the presence of the poor. In both cases, the ways of the world outside of the Christian community were being carried into the church. Jesus told the disciples that "the rulers of the Gentiles lord it over them; and those in authority over them are called benefactors. But not so with you."[36] Paul warned the Corinthians that the "wisdom of this age" and the "rulers of this age . . . are doomed to perish."[37] Is there a better way?

---

33. Theissen, *Social Setting*, 148–60.

34. Smith, *Symposium*, 45, quoting Martial, *Epigrams*, 3.60.

35. For discussions of status, deSilva, *Honor, Patronage, Kinship & Purity*; Hellerman, *Reconstructing Honor*; Clarke, *Secular and Christian Leadership*.

36. Luke 22:25–26.

37. 1 Cor 2:6.

The Cross of Christ from First to Last: The Strategy to Create Unity

The divisions (11:18) manifested in the Lord's Supper were not an isolated incidence of conflict among the Corinthians. In fact, Paul raises the problem of divisions in 1:10, immediately after the thanksgiving. The thematic statement that introduces the central issue of the letter is in 1:10,[38] where Paul writes, "Now I appeal to you, brothers and sisters, by the name of our Lord Jesus Christ, that all of you be in agreement and *that there be no divisions among you*, but that you be united in the same mind and the same purpose." *The goal of the letter is to create unity where division is the present reality.* So, what is Paul's primary strategy to achieve this unity among his children?

Before we get into Paul's principal approach to create harmony, I want to bring out a couple of details in 1 Cor 11, the immediate context, that correspond to strategies mentioned by Visser and Mamula in the introduction. First, notice how Paul closely *identifies* himself with the Corinthians, and the Corinthians with one another[39] by wrapping up his admonition with, "So then, my brethren," (v. 11:33).[40] The rebuke has been rather sharp, so Paul reminds them once again before he moves on that they are not only on the same side, but they are family. *Second*, in the same vein, I see Paul's move in 11:23 as an act of *"getting on the same side of the table,"* as Visser and Mamula put it. You might imagine it as the famous Leonardo da Vinci painting where Jesus and the disciples are all on the same side of the table. Here, Paul pulls up a chair next to them at the table, and they watch the Last Supper unfold before their eyes. Instead of looking at the *problem* together (as it was put in chapter one), they are looking at the *model* together, using the same slowed-down language typical for Last Supper descriptions (also descriptions of Jesus feeding the 5,000). Dramatically, they watch together as Jesus "takes bread . . . gives thanks . . . breaks it" (11:23–24).

---

38. Mitchell, *Paul and the Rhetoric*, 2, 297, emphasis added. Mitchell's thesis is that *the entire letter* of 1 Corinthians is deliberative rhetoric *designed to produce concord* among the Corinthians. She adduces an impressive array of parallels between 1 Corinthians and works of deliberative rhetoric from the Greco-Roman world.

39. See introduction for a discussion of identification as a strategy. "Identification means discovering and matching similarities between ourselves and others." This conflict is complicated because it is not only between two Corinthian groups—haves and have-nots—but multiple factions in the church (1:10–12), and between Paul and the church (4:10–13; 4:18–21)! Quite a mess!

40. Paul addresses them as "brethren" at strategic moments in the letter. See 1:10, the beginning of the thesis; 1:11; 1:26; 2:1; 3:1; 4:6, where he attaches it to a statement of their *benefit* (see Mitchell, *Paul and the Rhetoric*), "for you"; 7:24, 29; 10:1; 12:1; 14:6, 20; 15:1, 31; 15:58, "my beloved brethren"; 16:20, the last sentence in the letter.

For a few years I was a high school wrestling official. When the coach thought I made a bad call, he might "take me to the table," to use wrestling lingo. I would go to the table where he would proceed to explain (ahem) to me his argument. Here's the point: I was trained as an official not to stand face to face (or nose to nose!)[41] with the coach. Rather, I should position myself side by side with him and together look out onto the mat, where the incident in dispute took place. It is remarkable how effective this can be. It is not him against me; it is *he and I* discussing *that*, thinking this through together, both wanting the right call to be made.

Third, I see Paul *affirming* the Corinthians before *confronting* them. It is no coincidence that in 11:2 he says, "*I commend you* because you remember me in everything and maintain the traditions," when he will say in v. 17 (and v. 22) "*I do not commend* you in the following." When confrontation cannot be avoided, building trust by expressing praise first can be a powerful way to ease the tension. So, he begins by affirming them (v. 2), then pulling up a chair *beside* them (v. 23), and concludes by *identifying* with them (v. 33). That's wisdom.

Unfortunately, as Visser and Mamula observe in the introduction, though conflict is "normal," sometimes conflict is the result of sin. The examples given both apply to this situation: some have assumed a position of *superiority*, and they are acting *oppressively*. Therefore, Paul has no choice except to confront the sin head on. *For Paul, there can be no Band-Aid solution for this separation; it requires nothing short of transformation of mind and heart.* Coach Norman Dale was the new boys' basketball coach for the Hickory Huskers. One afternoon Opal Fleener, one of the team's most enthusiastic fans, said to Coach Dale, "Coach, tell me about the boys. You think you can bring 'em around?" Coach Dale replied, "Well, there's a lot of talent there. It's just raw and undisciplined." "What are you gonna do about that?" she asked. The coach responded, "*I'm gonna break 'em down, and then I'm gonna build 'em back up.*"[42] Paul's strategy to create unity among the Corinthian Christians is the same: he sets out to demolish their old ways of thinking and then creates a new way of understanding by means of the Word of the Cross.[43]

---

41. Note the difference in Paul's posture in Gal 2:11 where Paul confronted Peter, "opposed him to his face" (*kata prosōpon autō antestēn*).

42. From *Hoosiers* (the finest sports movie ever produced, followed closely by *The Natural*). Coach Dale is played by Gene Hackman, Opal Fleener by Fern Persons.

43. Extensive discussions in Clarke, "Equality or Mutuality?," 151–64; Clarke, *Secular and Christian Leadership*; Clarke, *Pauline Theology of Church Leadership*.

Alexandra Brown has demonstrated that 1 Cor 1:10—2:16 functions as the foundation of Paul's argument in the epistle.[44] The key word in this section is "mind" (*nous*). In 1:10 Paul urges them have the "same mind." In 2:16 he states that "we have the mind of Christ." The aim of Paul's words between 1:10 and 2:16 is to transform the Corinthians from "the alienated and divided *nous* (mind) to the unified and reconciling *nous tou Christou* (mind of Christ)."[45] The way they see the whole world must change.[46] Paul's strategy is to juxtapose the way of the world—everything that makes sense according to Corinthian culture—with the way of God revealed in the cross of Christ. The world around them values pride, wealth, pedigree, eloquence, strength, status; the Word of the Cross exalts self-sacrifice, humility, servanthood, mercy, and a crucified King. The course for the entire unit is set with the stark contrast laid out in v. 18:

> For the word of the cross is foolishness
> to those who are perishing,
> but to us who are being saved
> it is the power of God.

Paul proceeds in this way, line after line, deconstructing the present world that is "doomed to pass away" (2:6) and urging them to fully participate in the world God is creating through the proclamation of the Word of the Cross attended by the life-giving Spirit of God. But had Paul not already preached this message to them? He founded the church. He had remained with them for eighteen months. In 2:2 he says that when he came to them he "decided to know nothing among you except Jesus Christ, and him crucified." One can imagine some in Corinth asking, "Why is Paul so hung up on the cross?" Does the church need to be re-evangelized? The opening of the letter indicates that Paul believes them to be genuine believers who have faith in Jesus the Messiah.

Anthony Thiselton describes Paul's message in these chapters as a "*re-proclamation* of the cross."[47] In chapter 11, Paul does not contend that the offenders have no standing to receive the Lord's Supper; he argues that the manner in which they are observing the fellowship meal is unworthy of its purpose. In other words, they are Christians, but there is a serious deficit in their walk. Brown states, "Paul seems to locate the Corinthian error in an

---

44. Brown, *Cross in Human Transformation*.

45. Ibid., 21.

46. On pages 24–25 Brown lists the perceptual terminology in the Greek vocabulary of chapters 1–2. She identifies over twenty-five separate words that fit into this category. Phil 2 reflects the same strategy as 1 Corinthians as a whole.

47. Thiselton, *First Epistle to the Corinthians*, 33–34. Emphasis added.

insufficient comprehension and experience of the cross.... For this congregation, then, a transformation of consciousness has already occurred. Yet, *the transformation has been incomplete*, as their quarreling and divisions now demonstrate."[48]

Paul's strategy to create unity among the Corinthians, especially around the Table of the Lord, is to raise before them *again* the cross of Jesus. Until their eyes are fully opened to the cruciform life in Christ, there can never be true unity and intimacy in Christ. The hymn of Phil 2:6–11 makes this abundantly clear, but it is also why in 1 Cor 11:23–26, Paul rehearses the tradition which they had already received from him:

> For I received from the Lord what *I also handed on to you*, that the Lord Jesus on the night when he was betrayed took a loaf of bread, and when he had given thanks, he broke it and said, "This is my body that is *for you*. Do this in remembrance of me." In the same way he took the cup also, after supper, saying, "This cup is the new covenant in my blood. Do this, as often as you drink it, in remembrance of me." For as often as you eat this bread and drink the cup, you *proclaim the Lord's death* until he comes.

The linchpin Paul's strategy in 11:17–34 is to restate to them what they already have heard many times before. The tradition of verses 23–25 had previously been handed on to them; it is a re-proclamation. When God's church at Corinth comes together for the Lord's Supper, the manner of observance ought to be a re-proclamation as well: "as often as" they consume the bread and the cup, they proclaim the Lord's death until he returns. Paul said to them in 2:1–2, "When I came to you, brothers and sisters, I did not come *proclaiming* the mystery of God to you in lofty words or wisdom. For I decided to know nothing among you except Jesus Christ, and him *crucified*."[49] Just as Paul proclaimed Christ crucified in his preaching, the Corinthians must proclaim Christ crucified in the manner of their meeting. Their proclamation misfires, however, if they do not relate to one another in a cruciform way. Brown comments on the proclamation of the meal, "The proclamation is not verbal, but rather issues forth from the concrete action of persons in the setting of the Supper. It is what they show, not what they say, that proclaims the Lord's death. Notice that what is shown is the death of Jesus."[50] It is only when the church lives in unity through the humility of cruciformity, that it proclaims the transforming Word of the Cross. For Paul if there is to be true reconciliation, which issues in gospel proclamation,

---

48. Brown, *Cross in Human Transformation*, 24, 32. Emphasis added.
49. 1 Cor 2:1–2.
50. Brown, *Cross in Human Transformation*, 102.

there can be no Band-Aid and there is no Plan B. It is the cross of Christ from first to last.

A Teachable Moment

I began this chapter by pointing out the *danger* the Corinthians faced if they refused to come to the table and humbly fellowship as a true family. Visser and Mamula also say that the other character in the Chinese word for conflict is "*opportunity.*" I want to suggest that a conflict such as this, which goes to the heart of the work of Jesus, is a wonderful opportunity to remind our people of the beauty of the gospel. In 2008, Barack Obama was elected President of the United States. Living in rural Oklahoma, most of our folks are conservative, and there are still, sadly, signs of racism in our town. I must confess, I did not vote for President Obama. I have always been conservative in my political opinions, e.g., I'm pro-life. The Sunday morning after the election, however, knowing the majority of my congregation voted for John McCain, when I began my message, the first image that appeared on the big screen behind me was President Obama standing in front of an American flag.[51] Next I showed a picture of a black man drinking from a "colored" water fountain, and I preached how thankful I am, whether Republican or Democrat, that we as a nation have come this far. My sermon had three points: 1) There is no room for racism in God's good *creation*; we all come from the one God, in whose image we are all made. 2) There is no room for racism in *redemption*. Jesus died for all people. 3) There is no room for racism in the *consummation*, for around the throne will be those from "every nation, from all tribes and peoples and tongues" (Rev 7:9). I preached the same message last year as the racial tensions had been escalating, because all God's children *must never forget that we are family*, and our fellowship at the Lord's Table is testimony to the grace of God through the cross of Christ.

Paul's Strategy for Unity and Today

Jeff Blair's concluding observations on preaching about racism in a conservative church perfectly sets up the concern I (Derwin Gray) have in Transformation Church, namely, to seek to embody a multiracial church in a world loaded with racism and classism. The disunity that Paul addresses in his first letter to the Corinthian church was also caused by ethnocentrism

---

51. Something like this image, http://wallpaperose.com/barack-obama-flagged.html.

and classism within the local body. In 1 Cor 11:17–22, Paul rebukes the church because they were eating in factions that reinforced and reflected the corrupted Corinthian social codes outside the church; they were not participating in the Lord's Supper (vv. 19–20).[52] The wealthy would bring their own food and wine and eat with their social class while excluding the poor. And they were getting drunk! The way they ate their meal reinforced the sinful social realities that God overcame in Christ as he birthed Abraham's family (Gal 3:26–29).[53] We will also be writing about the disunity described in Luke 22 caused by pride as the disciples argued about who would be the greatest among them: "Then a dispute also arose among them about who should be considered the greatest" (Luke 22:24, CSB). In this conclusion to our study on conflict in Corinth, my primary task will be to provide pastoral and practical insights into resolving conflict caused by disunity in the local church as it relates to ethnocentrism, classism, and pride.

To accomplish my task, first I will provide two examples from my pastoral experience as founding and lead pastor at Transformation Church when disunity has occurred in our fellowship due to these issues. Second, the Bible's larger narrative, God's covenant with Abraham, which was fulfilled through the work of Jesus, the Messiah, gives birth to a multiethnic, multiclass people of God and this helps explain Paul's mission to create churches not marked by worldly divisions. Third, I will remind us about the ethnocentrism and classism in Corinth and how it caused the disunity in the local church. Fourth, we turn to how Jesus teaches his followers the true nature of leadership and discipleship and how we integrate the concept of servant-leadership in the context of Transformation Church.

The Seeds of Disunity: Part I

During the early years of my family's ministry, God planted in our hearts the dream of planting a multiethnic, socioeconomically diverse church just like the New Testament model. My wife Vicky and I recognized that most of the churches where I preached during my years as a speaking pastor were homogenous and socioeconomically segregated. We recognized that something needed to change. On February 7, 2010, Transformation Church was launched, and amazingly 701 multiethnic, socioeconomically diverse people attended our two worship services. A miracle happened right before our eyes as a gospel-shaped, multiethnic church was born.

52. McKnight, "The New Perspective and the Christian Life," In McKnight and Modica, *Apostle Paul and the Christian Life*, 122.

53. Ibid.

A few years after the launch, a white businessman and member of our church, whom I will call Bob, had a conversation with an affluent white Christian businessman friend. During the conversation, Bob said his friend asked a question that deeply disturbed him: "Do you think you are going to lose influence if you attend a church like Transformation Church?"

What did this friend, who attended a predominately white, affluent church, mean when he asked this question? Charlotte, North Carolina, is an ethnically and socioeconomically segregated city. Recent research shows that "segregation is very much a part of how our city is laid out."[54] Incredible wealth and poverty can literally be a block from each other.[55] Nathaniel Hendren, an economics professor at Harvard University, quoted in this recent research, "For low-income kids, Charlotte is one of the worst places to grow up in the United States." What his friend was saying to Bob is this: "Do you think you are going to lose your business connections if you attend a church where poor, uneducated people attend and where the pastor is black?" Charlotte is a city gorging itself with banking money. Affluent, homogenous churches are places to be seen and to make business connections and where people can gather with others like themselves.

Sociologist Michael Emerson found that "homogenous local churches reproduce inequality, encourage oppression, strengthen racial division, and heighten political separation."[56] This friend was simply reinforcing what Emerson's research presented. As an affluent, white evangelical, reared on a Western, racialized, individualistic gospel, he was living by the organizing principle of his life. As Scot McKnight said, "The gospel we preach shapes the kind of churches we create. The kind of church we have shapes the gospel we preach."[57] Later in this chapter, I will share how Transformation Church engaged this disunity.

The Seeds of Disunity: Part II

As Transformation Church continued to be blessed by God and gain national recognition, not only as one of the fastest growing churches in America, but as a new voice leading the way on gospel-shaped multiethnic, socioeconomic local church issues, disunity reared its ugly face. A white gentleman, whom I will call David, was a recently retired CEO with seven thousand employees under his leadership. He decided that he should be an elder who

54. Khrais, "In Charlotte, It's Especially Tough."
55. Ibid.
56. Gray, *High Definition Leader*, 6
57. McKnight, *Community Called Atonement*, 5.

oversaw the finances of our church. David was wealthy and powerful, and he was a former elder over the finances at his past affluent, white Midwestern church. He did not agree with our church leadership model, which we discerned to be an elder-pastor led and governed local church (1 Tim 3:1–7, 5:17; Titus 1:7–9; Heb 13:17; 1 Thess 5:12–13; Acts 20:17–38).[58] He was accustomed to being an elder, and his participation in that office was more or less based on his money, power, and influence. He also did not agree with our position of having an Executive Leadership Team, which "is comprised of men and women who ensure that Transformation Church operates in accordance with the law while implementing best practices, policies, and procedures regarding business, finances, and facilities for a church of our size and complexity. The Executive Elders-Pastors, in conjunction with the Executive Leadership Team, are the governing body of Transformation Church."[59]

Not surprisingly, David wanted Transformation Church to function like a corporation where he would sit on an executive board and have power and influence of the church's elder-pastors, finances, and policies. His approach and divisiveness sowed so much discord and disunity that it blinded a faction of people in our fellowship to the miracle that was right before us. An overwhelming number of churches in America are racially homogenous or segregated and not growing by conversion growth, but by God's enabling power, Transformation Church was multiethnic, making disciples, impacting our community, and baptizing hundreds. This faction missed this great work of God because disunity blinded them. David's pride caused disunity.

The Gospel: What Is It?

When engaging conflict at Transformation Church our aim is always to go back to the gospel because at the heart of the gospel is reconciliation to God and to one another (2 Cor 5:17–21). Conflict resolution resides in the One who entered our conflict and overcame it with his blood on the cross and the power that flows from his resurrection, all empowered for us in the Holy Spirit. At Transformation Church, we equip our staff and congregation to engage and resolve conflict through the source of our reconciliation, the gospel. In Gal 3:8 Paul writes, "Now the Scripture saw in advance that God would justify the Gentiles by faith and proclaimed the gospel ahead of time to Abraham, saying, 'All the nations will be blessed through you'" (CSB).

---

58. Transformation Church, "Our Team." http://transformationchurch.tc/about/our-team/.

59. Ibid.

At the heart of the gospel was God's covenant with Abraham. God promised Abraham a family, and this family is multiethnic, multiclass, and comprised of Jews and Gentiles, slave and free, Scythian and barbarian (Col 3:11). Jesus, the Messiah, through his sinless life, atoning death on the cross, resurrection, ascension, and sending of the Spirit, keeps God's covenant with Abraham. Paul writes in Gal 3:14, "The purpose was that the blessing of Abraham would come to the Gentiles by Christ Jesus, so that we could receive the promised Spirit through faith" (CSB). Therefore, at Transformation Church the gospel is that the true King, the Lord Jesus has brought forth a new people of God comprised of Jews and Gentiles who exist for worship and witness and God's royal priest (Eph 2:15; 1 Pet 2:9). We start with the gospel-reality that we are a family, the household of God (Eph 2:19–20).

Disunity Then, Disunity Now

In the first-century Second Temple Jewish context in the Greco-Roman world, disunity based on ethnicity, class, and gender was very much alive just as it is today in our world and far too often in the church. For example, the Roman philosopher Cicero (106–43 BCE) wrote, "As the Greeks say, all men are divided into two classes—Greeks and barbarians."[60] Another Greco-Roman expression that predates the book of Galatians is this: "Thank you that I was born a man and not a woman."[61] In addition, faithful Jewish men would pray, "Yahweh, thank you that I am not a gentile, slave, or woman."[62]

In the prayers of antiquity, you see that the sins of ethnocentrism, classism, and sexism are both everywhere present and at the same time destructive barriers to human flourishing if God's covenant with Abraham is to be embodied in communities. Jews and Gentiles entering God's kingdom by faith in the Messiah had to be taught and transformed out of ethnocentrism, classism, and sexism (Gal 4:19). It is not by accident that Paul, under the inspiration of the Holy Spirit, wrote in Gal 3:27–29, "For those of you who were baptized into Christ have been clothed with Christ. Here is no Jew or Greek, slave or free, male and female; since you are all one in Christ Jesus. And if you belong to Christ, then you are Abraham's seed, heirs" (CSB). Because God kept his covenant with Abraham, by and through the work of Jesus, God's people are clothed in the Messiah. Thus, ethnocentrism,

60. Gray, *High Definition Leader*, 51.
61. Hayes, *From Every People and Nation*, 186.
62. Ibid.

classism, and sexism have been crucified in their union and incorporation to the Messiah. God's people share a oneness in Christ that obliterates these dark, demonic barriers. This belief is the starting point for us at Transformation Church in equipping the staff and congregation in how to engage and resolve conflict caused by disunity flowing from ethnocentrism, classism, or sexism.

We Don't Create Unity

It is also important to note that, as church leaders, we don't create unity. Jesus already created unity and unified his people because we are one in him (Gal 3:27–29), a new humanity reconciled through him by the cross (Eph 2:14–26) and unified by the Spirit (1 Cor 6:17). We teach that there is no need to fight for unity, but that we fight powers that try to divide the unity we already possess in Christ. We teach that God's *grace*[63] created a new race, "so that he might create in himself one new man from the two, resulting in peace. He did this so that he might reconcile both to God in one body through the cross by which he put the hostility to death" (Eph 2:15–16, CSB).

Servant Leadership

At Transformation Church, we teach that leadership is about love, humility, and servanthood because Jesus embodied servant-leadership (Phil 2:1–11). Our goal is not simply to be good people, but to be agents of reconciliation through the development of character. We want to cultivate, from elder-pastors to the staff to our congregation, what we call the "5 C's of Leadership": character, competency, catalytic, collaboration, and chemistry. I will focus here on the first, that is, on character. When we talk about developing our character, we are talking about learning how to walk in the power of the Holy Spirit so the Fruit of the Spirit will flow in us and through us as we engage conflict. The Fruit of the Spirit is displayed in our emotional maturity and emotional intelligence, and these, we teach, lead to being agents of reconciliation.

Ultimately, we want to equip our elder-pastors, our staff (deacons), and congregation to embody the great "One Anothers," which as well sustains our vision for reconciliation and multiracial churches. As we equip

---

63. I did this on purpose to emphasize that God's grace in Christ creates a new race (Eph 2:8–15). God's grace is not just about individual salvation but corporate salvation of a new race of people called the church, who celebrate unity in their diversity.

our elder-pastors, staff, and congregation we emphasize how God the Holy Spirit empowers us to know that we are members of one another (Rom 12:5), who are called to build one another up (1 Thess 5:11), to care for one another (1 Thess 5:15), to bear with one another in love (Eph 4:2), to bear one another's burdens (Gal 6:2), to be kind and compassionate to one another, forgiving one another as Christ forgave us (Eph 4:32), to submit to another (Eph 5:21), to consider one another better than oneself (Phil 2:3), to be devoted to another in love (Rom 12:10), and to live in harmony with one another (Rom 12:16; 15:6–9).[64] Keep in mind, all these texts are written to multiethnic, socioeconomically diverse local churches who were struggling with disunity as we do today.

As a team of elder-pastors, we can train our staff and congregation, but ultimately, only they can walk by the Spirit to live out the "One Anothers." We believe our equipping helps Transformation Church work through conflict caused by disunity. But like any local church, it can be messy. I am so glad Jesus loves to get into our messiness.

Conflict Resolution: So What Happened?

I sat down and talked with Bob about how he should engage his friend who asked, "Do you think you will lose influence if you attend a church like Transformation Church?" I walked Bob through what the gospel is, how God desires ethnocentrism, classism, and sexism to be crucified by the work of Jesus (Gal 3:26–29), and how Bob should pray and walk in the Spirit's power as he engaged his friend. I did not hear from Bob about how the conversation with Jim went. However, about a year later, Bob informed me that he and his family would be leaving Transformation Church to become members of an affluent, white church.

Several of our elder-pastors sat down to talk with David, the former CEO, who decided he should be an elder over our church's finances. Our elder-pastors walked him through the qualifications of an elder-pastor (1 Tim 3:1–7; 5:17; Titus 1:7–9; Heb 13:17; 1 Thess 5:12–13; Acts 20:17–38) and why our elder-pastors are leaders who tend to the flock and are not just wealthy businessmen. The elder-pastors showed how the church's finances were in order and the accountability of checks and balances in our system. Despite our best efforts to preserve the unity, David and about ten people from his small group decided to leave Transformation Church. And they all went to an affluent, white church.

---

64. McKnight and Modica, *Apostle Paul and the Christian Life*, 99.

Conclusion

We don't have to fight for unity, we only need to realize that Jesus already fights for unity on the cross and won it. God's people are unified through his life, death, resurrection, ascension, and sending of the Spirit. The good news is that Jesus gave Abraham his family, which is a multiethnic, socio-economically diverse family. This family is an eschatological foretaste of eternity. I conclude with the words of the Paul in Gal 3:8 and 3:14:

> Now the Scripture saw in advance that God would justify the Gentiles by faith and proclaimed the gospel ahead of time to Abraham, saying, "All the nations will be blessed through you."
> ... The purpose was that the blessing of Abraham would come to the Gentiles by Christ Jesus, so that we could receive the promised Spirit through faith (CSB).

Bibliography

Bartchy, Scott S. "Table Fellowship." In *Dictionary of Jesus and the Gospels,* edited by Joel B. Green and Scot McKnight, 796. Downers Grove, IL: InterVarsity, 1992.

Blue, Bradley B. "Food, Food Laws, Table Fellowship." In *Dictionary of the Later New Testament and Its Developments,* edited by Ralph P. Martin and Peter H. Davids, 377–78. Downers Grove, IL: InterVarsity, 1997.

Bock, Darrell L. *Luke.* Vol. 1, *1:1—9:50.* Baker Exegetical Commentary on the New Testament 3. Grand Rapids: Baker, 1994.

Boring, M. Eugene. *Mark, A Commentary.* Louisville: Westminster John Knox, 2006.

Brown, Alexandra R. *The Cross in Human Transformation: Paul's Apocalyptic Word in 1 Corinthians.* Minneapolis: Fortress, 1995.

Clarke, Andrew D. "Equality or Mutuality? Paul's Use of 'Brother' Language." In *The New Testament in Its First Century Setting: Essays in Honour of B. W. Winter on His 65th Birthday,* edited by P. J. Williams et al., 151–64. Grand Rapids: Eerdmans, 2004.

———. *A Pauline Theology of Church Leadership.* London: T&T Clark, 2008.

———. *Secular and Christian Leadership in Corinth: A Socio-Historical and Exegetical Study of 1 Corinthians 1–6.* Paternoster Biblical Monographs. Milton Keyes, UK: Paternoster, 2006.

Danker, Frederick W. "Associations, Clubs, Thiasoi." In *The Anchor Yale Bible Dictionary,* edited by David Noel Freedman, 501–3. New York: Doubleday, 1992.

DeSilva, David A. *Honor, Patronage, Kinship & Purity: Unlocking New Testament Culture.* Downers Grove, IL: IVP Academic, 2000.

Esler, Philip F. *Community and Gospel in Luke-Acts: The Social and Political Motivations of Lucan Theology.* Society for New Testament Studies Monograph Series 57. Cambridge: Cambridge University Press, 1987.

Gray, Derwin L. *The High Definition Leader: Building Multiethnic Churches in a Multiethnic World.* Nashville: Thomas Nelson, 2015.

Hayes, J. Daniel. *From Every People and Nation: A Biblical Theology of Race*. Downers Grove, IL: IVP Academic, 2003.

Hellerman, Joseph H. *Reconstructing Honor in Roman Philippi: Carmen Christi as Cursus Pudorum*. Society for New Testament Studies Monograph Series 132. Cambridge: Cambridge University Press, 2005.

Khrais, Reema. "In Charlotte, It's Especially Tough to Climb the Economic Ladder." *Marketplace*, December 21, 2016. https://www.marketplace.org/2016/12/21/economy/charlotte-economic-mobility-among-worst-country.

Levine, Baruch A. *Leviticus*. The JPS Torah Commentary. Philadelphia: Jewish Publication Society, 1989.

Lewis, C. S. *The Four Loves*. New York: Harcourt Brace Jovanovich, 1960.

MacMullen, Ramsay. *Enemies of the Roman Order*. Cambridge: Harvard University Press, 1966.

Marshall, I. Howard. "Lord's Supper." In *Dictionary of Paul and His Letters*, edited by Gerald F. Hawthorne, Ralph P. Martin, and Daniel G. Reid, 569–75. Downers Grove, IL: InterVarsity, 1993.

McKnight, Scot. *A Community Called Atonement*. Nashville: Abingdon, 2007.

McKnight, Scot, and Joseph Modica. *The Apostle Paul and the Christian Life: Ethical and Missional Implications of the New Perspective*. Ada Township, MI: Baker Academic, 2016.

Meeks, Wayne. *The First Urban Christians: The Social World of the Apostle Paul*. 2nd ed. New Haven: Yale University Press, 2003.

Mitchell, Margaret M. *Paul and the Rhetoric of Reconciliation: An Exegetical Investigation of the Language and Composition of 1 Corinthians*. Louisville: Westminster John Knox, 1992.

Mumford, Lewis. "Closing Statement." In *The Ecological Conscience*, edited by Robert Disch, 96. Englewood Cliffs, NJ: Prentice-Hall, 1970.

Murphy-O'Connor, Jerome. *St. Paul's Corinth: Texts and Archaeology*. Wilmington: Glazier, 1983.

Nolland, John. *Luke 18:35—24:53*. Word Biblical Commentary 35c. Dallas: Word, 1998.

Smith, Dennis E. *From Symposium to Eucharist: The Banquet in the Early Christian World*. Minneapolis: Fortress, 2003.

———. "Meals and Morality in Paul and His World." *Society of Biblical Literature Seminar Papers* 20 (1981) 319–39.

———. "Table Fellowship." In *The Anchor Yale Bible Dictionary*, edited by David Noel Freedman, 303. New York: Doubleday, 1992.

Spencer, F. Scott. *The Gospel of Luke and Acts of the Apostles*. Interpreting Biblical Texts. Nashville: Abingdon, 2008.

Talbert, Charles. *Reading Luke*. New York: Crossroad, 1988.

Theissen, Gerd. *The Social Setting of Pauline Christianity: Essays on Corinth*. Edited and translated by John H. Schütz. Eugene, OR: Wipf & Stock, 2004.

Thiselton, Anthony C. *The First Epistle to the Corinthians: A Commentary on the Greek Text*. New International Greek Testament Commentary. Grand Rapids, MI: Eerdmans, 2000.

Witherington, Ben, III. *Conflict and Community in Corinth: A Socio-Rhetorical Commentary on 1 and 2 Corinthians*. Grand Rapids, MI: Eerdmans, 1995.

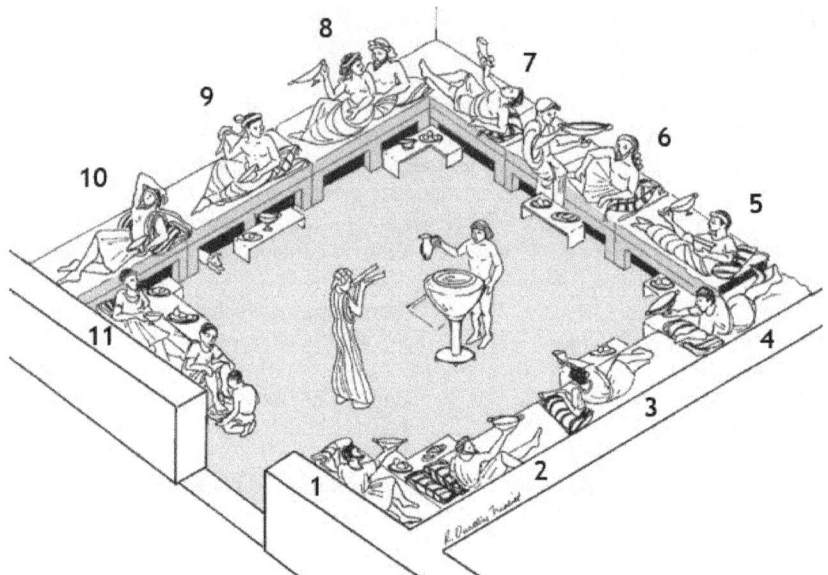

Figure 7.1: Reconstruction of a Greek Symposium

Sketch of Asclepius Sanctuary at Corinth. The couches have been numbered according to their most likely ranking, since the ranking order proceeds from left to right. (Except where otherwise indicated, the figures pictured here are all taken from classical-period Greek vase paintings and funerary reliefs that feature symposium scenes.)

The diners at couches 1, 2, 3, and 4 have raised their drinking vessels in apparent toast, a typical gesture in ancient banquet depictions.

The diner at couch 5 is positioning his cup for *kottabos*, the game in which the diners would compete to see who could hit a target with the last dregs of wine in their cups. Diner 6 is being served wine by a female companion; she is shown in a pose indicating she most likely was a courtesan. The diner at couch 7 is pictured drinking from the tip of a horn shaped *rhyton* (the pose is conjectured).

The female companion sharing an amorous embrace with diner 8 is clearly pictured as a courtesan. The diner at couch 9 is arranging the festive headband he wears for the occasion. There is also a dog under couch 9, ready to clean up any crumbs that might fall; dogs were often pictured in such poses in banquet scenes. Diner 10 is shown leaning back as if he will soon fall asleep.

The diner at couch 11 is holding out his cup to be served more wine. He is looking toward the servant in the center of the room, who is dipping wine out of a *dinos*, a large bowl for mixing and serving wine. Also in the center of the room is a flute girl, who is providing the entertainment for the evening. Near the door, a late-arriving guest is having his feet washed (the pose is conjectured); he will be sharing couch 1 with the diner already reclining there.

Figure 7.2: Reconstruction of a Roman Banquet in a Triclinium

The scene pictured here is arranged on a mosaic floor from a Roman-period dining room (the mosaic is now on display at the Pergamon Museum in Berlin). The design of the mosaic marked the area along the walls where the couches were to be arranged in the typical Pi shape of a Roman triclinium or three-couch room. The couches in this style of dining room were able to accommodate at least three diners each. The room would therefore normally hold nine diners, as pictured here. The couch on the right was designated *locus summus*, meaning "highest position"; the middle couch was called *locus medius*, or "middle position"; and the couch on the left was *locus imus*, or "lowest position." These designations indicated general ranking around the table, with some exceptions. As customs evolved, the highest-ranking became position 3 at *locus medius*, located where it joins *locus imus*; this position was designated *locus consularis*, "the consuls position" (Plut., *Quaest. Conv.* 1.3). The host could be placed at position 1 on *locus summus*, as in Petronius's depiction of the banquet of Trimalchio (*Sat.* 31.8; Smith, *Cena Trimalchionis*, 66–67), or, more commonly, at position on *locus imus*, located where this couch joins *locus medius*, and thus in close proximity to *locus consularis*. In our reconstruction, the three diners on *locus imus* are all women. They have been placed here in imitation of a reference in Lucian's *Symposium* in which the women present at a wedding banquet were all arranged on the same couch (Luc. Symp. 8). The musicians providing the entertainment and the style of the tables in front of the couches have been copied from the fifth-century CE Roman banquet scene.

8

Mission in Tension
Paul as Ministry Advocate

GALATIANS 2:1–10

By Brett Sanner and Paul Trainor

Introduction

The early Christian movement comprised of a Jewish sect that had come to believe Jesus of Nazareth, crucified by the Romans in Jerusalem circa 30 CE, was vindicated by the God of Israel having been resurrected from the dead and thus was the long awaited Jewish Messiah. The earliest Christian mission was within this one ethnic group comprising of Palestinian and Hellenistic Jews, both within the land of promise and scattered throughout the Diaspora. Yet, by divine fiat in a relatively short time the witness of this Jewish announcement expanded to include Gentiles, initiated by the Holy Spirit through two significant events involving two of Christianity's greatest witnesses. First, the call and commissioning of Paul to his Gentile mission (Acts 9:3–6, 15–16; Gal 1:15–16); and second, a vision (Acts 10:9–16) of Gentile acceptability leading to the first recorded Gentile conversions of the new creation (Acts 10:44–48). These two men represent two early

Christian missions; Paul the Gentile mission and Peter the Jewish mission (Gal 2:7–8). The conversion of Cornelius and his household launches what has been commonly called a "Gentile or second Pentecost" and with this breakthrough came conflict and tension in early Christian mission.

The potential firestorm for the early church concerned the practice of circumcision and whether Gentile male believers should be required to face the knife and obey the Mosaic Law (Gal 5:3)? This is not the gospel Paul had received since he was preaching a circumcision and therefore law free gospel, but not everyone agreed. Paul addresses the conflict in his epistle to the Galatians in an autobiographical section (Gal 1:11—2:14) and views it as a perversion of the true gospel (Gal 1:7). The purpose of this chapter is to address how Paul handled this conflict in Gal 2:1–10. It is important to note and emphasize the tension this caused for the early church and maybe more importantly the damage that was avoided. Dunn explains, referencing the Jerusalem conference (Acts 15:1–29),

> Nor should we miss the fact that the ruling reached here was one of the most important ever made in Christianity. On the outcome of the Jerusalem consultation hung the whole future of the infant faith: whether Paul's mission would become an independent movement, or whether it would remain in fellowship with the Judean churches; whether the Nazarenes would remain a sub-sect within Judaism or be able to retain within the same body divergent emphases, both traditional and liberalizing; whether the Jewish covenant heritage was to be maintained unquestioningly, abandoned altogether, or retained as a critical factor in Christianity's own make-up. Even allowing for subsequent setbacks, the decision here probably prevented a ruinous schism within Christianity.[1]

Paul believed the "truth of the gospel" (Gal 2:5) hung in the balance of this conflict. Before considering his response we will take a brief look at Jewish conversion requirements for proselytes during the Second Temple period. This is necessary since the mission tension under review is a Jewish conflict, all the participants are ethnic Jews.[2]

Reaching integrative solutions in conflict mediation requires having an awareness of the situation at hand. As information is being gathered mediators help those involved in the conflict become aware of their own

---

1. Dunn, *Epistle to the Galatians*, 105.
2. Jewish identity in the middle of the first century was not distinct from Christianity like it would become less than one hundred years later. Conflicts in Paul's day were intra-Jewish and not inter-religious disputes. Campbell, *Paul and the Creation*, 42.

interests, feelings, views, and needs to best understand why solutions up to the point of conflict have not resolved the issue. Understanding each party's view, history, and perspective of the situation helps focus the mediation process. In order to reach reconciliation, the solution must be efficient and respect the interests of the parties involved while respecting all available facts. What follows is an example of an inventory of first century interests, facts, and cultural elements that need to be squared so that Paul, the other apostles, Peter, Jewish Christians, and gentile Christians can reach lasting ministry reconciliation.

Jewish Conversion Rites

Circumcision was a big deal, given the backdrop of both the Abrahamic and Mosaic covenants (Gen 17:9–14; Lev 12:13). The mind-set of first century Jews and likely some who followed Jesus is revealed by literature from the Second Temple period. During this time covenant and circumcision became synonymous under the Maccabeans (2nd century BCE). Mattathias's revolt was largely due to the ban of circumcision by Antiochus IV (1 Macc 1:48, 60–63; cf. 2 Macc 6:10; 4 Macc 4:25; Josephus, *Ant.* 12:253–56; *J.W.* 1:34). Apostates were particularly viewed with contempt (1 Macc 1:13–15; cf. Josephus, *Ant.* 12.241).[3] The sentiment of Jubilees gives one the sense of the expectation and requirement calling those who neglect or ignore circumcision "children of destruction" or "sons of Beliar" (*Jub.* 15:26, 33).

The process of conversion for proselytes in the Second Temple period included circumcision, baptism, and sacrifice before the destruction of the Temple (70 CE). This consensus of scholarship is derived from second and third century Rabbinic sources.[4] The question remains, was it true in the first century or before? We will limit our discussion to circumcision in this section.

Outside of Achior in Judith 14:10, circumcision is not mentioned without questions for any conversions until Josephus mentions some gentile men were circumcised out of fear (*J.W.* 2.454; *Ant.* 11.285).[5] Yet, circumcision had social implications and was a marker of ethnic distinctions. Gentiles who were circumcised immediately identified with the covenant people having partaken in the sign of the covenant (Lev 12:3). During the

---

3. Bernat, "Circumcision," 472.

4. Cohen, *From the Maccabees to the Mishnah*, 44; McKnight, *Light Among the Gentiles*, 78.

5. McKnight, *Light Among the Gentiles*, 79–80.

Hasmonean period,⁶ the high priest Hyrcanus required Idumeans to be circumcised to remain in their own land (Josephus, *Ant.* 13.257–58). Josephus mentions other forced circumcisions (*Ant.* 20.139, 145–46). The Roman poet Juvenal understood it to be the distinctive action of a convert (*Sat.* 14.96, 99, 101).⁷ Additionally, the Roman historian Tacitus also mentions circumcision was the Jewish practice to set themselves apart from other men. "Converts adopt the practice, while they are taught to despise the gods, to disown their countrymen and set at nought parents, children, and brethren" (*Tac. Hist.* 5.5).⁸ McKnight concludes,

> It seems probable to me that circumcision was seen as an act whereby the male convert demonstrated his zeal for the law and his willingness to join Judaism without reservation. I hesitate to conclude that circumcision was a requirement throughout Second Temple Judaism, because the evidence is not completely unambiguous and there may well have been some diversity on the matter. Circumcision was probably required for male converts most of the time and in most local expressions of Judaism. It was the ritual that separated the Jew from the Gentile (at least in Jewish perception), and therefore it would have been the act that permitted the would-be convert to cross the boundary and enter the community.⁹

Later for the Apostle Paul this act of identification led to Torah observance and all the expectations of the Mosaic covenant requirement (Gal 5:3). Thus, circumcision was a clear conversion indicator of proselyte action.

Gentile conversion to Judaism by circumcision was the gold standard for Jewish acceptance into the community. It's possible that Paul practiced and approved of circumcising gentiles prior to his recognition and acceptance of Jesus as Messiah. Engaging his interlocutors later in the Galatian letter he continues his argument alluding to his "still proclaiming circumcision" (*ei peritomen eti kerusso*) as potentially something in his past (Gal 5:11). This is argued from Paul's use of the temporal adverb *eti* (still, yet) pointing to action in the past.¹⁰ Nevertheless, the gospel for Paul has

---

6. Collins sees this period as the only possible evidence of any Jewish proselytizing movement. In his view no other evidence of Jewish missionaries sent out to the Greco-Roman world existed. Collins, *Between Athens and Jerusalem*, 262.

7. Fredriksen, "Judaism," 536.

8. Tacitus, *Annals and the Histories*, 295.

9. McKnight, *Light Among the Gentiles*, 82.

10. It is generally agreed Paul preached circumcision in his past, see Longenecker, *Galatians*, 233; Donaldson, *Paul and the Gentiles*, 278–84; Dickson, *Mission-Commitment*, 46–49. How that is interpreted within the Galatian argument is debated either as

superseded past expectations and mission practices. Circumcision was no longer an expectation for gentile loyalty in this Jewish Pharisees' view. The good news that Jesus is Israel's Messiah has changed that for him and he was uncompromising in his rejection of practicing circumcision for gentile inclusion.

The Triumph of the Gospel

The mission tension in the early church surrounded the gospel of Jesus Christ, but for the apostles the content of the gospel was never an issue. That is to say, there were no disagreements that Jesus was Israel's Messiah and the true Lord of the world, and they were commissioned to proclaim that throughout creation. The issue was mission practice, specifically Gentile mission practice. This is a very specific interest that has to be clearly identified if the conflict is to be resolved. This is why Paul was so exercised in the Galatian letter. He understood the *missio Dei* and shared God's vision for the nations. The revelation he received convinced him of Jesus' identity and that the gospel was inclusive of Gentiles freely without any Jewish conditions.[11] Hence, Paul's mission goal was clear, he wanted to see the dividing wall between Jew and Gentile torn down and Gentiles added to God's covenant people (Rom 11:17; Eph 2:14; 3:5–6). McKnight states it clearly, "Paul's mission, not to reduce it to simplicities, was to get Gentiles saved and to get saved Gentiles to sit at table with saved Jews—and to like the arrangement at the table."[12] This was a radical idea for first-century people. Segal agrees and writes, "From a legal perspective Paul may not have startled the Jewish Christian community so much by saying circumcision was unnecessary for gentile salvation per se, as claiming that the saved Jews and Gentiles could form a single new community and freely interact."[13] Paul understood the restoration of all things included ethnic, social, and gender reconciliation as the heart and truth of the gospel (Gal 3:28). To require circumcision was a step backward and created unnecessary boundaries for new gentile converts to Christianity. If the conflict were going to be resolved all the groups involved would have to understand the gospel that united them. This is why there is such urgency in Paul's letter to the Galatians. He views the gospel as under attack from hostile and destructive forces that are requiring gentile

---

Paul's response to his accusers claim of inconsistency or Paul's reference to a past action no longer conducted.

11. Bird, *Anomalous Jew*, 131.
12. McKnight, "I Am the Church," 217.
13. Segal, "Costs of Proselytism and Conversion," 363.

circumcision for full participation in the Christian community. It is to this letter that we now turn.

Galatians 2

Paul continues his autobiographical account and highly charged polemical argument with further reference to his interaction with church leadership in Jerusalem in what he calls a private meeting. By Paul's own account in Galatians this is his second visit to Jerusalem. Paul's reference to fourteen years since his last visit (Gal 2:1) reckons either from his first visit with Peter (1:18-20) or from his call/conversion (1:15). Most scholars agree it is the latter and view the three (1:18) and the fourteen (2:1) years as concurrent and not consecutive.[14] Nonetheless, his second visit to Jerusalem likely emanated from Antioch,[15] taking along his fellow missionaries Barnabas and Titus.

Barnabas (Gal 2:1) played a role in both the Jewish and Gentile mission, having served in both. First in Jerusalem contributing to the needs of this new sect (Acts 4:36-37), followed by Luke's description of his mediating involvement with the Jerusalem church/apostles and Saul's (Paul) first visit back to Jerusalem post his conversion (Acts 9:26-27). He is next sent by leadership in Jerusalem to Antioch (Acts 11:22) because of the mission work done there by believers from northern Africa and Cyrpus (Acts 11:20-21). It is Barnabas who recruits Paul to join him in Antioch and they spend a year there pastoring and teaching a mixed group of Jewish and Gentile believers (Acts 11:25-26). They only leave Antioch because they are sent back to Jerusalem with relief funds for the church there (Acts 11:29-30). Agabus' prophecy in Acts 11:28 corresponds well with Paul's reason for going to Jerusalem in response to a revelation (Gal 2:2).[16] Barnabas is later connected with the Gentile mission serving with Paul on his first missionary journey

---

14. Longenecker, *Galatians*, 45; Martyn, *Galatians*, 189; Schreiner, *Galatians*, 119.

15. The church at Antioch circa 40 CE was progressive and a bit ahead of its time concerning these questions. Jewish and Gentile followers of Jesus dined together and experienced genuine fellowship there as it is attested by Paul before the men from James came to Antioch (Gal 2:12). Bockmuehl recounts the Jews in Antioch were more numerous and prosperous than Jews in Jerusalem in the first century and their relationship with the Gentile majority was not strained or politically encumbered. He further notes Josephus's claim that Greeks had become sympathetic to the central Jewish synagogue in Antioch. Bockmuehl, *Jewish Law*, 56-57.

16. Gal 2:1-10 may refer to this visit (Acts 11:30; 12:25) or to the Jerusalem conference in Acts 15, for a detailed discussion see Dunn, *Beginning from Jerusalem*, 376-77; McKnight, *Galatians*, 87-89; Schnabel, *Early Christian Mission*, 987-89.

(Acts 13–14) including mission in southern Galatia. Hence, Longenecker refers to him as "something of a bridge between the Christian mission to Jews and that to Gentiles."[17]

Seeking Unity

Paul seeks affirmation and unity for his Gentile mission vis-à-vis the Jewish mission proceeding from Jerusalem. Ultimately, the potential conflict between the two missions, one Gentile and one Jewish, was avoided and remained in harmony despite the social problem of a unified table fellowship (cf. Gal 2:11–14) caused by opposition Paul references in Gal 2:12. Paul's efforts help the church avoid the potential disaster of an early church split.

Assuming Paul's account in Gal 2 corresponds with his visit to Jerusalem in Acts 11:30 then Paul took occasion on that visit to have a private meeting with the Jerusalem leaders, including Peter, James, and John (2:9) to lay out (*anethemen*)[18] before them the gospel he preached for either their consideration or their consultation given the semantic range of the term. Paul seeks their recognition, he is not questioning the correctness of the content of his gospel. He is in need of the Apostles validation, so he can continue his ministry to the gentiles without requiring circumcision. He did not need human approval for what he had already received by direct revelation; rather, Paul knew the effectiveness of his mission efforts required unity of message with his Jewish brothers. However, good mediators like Paul sometimes require the validation from authoritative bodies to provide the foundation necessary to conduct their ministry. "The truth of the gospel included its continuity with and fulfillment of Israel's hope (Gal 3:8)."[19] F. F. Bruce clarifies this well,

> His commission was not derived from Jerusalem, but it could not be executed effectively except in fellowship with Jerusalem. A cleavage between his Gentile mission and the mother-church would be disastrous: Christ would be divided, and all the energy which Paul had devoted, and hoped to devote, to the evangelizing of the Gentile world would be frustrated.[20]

---

17. Longenecker, *Galatians*, 45.

18. Schnabel states *anethemen* "can mean to submit to a deliberative body for its consideration, but also to communicate something that is one's own, with a view to consultation and even to bring a dedicatory gift." Schnabel, *Early Christian Mission*, 991.

19. Dunn, *Beginning from Jerusalem*, 452.

20. Bruce, *Epistle to the Galatians*, 111.

Paul had inherent apostolic authority because of his calling and commissioning by Jesus on the Damascus road, but he is not some rogue authoritarian who is disinterested in unity. To not have the rest of the apostles recognize the gospel he preached was to have run in vain. Yet, when it came to circumcision he submits to the Galatians that even the apostles and leaders in Jerusalem did not equate the gospel with circumcision since Titus was not compelled to be (2:3) while there with Paul.

Before moving on it is helpful to understand Paul's expression in 2:2 translated in the NIV as "those esteemed as leaders." Paul does not downplay or diminish those he privately met with. Longenecker explains, "The expression . . . 'those reputed to be important' . . . was part of the political rhetoric of the day, being used both positively and derogatorily or ironically."[21] This expression is used four times (2:2, twice in 2:6, and in 2:9) in the narrative of his visit to Jerusalem and we believe positively except possibly in 2:6, see below. Good mediation values the relationships and interests of the parties involved. Paul demonstrates that he respects the leadership in Jerusalem. This provides him the foundation necessary to bridge the distance between Jerusalem Christian leadership and the gentile mission.

Paul does not stop in verse three with his account of his second visit and this private meeting. He has clarified for the Galatians the gospel has triumphed and was circumcision free.[22] He diverts a moment from his argument[23] to say the victory was not easy because of the "false brothers." Dunn sees the false brothers as the sect of the Pharisees (Acts 15:5).[24] While Paul refers to them as the circumcision party (Gal 2:12). Whoever they were they are traveling and dogging Paul in Jerusalem and Antioch. Paul states, "They were sent in to spy out our freedom" (2:4) indicating circumcision was not the norm among Gentile believers anywhere. There was no compromise by Paul's team (Barnabas and Titus), "We did not give into them even for a moment, so that the truth of the gospel might be preserved for you" (2:5). Paul seems to return to the specific narrative of his visit in 2:6. Clearly articulating opposing viewpoints helps focus the mediation process.

Paul is not impressed with status and concludes the story of his private meeting in Gal 2:6–10:

> As for those who were held in high esteem—whatever they were makes no difference to me; God does not show favoritism—they

---

21. Longenecker, *Galatians*, 48.

22. DeBoer, *Galatians*, 111.

23. V. 4 begins with a grammatical anacoluthon, for explanation see Longenecker, *Galatians*, 50.

24. Dunn, *Epistle to the Galatians*, 98.

added nothing to my message. On the contrary, they recognized that I had been entrusted with the task of preaching the gospel to the uncircumcised, just as Peter had been to the circumcised. For God, who was at work in Peter as an apostle to the circumcised, was also at work in me as an apostle to the Gentiles. James, Cephas and John, those esteemed as pillars, gave me and Barnabas the right hand of fellowship when they recognized the grace given to me. They agreed that we should go to the Gentiles, and they to the circumcised. All they asked was that we should continue to remember the poor, the very thing I had been eager to do all along. (NIV)

This affirms his gospel against further challenges that Paul was out on a limb doing his own thing against any authoritative acknowledgment. The "just as" in 2:7 "invokes complimentary not contradictory"[25] comments. Peter, James, and John did not add to Paul's gospel; rather, they affirmed and recognized his mission to Gentiles extending to him and Barnabas "the right hand of fellowship" (2:9). This expression is technical, indicating a formal agreement.[26] After identifying the parties involved, articulating their interests, bringing to light facts of the conflict, Paul is now able to present an integrated solution that is wise, efficient, and strengthens the relationships of those involved. This is the goal of modern mediation.

Implications and Applications

The example of Peter and Paul's conflict in Gal 2:1–10 offers the church some helpful guardrails for navigating ministry tensions today. Consider a scenario that plays itself out in the strategic planning of evangelical churches across American. Jon is thirty-nine years old. Originally from Iowa, Jon now lives and works in Quincy, a small city in west-central Illinois along the banks of the Mississippi River. Jon attended Iowa State University for his undergraduate degree, before heading to Chicago for a master's degree in Health Management and Patient Safety at Northwestern University. Jon and his family have lived in Quincy for five years, coming to Quincy for an administrative position at Blessing Hospital, the largest employer in the region.

Jon is married with two young children. Jon's marriage and children are his world. He met his wife Michelle, a part-time accountant, at Iowa State. They were married in 2007. Jon and Michelle spend a lot of their time

25. Schnabel, *Early Christian Mission*, 997.
26. Dunn, *Epistle to the Galatians*, 110.

with the family—soccer games, travel, school-related events. Jon is saving for a lake house, what he hopes will be the perfect weekend get-away for the family. Jon and Michelle have not been a part of a church for a long time. Jon grew up going to church with his family, but has not been back regularly since his freshman year of high school. Michelle was active in her high school youth group, but fell out of the habit during college. They are not opposed to church, but really do not think of it much. They have had some marital conflict over the last year (mostly around unfulfilled expectations and parenting styles), but they would not feel comfortable opening up about that to a pastor. Last week, though, Michelle's coworker mentioned a new teaching series at her church called, "It's Just a Phase," on parenting and family life. For the first time since their wedding day, Michelle found herself talking to Jon about going to church.

With just a few different details, Jon and Michelle's story could be the story of a dozen different families at my church. The only difference is that Jon and Michelle are not real. They are what is often called a target audience profile. Jon and family are used at LifePoint Church, where I serve, to help us empathize and understand our neighbors. While programming and content are not driven by this fictional family, the profile does help our staff to ensure that the service is accessible and compelling to an unbeliever or outsider.[27] What words or concepts would be incomprehensible to someone uninitiated in the Scriptures? How does the service and message address questions and doubts that Jon and Michelle might have about the Scripture or topic at hand? Jon and family help us move beyond our own personal preferences in service planning—and steward well the evangelistic opportunity present in our worship gatherings. This is certainly nothing unique to LifePoint. Such profiles are prolific in the church today. Willow Creek, Saddleback, and North Point, some of the most influential churches in America, as well as countless church growth consultants, have championed such an approach.

While we likely ask whether such an approach works, we should not neglect to ask whether it is good, healthy, and biblical. Is the nature of ministry (especially ministry in the local church) such that a pastor or church should say, "I am going to focus my ministry to reach a particular group in my community"? Is this effective and faithful contextualization of the mission, or simply the propagation of racist, classist, or otherwise segregated systems? To these questions, I believe that we will find the answer to be both a hardy yes and a resolute no.

---

27. In 1 Cor 14:16, 23–25, Paul seems genuinely concerned that the gathering of the church be accessible and comprehensible to an unbeliever, that he or she would be convicted and led to worship God.

Navigating Tensions

I cannot imagine a local church that does not at times find its mission in tension—whether that tension is between departments within the church, other churches in the community, or with nonprofit or parachurch organizations. The tension around the mission is not theoretical. Ask any local pastor. Mission clarity is often challenged, even compromised, by departmental silos, unclear principles for partnering with other organizations, and competition (implicit or otherwise) between local congregations. These challenges underlie the tension between different callings and focus areas within the mission of the church. Even when a church is clear about its place in the mission, the organizational discipline required and relational stress induced by these tensions can be exhausting for a pastor to navigate.

The account of Peter and Paul navigating conflict provides the church a powerful example. These leaders in the burgeoning Christian community are willing to recognize the validity of each other's ministry, as well as the unique calling that God had placed on each one: Peter's mission to the Jews and Paul's to the gentiles. This is a needed reminder in the life of the local church. The mission of the church is not a zero-sum/either-or proposition. Nonetheless, you can easily pick up the unspoken tension in many churches: "You work toward our expression of the mission, or you are not *really* doing kingdom work." The truth is that a local church can far too easily reflect a sort of fiefdom rather than the kingdom. The fiefdom-oriented church works toward their own mission with willful ignorance or even distrust toward other kingdom realities beyond their local church. This should not be.

The context of Galatians finds Paul quick to assert the independence of his gospel. Its source is not with man, even the pillars of the Jerusalem church, but God Himself. Paul's opponents cannot demand that he submit to Jerusalem. His gospel and ministry find their source in Christ Himself. And it is this strong foundation that gives Paul the self-confidence and kingdom-orientation needed to recognize the validity of Peter's ministry—and vice versa. The foundation of a unity—even partnership—beyond fiefdom Christianity is found in the bigness of the gospel.

A Shared Foundation

If it is a shared gospel that allows Peter and Paul to endorse one another's work, and later a perceived betrayal of gospel application that leads to Paul's confrontation of Peter in Gal 2:11–14, we must consider carefully what constitutes a gospel-issue in the church. There is no greater source of unity for the church than a clear and corporate gospel. For this reason, we can celebrate the contemporary resurgence of interest in the gospel. In fact, the contemporary buzz has gone beyond a resurgence of interest to a sort of gospel-infatuation, a near preoccupation with slapping the term in front of every ministry, department, and activity in the church. I am all for gospel-centrality, but only so far as we have a clear understanding of the term. For all its use in the blogosphere and Christian publishing, I am afraid that the church has a sickly gospel.

While it is not within the scope of the current work to lay out an answer to this problem in full, a starting point may be simply to identify what constitutes the gospel proper within the New Testament, as compared to what may be described as implications or applications of the gospel. The gospel proper is the story of Jesus—a story rightly read in the context of the story of Israel.[28] Using the term gospel as a shorthand for justification by faith alone, Reformed systematics, or even Protestantism in general is neither accurate nor helpful. The good news of Christianity is the story of Jesus. The implications of this power-releasing (Rom 1:16) story, then, are the freedom, salvation, and hope that are often confused for the good news itself. The application of the gospel may be understood as our union with Christ through faith and expressed in baptism, the Eucharist, and even our cruciform living. Point being simply that it will be hard to establish—and harder yet to maintain—a unity on the foundation of the gospel if we have a fuzzy or incomplete gospel. Pastors must do the hard and intentional work of thinking carefully about biblical categories before presupposing such unity.

Peter and Paul could each acknowledge the validity of the other's ministry because of their shared foundation in the gospel. On the other side of this tension, however, these early apostles also displayed a willingness to acknowledge each one's unique calling or mission within the ministry of that shared gospel. In other words, a shared gospel does not imply that we will always have a shared mission—at least in its localized expression. If some local churches cannot seem to transcend their fiefdoms, others may suffer from the opposite ailment; these churches have no ministry focus whatsoever. They may tend to send $10 to any global work, "partner" with every local parachurch, or subscribe to the strategy-of-the-month approach within the church itself.

---

28. See McKnight, *King Jesus Gospel*; and Bates, *Salvation by Allegiance Alone* for a framing of the story of Jesus within Israel, as preached by Jesus, the early apostles, and Paul.

Own-Catalyze-Bless

A shared gospel is essential, but we can—and should—recognize different callings. Modern conflict mediators can learn from Paul. By having his ministry to the Gentiles validated by the apostles, Paul's interests are being met. The furtherance of the gospel meets the interests of the Jerusalem leadership and Jewish Christians. Not requiring circumcision meets the interests of the gentile Christians. Meeting each interest is what creates integrated solutions. Paul had been graced with (or gifted for) a particular mission to the gentiles (Gal 2:9). Peter does not begrudge Paul his calling. Instead, Peter and the pillars of the Jerusalem church extend to Paul and Barnabas the right hand of fellowship, while simultaneously endorsing their unique mission. Pastors and church leaders need not "own" a particular mission or ministry focus in order to bless it. At LifePoint, for example, we have found the "own-catalyze-bless" grid to be a helpful tool to think through discussions related to discerning how our church interacts with the variety of distinct missions and callings that we encounter in our city, our church, or even globally.[29]

The "own" category refers to ministries that we conceive, resource, and staff as a church. This may refer to something like our "Love Your Neighborhood" campaign: our staff produces the teaching curriculum, video resources, and promotional materials; our lead team nurtures relationships with community leaders and seeks service opportunities; LifePoint volunteers organize opportunities to serve and donate within the community. Like our Sunday services, this campaign is an expression of our mission as a church organized and led by the church itself.

On the other end of the spectrum is the "bless" category of ministries. These are ministries (local, foreign, or even developed by someone within the church) that we do not directly resource or promote. Instead, a pastor may simply pray for the ministry or encourage the leader. LifePoint is recognizing the validity of the mission, but we are not directly involved in the oversight, resourcing, or execution of the work. An example of a ministry that we may "bless" would be an individual who wants to write notes with an encouraging verse of Scripture to the teachers of a local elementary school. We may likewise bless and even celebrate many great works across the city without leveraging our resources to help accomplish them.

The category of cooperation is to "catalyze." These are ministries that LifePoint will help resource—whether in terms of finances, volunteers, or ministry strategy—but the oversight and leadership of the work is owned by

---

29. Adapted from Greear, *Gaining by Losing*.

another. In our context, this means strategic partnerships like a feeding or drug rehabilitation ministry. It can also mean coming alongside a LifePoint member and helping her realize her call to start a community garden in an under-resourced neighborhood of our city. Whether due to lack of specialized training or differences in mission focus, it would be inappropriate for our church to "own" these unique mission expressions—but it would likewise feel inappropriate to merely "bless" these ministries without leveraging some of our God-given resources to help make it happen.

Certainly the "own-catalyze-bless" grid will not solve all tensions around how to relate to other valid expressions of gospel ministry, but it has proved to be a helpful tool that has allowed our church to think intentionally about how our mission relates to the unique callings of others. That, after all, is our main take-away from Gal 2:1–10. Paul is not seeking to provide the church with a universal and timeless paradigm for resolving mission tension. Paul's account here seems to be descriptive, not prescriptive. That said, contemporary churches would be wise to notice that the weight of some conflicts (whether theological or personal) demand an intentional and direct approach. We cannot leave gospel and mission clarity to chance.

To that end, Fisher and Ury's principles of effective negotiation apply well here: 1) take the personalities out of it; 2) think interests, not sides; 3) generate options, not ultimatums; and 4) agree upon objective criteria.[30] As you navigate mission tension in your own context, these principles may serve you well in fostering the direct and intentional conversations that Paul embodies in Gal 2:1–10. While far from a silver bullet, this approach offers an effective first step toward opening a dialogue, bringing clarity, and creating alignment in what can often be emotionally charged or relationally complicated situations.

Conclusion

While I (Brett) was in high school, God put what I can only describe as a unique and specific call on my life: love and serve Muslims in the name of Jesus. I have devoted more than fifteen years of my life to this call, which has taken me overseas and into conflict zones, compelled me to learn new languages and cultures, and threatened my safety and comfort. From the text and my own personal experience, I do not have problem believing that God may give one a call to reach a particular group or culture. I do not think that a target audience profile is necessarily bad theology or mission contextualization. This can be an effective means for developing understanding

---

30. Fisher, Ury, and Patton, *Getting to Yes*.

and empathy, while also giving us fresh eyes on practices and language that may become unnecessary obstacles to our neighbors' ability to understand and respond to the gospel. The challenge is not in the principle, but in the practice. Too often our target audience and ministry focus is less about a call from God and more about the people with whom we feel comfortable surrounding ourselves. In short, too often mission strategies reflect cultural preferences over divine call. This is an affront to the gospel. Baptizing our social preference with the language of theology makes for a compromised gospel and mission. This is just the sort of hypocrisy that enrages Paul in this letter to the Galatians.

Do not be deceived by what seems to be a very focused call on Paul's life to the gentiles. Even as Paul took the gospel to the gentiles, he almost always started in a diaspora synagogue and seemed to find his greatest success with God-fearing gentiles (a sort of pre-evangelized subset of gentile). And as his letter to the Galatians indicates, Paul's vision for the church was not simply to see gentiles converted, but to see converted gentiles sharing in a Messianic banquet with gospel-shaped Jews. Paul's end was not simply to engage with gentiles to the exclusion of Jews. Such a mission-focus would have likely been inconceivable to Paul and other early Christians. Rather, Paul seems to envision a great social experiment in the church—a coming together of statuses and ethnicities by the power of the gospel. Whether our call leads to a mission among Afghan refugees or suburban soccer moms, we must remember that this is not an end unto itself but a part of God's unfolding story of a new creation and new family in Christ.

Bibliography

Bates, Matthew. *Salvation by Allegiance Alone*. Grand Rapids, MI: Baker, 2017.
Bernat, David A. "Circumcision." In *The Eerdmans Dictionary of Early Judaism*, edited by John J. Collins and Daniel C. Harlow, 471–74. Grand Rapids, MI: Eerdmans, 2010.
Bird, Michael F. *An Anomalous Jew: Paul Among Jews, Greeks, and Romans*. Grand Rapids, MI: Eerdmans, 2016.
Bockmuehl, Markus. *Jewish Law in Gentile Churches: Halakhah and the Beginning of Christian Public Ethics*. Grand Rapids, MI: Baker Academic, 2003.
Bruce, F. F. *The Epistle to the Galatians: A Commentary on the Greek Text*. The New International Greek Testament Commentary. Grand Rapids, MI: Eerdmans, 1982.
Campbell, William S. *Paul and the Creation of Christian Identity*. T & T Clark Biblical Studies. London: T & T Clark, 2008.
Cohen, Shaye J. D. *From the Maccabees to the Mishnah*. Louisville, KY: Westminster John Knox, 2006.
Collins, John J. *Between Athens and Jerusalem: Jewish Identity in the Hellenistic Diaspora*. Biblical Resource Series. Grand Rapids, MI: Eerdmans, 2000.

DeBoer, Martinus C. *Galatians: A Commentary*. The New Testament Library. Louisville, KY: Westminster John Knox, 2011.

Dickson, John. *Mission-Commitment in Ancient Judaism and in the Pauline Communities*. Wissenschaftliche Untersuchungen Zum Neuen Testament. Tübingen: Mohr Siebeck, 2003.

Donaldson, Terence L. *Paul and the Gentiles: Remapping the Apostle's Convictional World*. Minneapolis: Fortress, 1997.

Dunn, James D. G. *Beginning from Jerusalem*. Christianity in the Making 2. Grand Rapids, MI: Eerdmans, 2009.

———. *The Epistle to the Galatians*. Black's New Testament Commentary. Peabody, MA: Hendrickson, 1993.

Fisher, Roger, William Ury, and Bruce Patton. *Getting to Yes: Negotiating Agreement Without Giving In*. 3rd ed. New York: Penguin, 2011.

Fredriksen, Paula. "Judaism, the Circumcision of Gentiles, and Apocalyptic Hope: Another Look at Galatians 1 and 2." *Journal Of Theological Studies* 42 (October 1991) 532–64.

Greear, J.D. *Gaining by Losing*. Grand Rapids, MI: Zondervan, 2016.

Longenecker, Richard N. *Galatians*. Word Biblical Commentary. Waco, TX: Word, 1990.

Martyn, J. Louis. *Galatians: A New Translation with Introduction and Commentary*. The Anchor Bible 33A. New York: Doubleday, 1997.

McKnight, Scot. *Galatians: From Biblical Text—to Contemporary Life*. The NIV Application Commentary. Grand Rapids, MI: Zondervan, 1995.

———. "I Am the Church: Ecclesial Identity and the Apostle Paul." *The Covenant Quarterly* 72 (August 2014) 217–32.

———. *The King Jesus Gospel: The Original Good News Revisited*. Grand Rapids, MI: Zondervan, 2011.

———. *A Light Among the Gentiles: Jewish Missionary Activity in the Second Temple Period*. Minneapolis, MN: Fortress, 1991.

Schnabel, Eckhard J. *Early Christian Mission*. Downers Grove, IL: InterVarsity, 2004.

Schreiner, Thomas R. *Galatians*. Zondervan Exegetical Commentary Series: New Testament. Grand Rapids, MI: Zondervan, 2010.

Segal, Alan F. "The Costs of Proselytism and Conversion." *Society of Biblical Literature Seminar Papers* 27 (1988) 336–69.

Tacitus, P. Cornelius. *The Annals and the Histories*. Great Books of the Western World. Translated by Alfred John Church and William Jackson Brodribb. Chicago: William Benton, 1952.

9

Addressing False Teaching and Heresy
Paul as Guardian of the Gospel

1–2 Timothy and Titus

By Kristen Bennett Marble and Jared Willemin

Introduction

As a pastor starting at a new ministry appointment, I have often cleaned out overstuffed closets, neglected Sunday school classrooms, and forgotten church libraries. Cleaning, sorting and decluttering the broken pencils, old hymnals, leftover VBS decorations and discarded books has become an energizing way to start fresh. With each cleaning, quality items receive new life, garbage is dumped and reusable goods are donated—except for a certain set of books. I readily admit to throwing away—rather than donating—a particular book series, trying to prevent the fictional novels, often passed off as biblical truths, from ending up in someone's hands. Some may not agree with such handling of these books, but my approach represents my one small attempt to limit the spread of false teaching!

Clearly though, as pastors and lay leaders, we cannot simply throw away everything that "stinks" of heresy or false teaching. If we could, our jobs might be a bit easier. But books, podcasts, blogs, television broadcasts, memes, and Facebook posts abound with theology and biblical teaching that make us cringe. Some Christian leaders have even begun to use their public platforms to call out such perceived heresies. "Farewell" tweets, attempted regulations of blog posts, public ridiculing, and establishment of "litmus test" issues represent contemporary responses to false teaching.

Other approaches address such challenges in more proactive ways, attempting to avoid reactionary responses. Church membership and discipleship classes educate parishioners about proper doctrine. Ordination and credentialing guidelines ensure proper clergy preparation. Pastoral learning communities facilitate guided discussions and support. Within Wesleyan traditions, the four-fold emphasis on Scripture, tradition, experience, and reason moderates shifts in doctrinal and biblical interpretation.

Challenges from false teaching and even heresy are not limited to the contemporary church. From the beginnings of the early church in Acts, maintaining proper teaching and practice has long been a focus. Paul's epistles frequently guided the early church in properly responding to the false teachers. While the particular nature of the false teaching may differ, Paul's guidelines offer helpful insights for church leaders who are looking to become, like Paul, guardians of the gospel. This chapter will explore passages about false teaching in Colossians, 1–2 Timothy, and Titus. It will consider the background of these Scriptures, the nature of the heresies faced by the early church, Paul's recommended responses, and an application of these responses to today.

Background to the Conflict at Colossae

In his letter to the Colossians Paul addresses the danger of false teaching spreading among the church there. There have been multiple proposals concerning the source of the false teaching that Paul warns against in Colossians. There is no real scholarly consensus on the issue, but there are some general possibilities that commentators tend to point to: various Jewish sources, syncretistic beliefs and practices, or teachings from a local mystery religion. There are clues in what Paul writes, but those are certainly not definitive. He warns the Colossians about "philosophy and empty deceit." Paul mentions "matters of food and drink," "observing festivals, new moons, or Sabbaths," "self-abasement," "worship of angels," "visions," and the regulations: "do not handle, do not taste, do not touch." He pejoratively describes these as "human commands and teachings," "self-imposed piety, humility, and severe treatment of the body."

Many of the elements that Paul mentions (Sabbaths, possible purity connections with the regulations of what to eat) lead one to suspect a Jewish source to this false teaching. N. T. Wright sees a play on the word *sylagogon* translated as "takes you captive" in 2:8. His argument is that Paul chooses this rare word because of its similarity to the word "synagogue." Wright interprets this passage as a call for the Colossians to not fall prey to those trying to convert Gentiles to Judaism as part of the Christian message in a way that echoes the problem in Galatians.[1] Other scholars have proposed other Jewish sources as base of the false teaching Paul addresses, including having proposed Jewish Gnosticism or Jewish mysticism.

There is also the possibility of a connection with the mystery religions of the Greco-Roman world or even neo-Pythagoreanism. Many scholars describe some type of syncretistic effort, with various sources providing a slightly different emphasis.[2] The "Colossian heresy" may be an inadvertent blend of Jewish laws with similar religious practices familiar to the Colossians from their pagan past. The result would not be a well-articulated "false teaching" or a deliberate syncretism, but a hodge-podge of practices based on an inadequate understanding of the gospel of Christ.[3]

Morna Hooker has argued that trying to match the false teaching with a particular first-century source is misguided. Her proposal is that instead of being tied to a specific situation, Paul's words are directed more generally and addressed to multiple congregations.[4] Again, it is difficult to make any conclusions because Paul does not provide exhaustive evidence. Another consideration that further complicates the question of source is whether Paul is accurate in his descriptions of the false teaching. His description of the false teaching could be a biased caricature in his appeal to the Colossians.[5] In the end, the things Paul mentions in the letter point to a Jewish foundation for the false teaching, but it is difficult to determine the exact source and to what extent it may be combined or influenced with other aspects of Greco-Roman culture in Colossae.

Conflict From Within or From the Outside?

Another critical question regarding this false teaching is whether its advocates are within the Christian community. Are the false teachers Christians

---

1. Wright, *Paul for Everyone*, 165–66.
2. Lincoln, "Colossians," 561.
3. Thompson, *Colossians and Philemon*, 64.
4. Hooker, "Were There False Teachers in Colossae?" 315–31.
5. Lincoln, "Colossians," 562.

within the Colossian church? Lincoln interprets v. 19 as describing the false teacher and since it refers to their "relation to the head," concludes that that person is a part of the Colossian body.[6] Garland, however, argues based on the strength of Paul's language in this passage that the threat is from the outside. He contrasts this language in vv.18–22 with that found in Rom 14 where the question of what to eat and not to eat also comes up. In Romans it is clear that the conflict is internal and consequently Paul's language is softened. Therefore, Garland concludes that the Colossians' conflict is an external one.[7] This opposing evidence leads to a more complicated situation than simply a question of an internal or external source to the teaching. The threat is an internal one in the sense that those promoting it have apparent influence on the community. They are "in" in that sense. Paul, however, portrays the teachers as outside the body and this is part of the conflict management strategy discussed below. Identifying the parties involved and their interests is the first step toward any conflict mediation process. It is important for him to present the false teachers as outsiders so that he can more easily identify with and affirm the Christian community separate from the false teaching. Also, if the teachers were fully in the community one would expect Paul to more clearly address them as such and to present a plan of action regarding those believers as he does with the sexually immoral man in 1 Cor 5. Paul sees this teaching as outside the bounds of those committed to following Jesus, so it has become primarily an outside threat, though most likely with internal origins.

Spiritual Forces vs. Basic Principles

A key phrase in Paul's denouncing of the false teaching that is subject to much debate is what the NRSV translates as "the elemental spirits of the universe" in vv. 8 and 20. The NIV translation itself has changed its own position in this debate. The 1984 translation encapsulated one view with its "basic principles of the world." The most recent edition of the NIV, however, is closer to the NRSV with "elemental spiritual forces of this world." The Greek phrase in question is *stoicheia tou kosmou*. Are these synonymous with the forces Paul rails against in Eph 6:12[8] or are they the principles that underlay a worldly view of things? Paul uses the same word in Gal 4:9. In that context in the previous verse he mentions "beings that by nature are not gods." It is difficult to settle the matter between spiritual forces and

---

6. Ibid., 567.
7. Garland, *Colossians and Philemon*, 174.
8. See particularly Col 2:15.

worldly teaching and principles because in the context of this passage Paul refers to both. Admittedly, his warnings seem to be heavily focused on human teaching and regulations. However, he also mentions the worship of angels in v. 18, which is itself a matter of some debate. Is Paul talking about people worshipping angels or people observing angels in the angels' act of worship? Thompson, following Bruce, is on the principles camp side.[9] The NIV change is evidence that most translations are moving in the opposite direction in favor of spiritual forces. Perhaps the best approach is to allow for both meanings since both angelic beings and human teachings and principle are described in the passage. Here, we are not as concerned with what Paul is specifically addressing as much as how he addresses it. It is to this concern that we now turn.

Although it is difficult to definitively settle the discussions presented above, there are some things we can be sure of. Practically, it appears that the false teaching promoted extra practices or regulations as a way to attain a higher spiritual experience.[10] Furthermore, though the exact nature and source of the teaching is unclear, Paul's reasoning against it is more easily grasped. Whatever the exact practices are and their roots, Paul sees them as attempting to replace what only Christ can accomplish. This is why in the intervening verses between when Paul directly addresses the false teaching, his focus is on Jesus and what he means for the Colossians. They "have come to fullness in him," they were circumcised in him, they "were buried with him in baptism, they "were also raised with him through faith," and they were made "alive together with him." Jesus's crucifixion brought about forgiveness for the Colossians and the defeat of the rulers and authorities. These are all the things that the Colossians are negating or putting in jeopardy by their preoccupation with the false teaching and traditions Paul is warning them about. According to Paul, the false teaching supposes that Jesus's actions are not enough and that more is required. In their attraction to this teaching they are demonstrating that they do not fully comprehend Christ's identity and the importance of the cross.[11]

---

9. Thompson, *Colossians and Philemon*, 53.
10. Ibid., 62.
11. Ibid., 61.

Conflict Management

General Thoughts

In one sense Paul's conflict management strategy in regard to false teaching is simple: do not fall prey to it. Where there is a difference from what Paul is teaching, correct it. In regard to the false teachers themselves, Paul certainly does not have a negotiation strategy or show any sense of compromise. He is not open to bargaining. What they are teaching is wrong, so do not listen to them. There is no appeal to bring them into the fold through argument. Paul portrays those whom he disagrees with as enemies. They are in line with human tradition and the world and set in contrast to Christ. The focus is on not allowing the false teachers to affect the Colossians in a negative way. Wilson summarizes Paul's approach to dealing with this conflict as following a pattern of affirmation, correction, and appeal.[12]

More specifically, Paul's arguments in this area are all centered on showing the inadequacy and inappropriateness of the false teaching for the Colossians, particularly in light of what Christ has done for them and in them. It is the work and person of Christ that makes up the majority of what Paul has to say on the issue. He appeals to the experiences they have had in receiving the gospel and that they had as Christians. Paul reminds the Colossians of who they are in Christ and emphasizes that Jesus' actions and their receiving him by faith is a game-changer. It is clear that Paul trusts that if the Colossians would take the nature of their experience in Christ seriously that would provide more than adequate defense against the deceptive false teaching. As Thompson phrases it, "Paul's antidote to deception is saturation in the gospel of Christ."[13] Everything about Jesus and what he accomplished for the Colossians makes the false teaching an out-of-bounds area. By following the false teaching they would call into question the very substance of what Christ has done as well as their faith in Christ.

Paul also emphasizes the ridiculous nature of the claims of the false teaching. He is able to do this through his attacking characterization of the teaching and the double meanings of words that he uses in that characterization. His summary of the regulations as "Do not handle! Do not taste! Do not touch!" in Col 2:21 are expressed in the way one would need to communicate to a child not to one who is on the verge of reaching new spiritual heights.[14] The humility that is being sought by the false teachers isn't a real

---

12. Wilson, *Hope of Glory*, 6.
13. Thompson, *Colossians and Philemon*, 54.
14. Ibid., 68.

humility but a false one and if anything it is more like humiliation.[15] Also, what the false teaching presents as worship has more to do with glorifying themselves according to Paul; it is "self-imposed worship."[16] Similarly, their focus on such things causes the teachers to be "puffed up" with a mind of the flesh—the very opposite of what they are setting out to achieve. It is fairly safe to assume that Paul's language has at least as much to do with the goal of his argument as with the actual positions of the false teachers. His aim is not to present an unbiased description of the opponents but to emphatically portray how they would lead the Colossians down the wrong road and toward a dead end.[17]

This ridiculous portrayal of the false teaching also serves to resolve a conflict implicit in the text. Paul's advice for the Colossians to not let anyone judge them in these matters[18] suggests that the false teachers are making the Colossians feel lower if they do not accept the teaching and regulations.[19] Paul addresses this conflict between the Colossians and the false teachers as well as what may be an internal conflict for the Colossians themselves, by showing that the false teachers who have put themselves in a judgment position have no legitimate reason to be in that position.

Another line of Paul's argument is targeted at a very practical level. The false teaching and regulation simply does not accomplish what it sets out to accomplish. Here he attacks the seemingly ascetic practices that the false teaching promoted. For all that those practices appear to achieve, ultimately, "they lack any value in restraining sensual indulgence."[20]

In Light of Present-Day Theories and Practices

Although Paul characterizes the false teaching in a negative way, he does not engage in a full-length attacking diatribe against the false teachers themselves. Certainly his emphasis is more heavily on presenting the correct, positive understanding of Jesus than in personally attacking the false teachers.[21] In that he is more concerned with the issue itself and how to deal with the real issue, Paul can be seen as using principled negotiation,

---

15. Ibid., 64.
16. Col 2:23.
17. Garland, *Colossians and Philemon*, 186.
18. Col 2:16.
19. Thompson, *Colossians and Philemon*, 67.
20. Col 2:23.
21. Garland, *Colossians and Philemon*, 164.

though, admittedly, without much room for negotiation on his part.[22] Paul practices a type of principled negotiation by separating the people from the problem. His focus is on the problem of the misrepresentation of the gospel, not on attacking those who are perpetuating that misrepresentation. He disentangles the poorly presented problem from the personalities of the false teachers. Paul knows the most important issues at stake in this conflict are the Colossians' relationship to God, the work of Christ, and the gospel itself. Thus, the gospel, or the mystery of Christ, functions as the legitimate outside authority that Paul uses to work toward agreement with the Colossians. These are all positive aspects of principled negotiation evidenced in Paul's letter to the Colossians in dealing with the conflict related to false teaching.[23]

On the other hand, Paul's methods serve as a good contrast to some of the aspects that Stone, Patton, and Heen describe in their *Difficult Conversations*.[24] Particularly, Paul would probably be found guilty of making the "truth assumption" that they say to avoid. Paul would have difficulty with the distinction between what is true and what is important. He certainly in Col 2 assigns intentions to the false teachers as wanting to deceive and capture the Colossians. He also squarely puts the blame on the teachers. However, in relation to conflict between the Colossians and Paul, he does not make these same steps. It is more like he separates the false teachers as the blame-takers, or scapegoats, in order to salvage the relationship with the Colossians themselves. This also connects with Lederach's caution against forming enemies in conflict resolution.[25] Paul does not make enemies of the Colossians but he certainly makes enemies of the false teachers. His primary concern is not on mending the relationship between the Colossians and the false teachers. Instead, the integrity of the church and of living in line with a proper understanding of the work of Christ is paramount.[26]

In regard to feelings, it is not apparent that Paul was in the practice of taking time to weigh the impact of feelings on an issue or argument. The identity conversation questions in *Difficult Conversations* would have been very foreign to Paul and he would be quicker to point to who was wrong, whereas authors discuss the importance of fostering learning conversations. Paul may have agreed that he could not change anyone, but he would have argued strongly that a person could be changed by God.

22. Fisher, Ury, and Patton, *Getting to Yes*.
23. Ibid., 134–36.
24. Stone, Patton, and Heen, *Difficult Conversations*.
25. Lederach, *Journey Toward Reconciliation*.
26. Christensen and Johnson, *Healing Church Strife*, 8–9.

Paul can also be viewed from a family systems theory of conflict and communication. This is particularly relevant because Paul uses the image of family or household in describing the people of God in his letters.[27] In Colossians, Paul is not writing as the founder of the church in Colossae, but he still adopts a position of parental power in his letter to the church there. Since we do not possess any letters of correspondence from the church back to Paul it is not possible to fully assess how open or closed the communication between the two parties is. It is clear, though, that Paul employs something similar to the strategies that Cosgrove and Hatfield identify as useful to pastors in interacting with their congregations according to family systems theory.[28] Paul uses insider language to connect himself with the Colossians. This is evident through the "us" and "our" language in the letter. He also emphasizes the joining work of Christ and how it puts them all in the same situation.[29] Paul's language here is also connected to another strategy Cosgrove and Hatfield mention: affiliation through positive identification. Paul does this in presenting his suffering as taking place for the sake of the Colossians.[30] Paul also demonstrates affirmation and identification in his writing to the Colossians as he remarks on their faith and love and how disciplined they are.[31]

Colossians Section Conclusion: Contemporary Application

In Colossians, Paul does not offer one go-to model for how to deal with false teaching that is exhaustively prescriptive for all times and places. Instead, Paul puts forward an example that can be generally applied by church leaders in their own contexts. Rather than a set of step-by-step instructions, one finds general principles to guide conflict management in regard to false teaching. This allows space for the consideration of present-day conflict management and communication strategies, while at the same time providing guidelines for a biblical approach.

One of these guidelines involves what is characterized as false teaching and worthy of reproach and attack. Paul does not set a precedent for demanding unity in all areas of belief and practice. He saw the need for some things to be determined by context. Yet, in Colossians it is clear that

27. Eph 2:19; 1 Tim 3.
28. Cosgrove and Hatfield, *Church Conflict*.
29. Col 1:13–14, 23.
30. Col 1:24; 2:1.
31. Col 1:4; 2:5.

there is one area where Paul does not compromise: things that diminish Christ's person and work. When a church is presented with teaching that questions the importance of Jesus and what he accomplished for those who trust in him it needs to be addressed head on. This is a helpful reminder for us today. Not all differences of opinion or practice should be characterized as false teaching, but when it explicitly or implicitly downplays the role and work of Christ churches must reject it.

This leads to the second and third guidelines evident in Paul's approach that relate to how the false teaching is addressed. Like Paul, the response today should be pastoral. Paul was concerned with keeping the Colossians in the fold. He affirmed them in areas and encouraged them in others. He did not make enemies of the Colossians. Pastors and leaders today need to likewise demonstrate pastoral sensitivity in addressing false teaching in their congregations. Yet, at the same time Paul did not hesitate in drawing a line of distinction and to call false teaching out for what it was. Pastors today should not let the cultural emphasis on inclusion keep them from drawing clear lines between orthodoxy and heresy. This requires pastors and leaders to follow Paul's example in both what constitutes false teaching and in how to pastorally address the issues.

Despite the different approaches taken in modern conflict mediation, the goal remains the same: settle the issue in a wise and efficient manner that strengthens, or at least maintains, the relationships of those involved. In this example from Colossians related to false teaching Paul demonstrates a similar goal. He identifies the problem in the misrepresentation of the gospel, describes steps needed for a resolution to the problem, and works to strengthen his relationship with the Colossians themselves. At the same time, his approach to the false teachers themselves leaves little room for reconciliation unless they completely abandon their false teaching. Pastors and church leaders today can feel confident in following Paul's example of dealing with conflict arising from false teaching when the centrality of the gospel is prioritized while also considering ways to strengthen and improve relationships among brothers and sisters in Christ.

Pastoral Epistles (PE)

Background of PE

The three letters of 1–2 Timothy and Titus, collectively known as the Pastoral Letters, "provide the opportunity to examine a mid-first century Christianity

ADDRESSING FALSE TEACHING AND HERESY

struggling with the purity of the Gospel."[32] The letters present stark dualisms of sound doctrine vs. false teaching, adherence to tradition vs. falling away, and virtues vs. vices.[33] In comparison to other Pauline epistles,[34] the Pastorals address individual church leaders Timothy and Titus, rather than entire church communities. They also uniquely focus on doctrine, church governance, and criteria for leaders. The Pastorals contain at least thirteen references to safeguarding sound doctrine and avoiding false teaching. All three contain "warning against false doctrine, exhortation to abide in the truth and lead a holy life [and] the organization, the doctrine and the life of the Christian Church."[35]

It is not clear whether the Pastorals have a singular unifying theme such as establishing church administration (1 Tim 3:15) or correcting false teachers (1 Tim 1:3), or are a collection of Paul's responses to a variety of topics and problems. However, the pastors represent Paul's intentionality in keeping the church as a "stronghold for the gospel of truth," and as such, this necessarily included "eradicating false doctrine."[36]

The Pastorals' vagueness has long stymied readers. Little consensus exists in regard to the identities of the false teachers, the nature of their specific heresies, and the extent their influence impacted the early Christian communities. Whereas some suggest the Pastorals do not represent a historical reality, but rather a generic paradigm for addressing heresy, Karris notes that to see them as "an apologetic *vademecum* for all possible antignostic battles in which the church leaders may engage—may go beyond the evidence."[37] Rather, the Pastorals do seem to address actual threats in Ephesus and Crete. Certainly, Ephesus had battled challenges from false teachers more than a decade before the Pastorals.[38] Less is known about the history of the church, and potential heresies, in Crete, but according to Cranford, both Ephesus and Crete faced the same heresies, albeit in different forms.[39]

---

32. Cranford, "Encountering Heresy," 26.

33. Brown, "Asceticism and Ideology," 77.

34. Identifying the author of the Pastorals lies outside the scope of this discussion and does not directly impact what follows, the author will simply be assumed to be Paul. While historically the Pastorals were widely attested as Pauline by the early church, their authorship has recently become the most widely disputed of any Pauline epistles. Keener, *IVP Bible Background Commentary*, 605.

35. Surburg, "Pastoral Epistles," 26–27.

36. Mappes, "Heresy Paul Opposed in 1 Timothy," 454.

37. Karris, "Background and Significance," 563.

38. See Acts 20:28–31 and Eph 4:14; 5:6–7.

39. Cranford, "Encountering Heresy," 26–27.

Considering Heresy

Church leaders know that throwing the words "heresy" and "heretics" around too loosely today can raise many red flags. Several colleagues recently reviewed a Bible study I was writing, and without fail, every single reviewer challenged my use of "heretic" when talking about Marcion, suggesting the word was perhaps too strong. The warning about these words' proper use is appropriate, and adds an element of significance to our discussion of the Pastorals.

In antiquity, *hairesis* did not originally possess a negative connotation. The neutral or positive term was used by Josephus and the author of Acts to refer to different parties or sects within Judaism. *Hairesis* is used nine times in the New Testament. It is translated seven times as "sects" (in Acts), twice as "factions" (1 Cor 11:19; Gal 5:20) and once as "heresies" (2 Pet 2:1). Even when translated as "factions," *hairesis* still denotes individuals within the Christian community, albeit as part of a potential schism (see 1 Cor 11:18). By the second century, starting with Ignatius' use of *hairesis*, the term had evolved to a negative term, representing sinful people and ideas that threatened the unity of the Body.[40]

The term *hairesis* is never used in the first century Pastorals, even though the Pastoral Letters are intended to address false teachers or heretics. Instead, the pastors employ more specific terms related to their false teaching such as *heterodidaskalein* (1 Tim 1:3) and *hairetikos anthropos* (Titus 3:10). In order to better understand the nature of these heresies, we now consider the identities of the false teachers, their specific teachings and the extent to which their ideas infiltrated the early Christian community.

False Teachers

Last week at church I overheard one of our members introducing himself and his wife to a first-time visitor. The member joked that he perhaps looked familiar because of his face being posted at the local post office. Identifying "bad guys" with photos and descriptions is a common response today to stopping crime and problems. Readers of the Pastorals have long desired to identify the false teachers in similar ways, but their efforts have failed. The Pastoral Letters provide just enough details to pique interest and justify Paul's response, but not enough to satisfy our curiosity. Traditionally, these false teachers were assumed to align with second century Gnostics, but that conclusion has since shifted as the interplay between and influence

---

40. Ibid., 25.

of (proto?) Gnosticism, Judaism and Greek culture are more broadly considered. Lemaire notes, "The heretics of the Pastorals are increasingly less connected with the Greek milieu and more with the Jewish."[41] The heretics were likely not connected to Galatia's Judaizing movement or even the fully developed second-century Gnosticism, but suggests their connection to Colossae, while not clear, was likely.[42]

Whether the false teachers were "Judaizing Christians with a Gnostic leaning, or gnosticizing Christians with a Judaizing tendency,"[43] they appear to be within the church and may have even been leaders or teachers (1 Tim 1:3; 6:3). Paul's depiction of a "mixed church" in 2 Tim 2:19–21 lends credence to this conclusion. But what exactly were these false teachers teaching? Before looking at their specific false teachings, we first consider the manner in which they are depicted.[44]

The Pastorals utilize a polemical schema similar to those used by philosophers against sophists.[45] The purpose of the schema was twofold: to associate the false teaching with false wisdom and create aversion for their teachings, and to disassociate the writers from the heretics and establish themselves as teachers of truth. This polemical schema was first utilized by Plato, and subsequently adopted by Aristotle, Philo, Tatian, Clement of Alexandria, and others. In applying the schema, authors often incorporated identical wording and standard charges against their opponents. Karris sees the Pastorals as also using this schema, and as such, suggests that many of the details and characteristics attributed to the false teachers in these Pastoral Letters may not necessarily indicate actual teaching, beliefs, or behaviors. Karris distinguishes between traditional "stock charges" of the schema and the unique charges against the Pastorals' false teachers, suggesting only the unique challenges should be interpreted as authentic.[46] Alternatively,

41. Mappes, "Heresy Paul Opposed in 1 Timothy," 454.
42. Cranford, "Encountering Heresy," 27.
43. Skarsaune, "Heresy and the Pastoral Epistles," 9.
44. In the uncontested Pauline epistles, Paul addresses the false teachers and "picks up their themes and argues against them on their own terms." Karris, "Background and Significance," 549. For example, consider Paul's approach in 2 Cor 10–13 and compare it to his responses in the Pastorals. In 2 Cor 11:13–15, Paul pointedly calls out his opponents, calling them "false apostles, deceitful workmen, masquerading as apostles of Christ." But his type of response can only be seen in 1 Tim 4:1–5. Perhaps different authorship (authentic Paul vs. contested Paul), the identity of the opponents (i.e., were the teachers outside or inside the church), or the nature of the letter (i.e., addressed to a church community or a single leader) might explain the differences in polemical response.
45. Ibid., 551.
46. Ibid., 563.

Cranford rejects Karris' conclusions, concerned it reflects a "modern affinity with ancient philosophers." He asserts the Pastorals' authenticity and emphases on truth and purity discredit Karris's conclusions about Paul's use of polemic.[47] Affinity or not, it seems reasonable that Paul may have been influenced by and thus used contemporary writing styles. Therefore, in keeping with Karris' conclusions, the greatest attention in discussing the Pastorals' false teaching will be those charges deemed unique from traditional polemical charges.

False Teaching

The false teaching challenged in the Pastorals fits within three large categories: improper teaching from or use of the Old Testament, asceticism, and an over-realized eschatology. The heretics were likely Jewish Christians and teachers of the Law (1 Tim 1:6–7; Titus 1:10) who taught Jewish myths and genealogies (1 Tim 1:3–4; Titus 1:14). Jewish practices appear to be a means for attaining a "super piety."[48]

Nielsen also sees improper use of the Old Testament in the Pastorals, but in a different way. Arguing primarily from silence, he suggests the Pastorals reject the Old Testament and other apostles, elevating Paul and his epistles alone. Nielsen understands the Pastoral Letters as scriptural evidence of pre-Marcionism. Wolfe agrees with Nielsen's conclusions that the Pastorals uniquely present Scripture, but not as Nielsen suggests. Rather, the Pastoral Letters not only hold up the Old Testament and other apostles, but may be the earliest, extant evidence of an expanding understanding of Scripture and tradition within the church.[49] Philip H. Towner, in Beale and Carson's comprehensive *Commentary on the New Testament Use of the Old Testament* also rejects Nielsen's conclusions. "The role of the OT in its Greek translation (LXX) within these letters is greater than often is perceived."[50]

If all Scripture is God-breathed (2 Tim 3:16), including extensive Old Testament genealogies, what was Paul challenging in 1 Tim 1:3–4? Perhaps he was faulting the use of genealogies to recreate distinctions between Jews and Gentiles or the allegorization of such genealogies. These may be at the heart of Titus' reference to their foolish, controversial use (Titus 3:9). Dewey notes the Pastorals challenged the heretics' "speculative use of the Old Testament creation material and stories about famous personages, from which

---

47. Cranford, "Encountering Heresy," 32.
48. Ibid., 29.
49. Wolfe, "Scripture in the Pastoral Epistles," 15.
50. Beale and Carson, *Commentary on the New Testament*, 891.

proof texts and spiritual lessons (or bizarre doctrines) were drawn."[51] Keener further notes, Philo and Josephus, among others, also challenged extrabiblical interpretations the Old Testament contained myths, and Paul's response may be heard as such.[52] While specific details about improper use of the Old Testament remain elusive, the Pastorals demonstrate the continuing importance of the Old Testament in the church, as well as the necessity of its proper interpretation.

Inappropriate practices also lie at the heart of false teaching about asceticism. The Pastorals challenge false teaching about abstaining from certain foods and the forbidding of marriage (1 Tim 4:3). But what about these practices was disconcerting? Then, as is true today, ascetic practices in Christianity certainly represent a "readily available route to spirituality."[53] Elsewhere in Scripture, Paul presents flexible and nuanced views on food abstention (1 Cor 10:23–33) and marriage (1 Cor 7:1–9). Again, the heresy of these ambiguous practices is not immediately discernible. But perhaps the false teachers presented these ascetic practices as necessary for faith or salvation, or suggested they produced a superior faith. Perkins also notes that by challenging these ascetic practices, the Pastorals "show that Christianity accomplishes what the philosophers and moralists thought was only the preserve of an elite few," establishing the church's ability to fit into a virtuous and pious society.[54]

The final area of false teaching relates to the resurrection. Gnostics would later deny Christ's divinity or resurrection and view the world dualistically, desiring to escape the evil, created world. These falsehoods do not appear to challenge the churches in Ephesus and Crete. Instead, the false teachers taught the resurrection already occurred and its followers were experiencing a fuller version of the eschaton. Mappes has identified a verbal link between 1 Tim 6:20–21 and 2 Tim 2:15–18, suggesting the gnosis relates to knowledge the resurrection had already come.[55] This "superior" faith resulting from an over-realized eschatology may closely resemble the setting in Corinth.[56] In 1 Corinthians, Paul challenges the community whose beliefs that the eschaton had already arrived were negatively impacting the community's interactions, particularly among women and slaves (1 Cor 4).

---

51. Newsom and Ringe, *Women's Bible Commentary*, 24.
52. Keener, *IVP Bible Background Commentary*, 608.
53. Cranford, "Encountering Heresy," 30.
54. Perkins, "Pastoral Epistles," 1431.
55. Mappes, "Heresy Paul Opposed in 1 Timothy," 457.
56. Towner, "Gnosis and Realized Eschatology," 95.

Extent of Impact

Last fall a fairly significant dispute arose between two individuals in my church—so much so that one actually ended up leaving the church. On the surface, the argument was over paper plates and a funeral dinner, but like most disputes in church, the real dispute went much deeper; it was over ministry territories, control, and power. After learning what happened, I needed to determine how far-reaching this dispute was. What was the extent of the impact? Similarly, as we read the Pastorals, and hear Paul's challenges to the heretics, we question the degree to which these false teachings permeated the communities in Ephesus and Crete. Not surprisingly, we are left with more unanswered questions than we would hope for. However, let us consider what can be concluded.

The immediate impact of ascetic practices being taught by the heretics was likely visible. Individuals were abstaining from certain foods and avoiding marriage. But even more than that, the false teaching impacted how people were living in the Christian community. The social norms and cultural authority structures were being disrupted, undermined, and ignored by those thinking they were already living in the eschaton (1 Tim 5:3–5; 2 Tim 3:6–7; Titus 1:11). As in Corinth, adherents of the false teaching flouted traditional societal roles, causing discord and strife. Women appear to either be intentional targets of the false teachers, or at least willing and eager recipients.[57] The false teachers may have even engaged in "missionary" type endeavors, attempting to recruit new members. They may have specifically targeted households in their outreach, or were at least effective in significantly impacting households.

More than disrupting societal expectations, the false teaching of the heretics was turning people away from the truth and corrupting the community's morality. Paul characterized the teachers as leading hypocritical lives (1 Tim 4:1–2), occupied with conceit and greed (2 Tim 3:2–5). Their conduct earned them the title of the worst of sinners (1 Tim 1:9–10), and even being handed over to Satan (1 Tim 1:20). How much of these descriptors represent actual realities is hard to determine, as many of them fit within the standard charges of the polemical schema previously discussed.

But, as the saying goes, the proof is in the pudding and as such, we see Paul intentionally addressing proper living in the Pastorals. Paul emphasizes godliness and instructs that godly living matters in the present and future. He also reminds his leaders that salvation was something of the past,

---

57. Karris, "Background and Significance," 563.

present, and future.[58] The reality of a now-and-not-yet salvation demanded lives significantly different than what existed within the communities of Ephesus and Crete. Simply living as if the eschaton had already arrived, with little regard for choices and morals was unacceptable and detrimental to the church. How, then, did Paul recommend the leaders respond? It is at this point in the discussion that the focus begins to shift from the historical to contemporary application for our churches today.

Addressing Heresies

Last year during our annual Pastor Resourcing Days, conference leaders and pastors took an honest look at the trajectories in attendance, membership, giving, conversions, and baptisms of our conference churches. In some cases, the statistics looked grim and could easily have generated despair and frustration. We tend to skip over the hard facts to more quickly focus on the solutions. But in order to make significant and effective changes, we first understand the underlying problems. So too is it with reading the Pastorals. Before launching into Paul's solutions for responding to heresies, we had to first focus on what questions the Pastoral Letters were answering.

The Pastorals represent Paul's three-fold response to guarding sound doctrine against heresies within the church, which severely threatened the gospel, the community's witness, and their continued effectiveness.

Paul's first focus in the Pastorals is the recruitment, training, and organization of effective church leaders and teachers. Today leadership workshops, books, trainings, and conferences respond to the need for professional development of leaders. This emphasis reflects the truth that in business, education, or ministry, an organization can only be as healthy as the leader. For this reason, each August I attend the Global Leadership Summit to learn from a great diversity of world leaders. While the guidelines for bishops and deacons in 1 Timothy receive much scrutiny today, particularly in regard to whether they intentionally exclude women from such leadership positions, Paul's intentions cannot be forgotten in such discussion. Paul wrote the Pastorals specifically to challenge and defeat heresy in Ephesus and Crete. His descriptions of leader qualifications and proper behavior, as well as attempts to establish structure and order, were a response to problems resulting from the false teachers. Paul hoped appointing particular teachers would help the communities reconnect with the truth.

Creating structures of healthy, strong leaders was critical in the Pastorals, and continues to be critical today. Capable leaders with high

---

58. Mappes, "Heresy Paul Opposed in 1 Timothy," 458.

qualifications serving within established organizations can respond to and ultimately prevent false teaching. Paul's instructions in Titus 1:5–9 demonstrate the value of training up strong leaders. The Pastorals not only provide guidelines for establishing healthy leadership in the future, they also address existing problematic leaders. Paul outlines a simple test for identifying false teachers, clarifying that anything beyond the teaching of Jesus and instructions for godly living should be rejected (1 Tim 6:3–4).

The Pastorals also outline specific methods for correcting or stopping false teachers. While Paul's goal was to protect the church from the heretics' influence, it is interesting to also note that his multifaceted approach always has a redemptive goal for the teachers in mind.[59] Paul encourages Timothy to treat wayward believers as family, respect his elders, be sensitive to his peers, maintain purity in relationships with females, and to not overextend his pastoral authority (1 Tim 6:1–2).[60] Further, in Titus 1:13, the rebukes are "so that they will be sound in the faith." In 2 Timothy, Paul hopes that God will grant them repentance leading them to a knowledge of the truth, and that they will come to their senses and escape from the trap of the devil, who has taken them captive to do his will" (2 Tim 2:25–26). The Pastorals' intentional focus on redemption should serve as an important reminder for us today as individual's restoration should undergird all our responses to false teaching and heresy.[61]

A first response to false teaching involves direct encounters. Paul instructs Timothy to gently instruct (2 Tim 2:25) and command false teachers to stop (1 Tim 1:3). Further, Titus is instructed to silence (Titus 1:11) and rebuke (Titus 1:13) the heretics. If these intentional encounters are unsuccessful, Paul then instructs Timothy and Titus to disassociate from the false teachers by making a definitive break from continued relationships.[62] Timothy is told to "turn away from godless chatter and the opposing ideas of what is falsely called knowledge" (1 Tim 6:20) and "have nothing to do with" the teachers (2 Tim 3:5). Similarly, Paul instructs Titus that after divisive people are given two warnings, he should "have nothing to do with them" for they are warped, sinful, and self-condemned (Titus 3:10–11).[63] Contin-

---

59. Cranford, "Encountering Heresy," 37.

60. Fee and Hubbard, *Eerdmans Companion to the Bible*, 688.

61. I concur with Keener's suggestion that Paul's experience of having been converted himself from blasphemy perhaps lies at the heart of his attempt to focus on false teachers' redemption in 1 Tim 1:12–17. Keener, *IVP Bible Background Commentary*, 610.

62. Cranford, "Encountering Heresy," 35.

63. Perkins notes Paul likely did not anticipate successfully restoring Crete's false teachers. In Titus 1:12, Paul employs a commonly used, derogatory phrase about

ued debate with false teachers over sound doctrine should be avoided for "it is of no value, and only ruins those who listen" (2 Tim 2:14–26). Finally, in what might be characterized as the most extreme response, unrepentant heretics may need to be handed over to Satan (1 Tim 1:19–20). Even then, however, one hopes God will punish and redeem the situation.[64]

The second focus of Paul concerns proper teaching. The Pastorals emphasize the importance of "develop[ing] strong congregations with capable leaders."[65] But churches staffed with capable leaders and operating within organized structures is not enough. People in the churches need instruction in God's truth. Individuals should hear "the sound instruction of our Lord Jesus Christ and . . . godly teaching" (1 Tim 6:3), for such teaching fosters godliness.[66] Paul instructs Timothy to "command and teach" the truths, devoting himself to "public reading of Scripture, to preaching and to teaching" (1 Tim 4:11, 13). This direct teaching enables individuals to distinguish between God's truth and human beliefs.[67]

In her published PhD thesis, "Pauline Communities as 'Scholastic Communities,'" Smith highlights the role of teaching as essential and relevant for all aspects of life. Teaching had the potential and "sought to transform belief and the whole of life."[68] In studying the role of teaching in the Pastorals and 1 Corinthians, she concluded teaching was the "normative value-laden designation for the communication of sound knowledge originating with God."[69] Today's shifting landscape of the western church would benefit from the Pastorals' emphasis on direct, intentional, sound teaching. Most churches no longer find themselves able to rely on the teaching originally reserved for weekly Sunday school, and Sunday and Wednesday night services. The popularity of small groups (often called life groups or home groups), particularly within larger churches, often successfully creates fellowship opportunities for individuals lost by the dissolution of Sunday school. However, these groups may or may not focus on direct teaching, potentially burdening the Sunday morning sermon as the sole vehicle for the type of instruction Paul suggests. In a society and church no less encumbered by false teaching than Ephesus and Crete, Paul's emphasis on the

---

Cretans found in ancient literature, "play the Cretan" or "to lie," to suggest such people shouldn't be allowed to teach. Perkins, "Pastoral Epistles," 1443.

64. Cranford, "Encountering Heresy," 37.
65. Ibid.
66. Ibid., 39.
67. See 1 Tim 1:9; 4:16; 6:20–21; and 2 Tim 2:15.
68. As described in Vegge, "Pauline Communities," 511.
69. Ibid.

important role of direct teaching speaks loudly. Churches need to intentionally determine how best to enhance and reemphasize his instructions today.

The final focus of Paul in the Pastorals relates to an emphasis on the importance of godliness in the lives of the leader and the people in the church. As we discovered with the heretics, false teaching leads to problematic living. Similarly, godly teaching leads to godly living. An undeniable connection exists between the life of the church and the characteristics of the teacher and teaching. The Pastorals thus offer a two-fold admonition in spiritual health. "The minister is to carefully supervise his own spiritual nourishment, as well as lead his people in spiritually profitable activities."[70]

Attending to one's spiritual nourishment and health as a church leader is critical. Paul instructs Timothy, "But you, man of God, flee from all this, and pursue righteousness, godliness, faith, love, endurance, and gentleness. Fight the good fight of the faith" (1 Tim 6:11–12a). Further, leaders' lives should be characterized by piety and morality and spiritual maturity, noting, "They must keep hold of the deep truths of the faith with a clear conscience" (1 Tim 3:9).

A fellow pastor recently shared an article by Crosswalk.com on Facebook titled, "15 Myths People Believe about Their Pastor." Aimed at laypersons, the article highlighted the realities and challenges of clergy health, referencing a recent study by the Schaeffer Institute. This study of 1,050 Reformed and Evangelical pastors exposed alarming statistics: 50 percent of pastors reported using pornography as a tension reliever; 37 percent admitted having inappropriate sexual relationships with parishioners; 70 percent of pastors regularly contemplate leaving the ministry because of moral failure, emotional health, or burnout; and 91 percent admitted to experiencing burnout.[71] Churches, leadership boards, denominations, and even seminaries cannot afford to overlook these trends. Spiritual health and maturity of clergy must be emphasized and the Pastorals offer some potential guidelines.

Secondly, churches must be intentionally led to pursue, practice, and prioritize spiritual growth themselves. Paul admonishes Titus to "remind everyone" of not only proper behavior, but also their own spiritual journeys of growth. In the end, Paul hopes, "Those who have trusted in God may be careful to devote themselves to doing what is good. These things are excellent and profitable for everyone" (Titus 3:1–11). Similarly, Timothy is instructed to "keep reminding God's people" of the truths of faith (2 Tim 2:1–14), so that they may "flee the evil desires of youth and pursue righteousness, faith,

---

70. Cranford, "Encountering Heresy," 35.
71. Gaultiere, "Pastor Stress Statistics."

love, and peace, along with those who call on the Lord out of a pure heart" (2 Tim 2:22). Paul commends Timothy to teach and accept that "godliness has value for all things, holding promise for both the present life and the life to come" (1 Tim 4:8).

Similar to challenges of directly teaching in today's church environment, problems also exist in pursuing spiritual growth and discipleship. Again, trends away from Sunday school and secondary worship services often result in limited opportunities for such engagement. Unless small groups intentionally address discipleship, these spiritual growth needs may go unmet. Even if small groups effectively disciple their members, how will children and non-participants in small groups grow? Where and how should individuals learn and practice spiritual disciplines? How should churches intentionally prioritize spiritual growth and discipleship among their congregants? These are vital questions to consider, and unless intentionally pursued, growth will not happen. Last summer I began ministering as lead pastor at an urban church. After six months of intentional discipleship and teaching in my church, I regularly heard from long-time church attenders that they had "grown more in the past six months than the past six years." These statements were not critical of the former pastor, but rather a reflection of how purposeful such instruction must be.

Conclusion

Conflict in the church is inevitable. Debates about proper teaching, worship, and beliefs have existed as part of the landscape of church from the very beginning. In today's society, heresy and false teachers continue to challenge leaders and congregations alike. The Pastorals provide valuable insights and guidelines for ministry leaders, particularly in regard to correct practices (use of Scripture, asceticism, interpretation of eschatology), church leadership guidelines, and church teaching. Certainly the particular nature of today's challenges may be unique from the Pastorals' original audiences and each situation necessitates a unique response. But, some general guidelines still apply. The Pastoral Letters could be preemptively heard and implemented as safeguards against potential threats. This is particularly important preventive work since the heretics in Ephesus and Crete came from within the body of faith and started as faithful believers.

Reaching negotiated integrative solutions requires identifying the parties, determining key interests, and searching for facts. In the pastoral epistles, the identified parties include the churches, Paul, and false teachers. The key interests included healthy congregations, a clear definition of the gospel, false teachings, and heresies. In searching for facts, mediators ask questions. Who are the false teachers? Where do they come from? What impact are they having? What is the context of each local church and the specific heresy being addressed? By identifying the parties, the issues, and as many facts as possible, mediators can begin helping create workable solutions. Paul does just that in establishing the steps forward for the congregations in the epistles.

In contemporary contexts, mediators need to trust this process. Identify all the parties involved in a conflict and their interests. What drives them? Why are they doing what they are doing and what motivates their responses? Dig deep and find as many facts about the parties, the responses, and the situation at hand as possible. Mediators also have to be aware of the cultural context of their environment. Paul clearly understood his churches' contexts and was immersed in his first-century Mediterranean Jewish-Christian culture. While we may not have all the background necessary to fully judge Paul's responses to the false teachers he was facing, modern mediators must know as much as possible about their *own* contexts so their solutions workably fit their context and culture. This is key for creating meaningful and lasting integrative solutions.

The importance of clergy and congregational training in areas of leadership, spiritual growth, and doctrinal truths in the Pastorals cannot be overstated. The recent trend to minimize the value of seminary education and over-emphasize experience and the leading of the Spirit contradicts Paul's instructions. A leader's ability to understand and teach sound doctrine plays a critical role in the health and vitality of the church. Continuing education opportunities, pastoral accountability groups, regularly scheduled sabbaticals, and intentional focus on clergy spiritual health would be beneficial for leaders and churches alike. Paul's instructions may also strengthen leaders susceptible to burnout or moral fall-out.

One specific area of necessary clergy and congregational training relates directly to an issue in the Pastorals—namely, correctly reading and interpreting the Old Testament. The Pastoral Letters briefly describe how the heretics have falsely understood Jewish myths and genealogies. Devotion to such teaching "promotes controversial speculations rather than advancing God's work—which is by faith" (1 Tim 1:4). Further, the false teachers' asceticism may also have stemmed from improperly interpreting Old Testament texts. Alternatively, the Old Testament cannot be rejected or ignored as too commonly happens today within the church. Paul emphasizes "*all Scripture* is God-breathed and is useful for teaching, rebuking, correcting and training in righteousness, so that the servant of God may be thoroughly equipped for every good work" (2 Tim 3:16–17, emphasis added).

Good works and right living are also at the heart of the Pastorals. False teaching leads to false living, and conversely, godly teaching leads to godly living. While the specific ascetic practices have previously been discussed, an essential take-away warrants further discussion. Paul challenged the heretics' abstention from certain foods in Ephesus, yet also chastised the Corinthians for their lack of dietary restraint. Similarly, the Pastorals correct the false teachers' prohibition of marriage, but also encouraged the Corinthians that it was good to stay single. These "contradictions" can be explained away by Paul responding to unique situations in Ephesus vs. Corinth or as evidence that the Pastorals were not authored by Paul. However, another explanation warrants consideration. The Pastorals' focus on safeguarding sound doctrine and refuting false teaching suggests an alternative.

While the outgrowth of heresy is addressed and corrected, it is the false teaching itself that ultimately matters. Even if false teaching leads to "good living," the teaching is problematic. What Paul challenged in the Pastorals was primarily the false teaching. This reality challenges us to think about heresies today in the church. The prosperity gospel, for example, is too often ignored and disregarded among believers. After all, the reasoning goes, such teaching can increase individuals' faith and produce generosity in believers. Paul would disagree. Regardless of potential neutral or positive outcomes, any teaching based upon a false understanding of the gospel also needs to be challenged.

False teaching related to salvation and eschatology also has immediate consequences in the western church. Although an over-realized eschatology may not impinge primary doctrinal issues such as Christ's identity and resurrection, such false teaching cannot persist uninhibited. "The over-realized outlook had upset the delicate balance between the 'already/not yet' in the community's thinking." As such, the Pastorals "aimed to restore the 'forward look' to a place of prominence . . . while at the same time underlining the requirements of perseverance and service in the present age."[72] Do our churches suffer from a similar misunderstanding of the eschaton today?

Bishop Todd Hunter, author of *Christianity Beyond Belief*, challenges our tendency to view Christianity as a secure death, rather than a vibrant life lived today for the sake of others. Hunter provides an important correction to our overly simplified understanding of salvation. Sometimes in an evangelical fervor of saving souls, the church has inadvertently reduced salvation to simply being about getting into heaven when we die. This has resulted in neglecting the "now" of living and thus abandoning the call to co-labor with God in bringing the Kingdom of God. If Paul were writing the

---

72. Towner, "Gnosis and Realized Eschatology," 114.

Pastorals today, this false teaching about salvation and eschatology would likely receive his attention.

Finally, Lucinda Brown raises two concerns that today's churches should guard against. These concerns relate to potentially negative impacts of the Pastorals on their original communities, and should also be heard today. First, Brown challenges the Pastorals' move toward solidifying hierarchical systems. By outlining criteria for bishops and deacons, while also maintaining societal norms for women and slaves, the Pastorals potentially create a system that maintains the status quo, fails to challenge inequality, and provides minimal opportunity for outside voices to contribute. Brown notes,

> Authority to make decisions regarding the community's beliefs and practices was based on predetermined roles rather than on the actual intellectual, spiritual, or organizational abilities of the persons who filled those roles. . . . Authority was assumed only by those who filled roles at the top of the hierarchy, while those lower on the hierarchical leader were not only denied access to that authority but were dismissed as trouble-makers.[73]

While some may debate Brown's conclusions about authority and predetermined roles within the community, her caution should not be ignored. We would do well to heed her concern by asking questions of ourselves, our churches, and our denominational leaders. How are individuals' intellectual, spiritual, and organizational abilities evaluated, valued, and utilized within our system? Who is given authority, by whom, and based on what? How are other voices encouraged and heard? How are differing opinions respected and considered?

Brown's second concern relates to the Pastorals' emphasis on piety. By focusing on piety, Brown saw moderation and self-control being encouraged. This "served to strengthen the hierarchical social structure and to limit the creative exchange of ideas and sharing of power within the community."[74] Again, whether the historic realities of Brown's concerns are accurate, her point is well taken. In our attempts to disciple and foster godly living, are we silencing divergent voices? Does our desire for orderliness, structure, and piety result in erasing individuality, creativity and unique expressions of faith? Conversely, how do our churches encourage new ideas and shared power? How are repressive or unequal social structures dismantled and rebuilt? How can our churches be organized to be on the forefront of leading cultural change, rather than simply responding and defending against it?

73. Brown, "Asceticism and Ideology," 92.
74. Ibid., 93.

Viewed through the lens of conflict resolution, the Pastoral Letters helpfully respond to false teaching. They offer guidelines for addressing heretics themselves, as well as corrective measures for safeguarding sound doctrine, developing effective leaders and establishing healthy organizational structures. The Pastorals do more than simply defend against false teachers, however. As Erasmus wisely noted, "Prevention is better than cure." The Pastorals provide church leaders much more than simply cure. They specifically address preventative measures against future heresy that churches today would do well to implement.

In the world of church conflict, perhaps no greater conflicts exist than whether our churches are properly handling and teaching the truths of Christ. These passages from Colossians and the Pastorals provide helpful guidelines in identifying and responding to potential heresy.

At the heart of the false teaching challenged by Paul lies a Christ-plus faith. Whether accomplished through prescribing additional restrictions or through following ascetic practices, Christ's work became the starting place, rather than entirety of a faith-filled life. As a result of the extra practices or knowledge, the heretics developed a faith marked by a superiority complex, which suggested their new ways of engaging faith exceeded the others'. These challenges are not too far afield from claims today by individuals and denominations to be the only "true Christians" who possess the proper doctrine and practices.

As leaders we must honestly assess and guard against such conclusions. How might we be elevating ourselves and our practices above others, suggesting our church is the better, more faithful way? Further, as we implement and teach spiritual practices and disciplines in our faith communities, what is the motivation behind these practices? Are they intended to point the church to Christ, and allow his transforming work to be accomplished in and among us? Or are they supplementing Christ's already-accomplished work? Are these practices helpful tools in our journey together as a community, or do they create boundary markers, barriers to inclusion or even additional requirements necessary for salvation?

Paul's teaching also reminds church leaders that beliefs—both false and true—have real implications and practices. The importance of guarding both orthodoxy and orthopraxy is critical, as the two cannot be separated. Whereas the church today often focuses on rooting out false teaching, Paul's intentionality in also addressing the practices is significant. Heresy—and health—will be tied to both beliefs and practices.

Finally, when leaders do identify heresy within their churches, Paul's letters provide some important overarching guidelines. First, it is critical to remember one size does not fit all. Unique responses are required for each individual situation. Secondly, our responses to false teaching need to be pastoral. As leaders, our actions should be grounded in a desire and intention that these individuals would remain in community, and their faith would be restored. Finally, being guardians of the gospel and addressing conflicts of heresy and false teaching is less about protecting or defending against outside "attacks" and more about strengthening our communities of faith in living into Christ's work.

Bibliography

Beale, G. K., and D. A. Carson, eds. *Commentary on the New Testament Use of the Old Testament*. Grand Rapids: Baker Academic, 2007.

Brown, Lucinda A. "Asceticism and Ideology: The Language of Power in the Pastoral Epistles." *Semeia* 57 (1982) 77–97.

Christensen, James, and Thomas F. Johnson. *Healing Church Strife in the New Testament and Today Beyond Matthew 18:15–17*. Eugene, OR: Wipf & Stock, 2016.

Cosgrove Charles H., and Dennis D. Hatfield. *Church Conflict: The Hidden Systems Behind the Fights*. Nashville: Abingdon, 1994.

Cranford, Lorin. "Encountering Heresy: Insight from the Pastoral Epistles." *Southwest Journal of Theology* 22 (1980) 23–40.

Fee, Gordon D., and Robert L. Hubbard Jr., eds. *The Eerdmans Companion to the Bible*. Grand Rapids: Eerdmans, 2011.

Fisher, Roger, William L. Ury, and Bruce Patton. *Getting to Yes: Negotiating Agreement Without Giving In*. 3rd ed. New York: Penguin, 2011.

Garland, David E. *Colossians and Philemon*. The NIV Application Commentary. Grand Rapids: Zondervan, 1998.

Gaultiere, Bill. "Pastor Stress Statistics." Soul Shepherding, November 11, 2009. http://www.soulshepherding.org/2009/11/pastors-under-stress/.

Hooker, Morna D. "Were There False Teachers in Colossae?" In *Christ and Spirit in the New Testament*, edited by B. Lindars and S. S. Smalley, 315–32. Cambridge: Cambridge University Press, 1973.

Karris, Robert J. "The Background and Significance of the Polemic of the Pastoral Epistles." *Journal of Biblical Literature* 92 (1973) 549–64.

Keener, Craig S. *The IVP Bible Background Commentary: New Testament*. Downers Grove: InterVarsity, 1993.

Lederach, John Paul. *The Journey Toward Reconciliation*. Scottdale, PA: Herald, 1999.

Lincoln, Andrew T. "Colossians." In vol. 11 of *The New Interpreter's Bible*, edited by J. Paul Sampley, 553–669. Nashville: Abingdon, 2000.

Mappes, David A. "The Heresy Paul Opposed in 1 Timothy." *Bibliotheca Sacra* 156 (1999) 452–58.

Newsom, Carole A., and Sharon H. Ringe. *The Women's Bible Commentary*. Louisville: Westminster John Knox, 1995.

Perkins, Pheme. "Pastoral Epistles." In *Eerdmans Commentary on the Bible*, edited by James D. G. Dunn and John W. Rogerson, 1428–47. Grand Rapids: Eerdmans, 2003.

Skarsaune, Oskar. "Heresy and the Pastoral Epistles." *Themelios* 20 (1994) 9–14.

Stone, Douglas, Bruce Patton, and Sheila Heen. *Difficult Conversations: How to Discuss What Matters Most*. New York: Penguin, 1999.

Surburg, Raymond F. "The Pastoral Epistles and Sound Doctrine." *Springfielder* 25 (1961) 26–30.

Thompson, Marianne Meye. *Colossians and Philemon*. Grand Rapids: Eerdmans, 2005.

Towner, P. H. "Gnosis and Realized Eschatology in Ephesus (of the Pastoral Epistles) and the Corinthian Enthusiasm." *Journal for the Study of the New Testament* 31 (1987) 95–124.

Vegge, Tor. "Pauline Communities as 'Scholastic Communities': A Study of the Vocabulary of 'Teaching' in 1 Corinthians, 1 and 2 Timothy and Titus." *Zeitschrift Für Antikes Christentum* 18 (2014) 509–59.

Wilson, Walter T. *The Hope of Glory: Education and Exhortation in the Epistle to the Colossians*. New York: Brill, 1997.

Wolfe, B. Paul. "Scripture in the Pastoral Epistles: Premarcion Marcionism?" *Perspectives in Religious Studies* 16 (1989) 5–16.

Wright, N. T. *Paul for Everyone: The Prison Letters: Ephesians, Philippians, Colossians and Philemon*. Louisville: Westminster John Knox, 2004.

www.ingramcontent.com/pod-product-compliance
Lightning Source LLC
Chambersburg PA
CBHW031432150426
43191CB00006B/482